FORWARD/COMMENTARY

The National Institute of Standards and Technology (NIST) is a measurement standards laboratory, and a non-regulatory agency of the **United States Department of Commerce**. Its mission is to promote innovation and industrial competitiveness. Founded in 1901, as the National Bureau of Standards, NIST was formed with the mandate to provide standard weights and measures, and to serve as the national physical laboratory for the United States. With a world-class measurement and testing laboratory encompassing a wide range of areas of computer science, mathematics, statistics, and systems engineering, NIST's cybersecurity program supports its overall mission to promote U.S. innovation and industrial competitiveness by advancing measurement science, standards, and related technology through research and development in ways that enhance economic security and improve our quality of life.

The need for cybersecurity standards and best practices that address interoperability, usability and privacy has been shown to be critical for the nation. NIST's cybersecurity programs seek to enable greater development and application of practical, innovative security technologies and methodologies that enhance the country's ability to address current and future computer and information security challenges.

The cybersecurity publications produced by NIST cover a wide range of cybersecurity concepts that are carefully designed to work together to produce a holistic approach to cybersecurity primarily for government agencies and constitute the best practices used by industry. This holistic strategy to cybersecurity covers the gamut of security subjects from development of secure encryption standards for communication and storage of information while at rest to how best to recover from a cyber-attack.

Why buy a book you can download for free?   We print this so you don't have to.

Some are available only in electronic media. Some online docs are missing pages or barely legible.

We at 4th Watch Publishing are former government employees, so we know how government employees actually use the standards. When a new standard is released, an engineer prints it out, punches holes and puts it in a 3-ring binder. While this is not a big deal for a 5 or 10-page document, many NIST documents are over 100 pages and printing a large document is a time-consuming effort. So, an engineer that's paid $75 an hour is spending hours simply printing out the tools needed to do the job. That's time that could be better spent doing engineering. We publish these documents so engineers can focus on what they were hired to do – engineering. It's much more cost-effective to just order the latest version from Amazon.com

If there is a standard you would like published, let us know. Our web site is usgovpub.com

1
2

Draft NIST Special Publication 800-77
Revision 1

3

Guide to IPsec VPNs

4
5

6 Elaine Barker
7 Quynh Dang
8 Sheila Frankel
9 Karen Scarfone
10 Paul Wouters

11
12
13
14
15
16
17
18
19

20 C O M P U T E R   S E C U R I T Y

21
22

National Institute of
Standards and Technology
U.S. Department of Commerce

23
24

Draft NIST Special Publication 800-77
Revision 1

25
26

Guide to IPsec VPNs

27
28
29
30
31
32
33
34
35
36
37
38
39
40
41
42
43
44

Elaine Barker
Quynh Dang
Sheila Frankel
Computer Security Division
Information Technology Laboratory

Karen Scarfone
Scarfone Cybersecurity
Clifton, VA

Paul Wouters
No Hats Corporation
Toronto, ON, Canada

45
46
47

July 2019

48
49
50
51
52
53
54
55

U.S. Department of Commerce
Wilbur L. Ross, Jr., Secretary

National Institute of Standards and Technology
Walter Copan, NIST Director and Under Secretary of Commerce for Standards and Technology

Authority

This publication has been developed by NIST in accordance with its statutory responsibilities under the Federal Information Security Modernization Act (FISMA) of 2014, 44 U.S.C. § 3551 *et seq.*, Public Law (P.L.) 113-283. NIST is responsible for developing information security standards and guidelines, including minimum requirements for federal information systems, but such standards and guidelines shall not apply to national security systems without the express approval of appropriate federal officials exercising policy authority over such systems. This guideline is consistent with the requirements of the Office of Management and Budget (OMB) Circular A-130.

Nothing in this publication should be taken to contradict the standards and guidelines made mandatory and binding on federal agencies by the Secretary of Commerce under statutory authority. Nor should these guidelines be interpreted as altering or superseding the existing authorities of the Secretary of Commerce, Director of the OMB, or any other federal official. This publication may be used by nongovernmental organizations on a voluntary basis and is not subject to copyright in the United States. Attribution would, however, be appreciated by NIST.

National Institute of Standards and Technology Special Publication 800-77 Revision 1
Natl. Inst. Stand. Technol. Spec. Publ. 800-77 Rev. 1, 161 pages (July 2019)
CODEN: NSPUE2

Certain commercial entities, equipment, or materials may be identified in this document in order to describe an experimental procedure or concept adequately. Such identification is not intended to imply recommendation or endorsement by NIST, nor is it intended to imply that the entities, materials, or equipment are necessarily the best available for the purpose.

There may be references in this publication to other publications currently under development by NIST in accordance with its assigned statutory responsibilities. The information in this publication, including concepts and methodologies, may be used by federal agencies even before the completion of such companion publications. Thus, until each publication is completed, current requirements, guidelines, and procedures, where they exist, remain operative. For planning and transition purposes, federal agencies may wish to closely follow the development of these new publications by NIST.

Organizations are encouraged to review all draft publications during public comment periods and provide feedback to NIST. Many NIST cybersecurity publications, other than the ones noted above, are available at https://csrc.nist.gov/publications.

Public comment period: *July 2, 2019* through *October 8, 2019*

National Institute of Standards and Technology
Attn: Computer Security Division, Information Technology Laboratory
100 Bureau Drive (Mail Stop 8930) Gaithersburg, MD 20899-8930
Email: revision_of_SP800-77@nist.gov

All comments are subject to release under the Freedom of Information Act (FOIA).

94   **Reports on Computer Systems Technology**

95   The Information Technology Laboratory (ITL) at the National Institute of Standards and
96   Technology (NIST) promotes the U.S. economy and public welfare by providing technical
97   leadership for the Nation's measurement and standards infrastructure. ITL develops tests, test
98   methods, reference data, proof of concept implementations, and technical analyses to advance
99   the development and productive use of information technology. ITL's responsibilities include the
100   development of management, administrative, technical, and physical standards and guidelines for
101   the cost-effective security and privacy of other than national security-related information in
102   federal information systems. The Special Publication 800-series reports on ITL's research,
103   guidelines, and outreach efforts in information system security, and its collaborative activities
104   with industry, government, and academic organizations.

105

106   **Abstract**

107   Internet Protocol Security (IPsec) is a widely used network layer security control for protecting
108   communications. IPsec is a framework of open standards for ensuring private communications
109   over Internet Protocol (IP) networks. IPsec configuration is usually performed using the Internet
110   Key Exchange (IKE) protocol. This publication provides practical guidance to organizations on
111   implementing security services based on IPsec so that they can mitigate the risks associated with
112   transmitting sensitive information across networks. The document focuses on how IPsec
113   provides network layer security services and how organizations can implement IPsec and IKE to
114   provide security under different circumstances. It also describes alternatives to IPsec and
115   discusses under what circumstances each alternative may be appropriate.

116

117   **Keywords**

118   communications security; Internet Key Exchange (IKE); Internet Protocol (IP); Internet Protocol
119   Security (IPsec); network layer security; networking; virtual private network (VPN).

120

121   **Acknowledgments**

122   The authors, Elaine Barker, Quynh Dang, and Sheila Frankel of NIST, wish to thank everyone
123   who has contributed to this revision of Special Publication (SP) 800-77, particularly Andrew
124   Regenscheid, David Waltermire, and Lily Chen of NIST, and Dorothy E. Cooley and James
125   Banoczi of the National Security Agency (NSA).

126   The authors acknowledge the following individuals (with their original affiliations) and
127   organizations that assisted in the development of the original SP 800-77:

128   •   The authors of the original version: Sheila Frankel of NIST, and Karen Kent, Ryan
129   Lewkowski, Angela D. Orebaugh, Ronald W. Ritchey, and Steven R. Sharma of Booz
130   Allen Hamilton
131   •   Bill Burr, Tim Grance, Okhee Kim, Peter Mell, and Murugiah Souppaya of NIST
132   •   Darren Hartman and Mark Zimmerman of ICSA Labs
133   •   Paul Hoffman of the VPN Consortium
134   •   Representatives from the Department of Energy, the Department of State, the
135   Environmental Protection Agency, and the U.S. Nuclear Regulatory Commission

136

137   **Audience**

138   This document has been created for network architects, network administrators, security staff,
139   technical support staff, and computer security program managers who are responsible for the
140   technical aspects of preparing, operating, and securing networked infrastructures. The material in
141   this document is technically oriented, and it is assumed that readers have at least a basic
142   understanding of networking and network security.

143

144   **Trademark Information**

145   All names are registered trademarks or trademarks of their respective companies.

146

147   **Call for Patent Claims**

148   This public review includes a call for information on essential patent claims (claims whose use
149   would be required for compliance with the guidance or requirements in this Information
150   Technology Laboratory (ITL) draft publication). Such guidance and/or requirements may be
151   directly stated in this ITL Publication or by reference to another publication. This call also
152   includes disclosure, where known, of the existence of pending U.S. or foreign patent applications
153   relating to this ITL draft publication and of any relevant unexpired U.S. or foreign patents.

154   ITL may require from the patent holder, or a party authorized to make assurances on its behalf,
155   in written or electronic form, either:

156   a) assurance in the form of a general disclaimer to the effect that such party does not hold
157   and does not currently intend holding any essential patent claim(s); or

158   b) assurance that a license to such essential patent claim(s) will be made available to
159   applicants desiring to utilize the license for the purpose of complying with the guidance
160   or requirements in this ITL draft publication either:

161   i.   under reasonable terms and conditions that are demonstrably free of any unfair
162   discrimination; or
163   ii. without compensation and under reasonable terms and conditions that are
164   demonstrably free of any unfair discrimination.

165   Such assurance shall indicate that the patent holder (or third party authorized to make assurances
166   on its behalf) will include in any documents transferring ownership of patents subject to the
167   assurance, provisions sufficient to ensure that the commitments in the assurance are binding on
168   the transferee, and that the transferee will similarly include appropriate provisions in the event of
169   future transfers with the goal of binding each successor-in-interest.

170   The assurance shall also indicate that it is intended to be binding on successors-in-interest
171   regardless of whether such provisions are included in the relevant transfer documents.

172   Such statements should be addressed to: revision_of_SP800-77@nist.gov.

173 **Executive Summary**

174 Internet Protocol Security (IPsec) is a suite of open standards for ensuring private
175 communications over public networks. It is the most common network layer security control,
176 typically used to encrypt IP traffic between hosts in a network and for creating a virtual private
177 network (VPN). A VPN is a virtual network built on top of existing physical networks that
178 provides a secure communications mechanism for data and control information transmitted
179 between computers or networks. IPsec is also used as a component that provides the security for
180 many other internet protocols. The User Datagram Protocol (UDP) usage guidelines [1] specify
181 IPsec as one of the methods to secure UDP.

182 The Internet Key Exchange (IKE) protocol is most commonly used to establish IPsec-based
183 VPNs. The terms IKE and IPsec are often used interchangeably, although that is not correct. In
184 practice, the terms "IPsec VPN," "IKEv2 VPN," "Cisco IPsec," "IPsec XAUTH," and
185 "L2TP/IPsec" all refer to IPsec-based VPN connections. Some examples of technologies and
186 protocols that use IKE and/or IPsec are:

187 • 3rd Generation Partnership Project (3GPP) mobile phone telephony standard (Long-Term
188   Evolution [LTE]/5th Generation [5G], Wireless Fidelity [WiFi] calling) [2], [3]
189 • Ethernet VPN (EVPN) and Virtual eXtensible Local Area Network (VXLAN) [4]
190 • Software-Defined Networking (SDN) and Software-Defined Wide Area Network
191   (SDWAN)
192 • Segment Routing [5]
193 • Data Center Network Virtualization Overlay (NVO3) Networks [6]
194 • Generic Network Virtualization Encapsulation (GENEVE) [7]
195 • Smart Grid [8]
196 • Constrained Application Protocol (CoAP)
197 • Low-Power Wireless Personal Area Network (6LowPAN) [9]
198 • Routing protocol protection [10] such as Border Gateway Protocol (BGP)/BGP
199   Monitoring Protocol (BMP) [11] and Open Shortest Path First (OSPFv3) [12]

200 VPNs protect communications carried over public networks such as the Internet as well as
201 private networks such as fiber networks or Multi-Protocol Label Switching (MPLS) networks. A
202 VPN can provide several types of data protection, including confidentiality, integrity, data origin
203 authentication, replay protection, and access control. The primary VPN architectures are as
204 follows:

205 • **Gateway-to-gateway.** This architecture protects communications between two specific
206   networks, such as an organization's main office network and a branch office network, or
207   two business partners' networks.

208 • **Remote access.** Also known as host-to-gateway, this architecture protects
209   communications between one or more individual hosts and a specific network belonging
210   to an organization. The remote access architecture is most often used to allow hosts on

211   unsecured networks, such as traveling employees and telecommuters, to gain access to
212   internal organizational services, such as the organization's email and Web servers.

213   • **Host-to-host.** A host-to-host architecture protects communication between two specific
214   computers. It can be used when a small number of users need to use or administer a
215   remote system that requires the use of inherently insecure protocols.

216   • **Mesh.** In a mesh architecture, many hosts within one or a few networks all establish
217   individual VPNs with each other.
218

219 The guide provides an overview of the types of security controls that can provide protection for
220 network communications that are widely used throughout the world. IP communications are
221 composed of four layers that work together: application, transport, network, and data link.
222 Security controls exist for network communications at each of the four layers. As data is
223 prepared for transport, it is passed from the highest to the lowest layer, with each layer adding
224 more information. Because of this, a security control at a higher layer cannot provide full
225 protection for lower layers, because the lower layers add information to the communications
226 after the higher layer security controls have been applied. The primary disadvantage of lower
227 layer security controls is that they are less flexible and granular than higher layer controls.
228 Accordingly, network layer controls have become widely used for securing communications
229 because they provide a more balanced solution.

230 IPsec is a network layer security protocol with two main components:

231   • **Encapsulating Security Payload (ESP)** is the protocol that transports the encrypted and
232   integrity-protected network communications across the network. If only integrity
233   protection is needed without encryption, the ESP protocol can use NULL encryption. An
234   older method for IPsec transport of non-encrypted data is to use the Authentication
235   Header (AH) protocol, but this method is no longer recommended by this guidance.

236   • **Internet Key Exchange (IKE)** is the protocol used by IPsec to negotiate IPsec
237   connection settings; authenticate endpoints to each other; define the security parameters
238   of IPsec-protected connections; negotiate session keys; and manage, update, and delete
239   IPsec-protected communication channels. The current version is IKEv2.
240

241 Optionally, IPsec can use the IP Payload Compression Protocol (IPComp) to compress packet
242 payloads before encrypting them, but this has not been widely used.

243 Only implementations of NIST-approved cryptographic algorithms specified in Federal
244 Information Processing Standards (FIPS) or NIST Special Publications (SPs) and contained in
245 FIPS-validated cryptographic modules shall be used in IPsec VPN deployments for compliance
246 with this guidance. The FIPS 140 [13] specification defines how cryptographic modules will be
247 validated. One requirement of FIPS 140 is that the module be capable of operating in a mode
248 where all algorithms are NIST approved. NIST-approved algorithms are specified in a FIPS
249 (e.g., FIPS 180, *Secure Hash Standard*) or in a NIST Special Publication (e.g., SP 800-56A,
250 *Recommendation for Pair-Wise Key Establishment Schemes Using Discrete Logarithm*

251 *Cryptography*). Some implementations can run in both FIPS mode and non-FIPS mode, so it is
252 important to set and verify the mode of operation of the IKE and IPsec modules.

253 The Cryptographic Module Validation Program (CMVP) is a joint effort between NIST and the
254 Communications Security Establishment (CSE) of the Government of Canada for the validation
255 of cryptographic modules against FIPS 140-2 [13]. The Cryptographic Algorithm Validation
256 Program (CAVP) provides validation testing of FIPS-approved and NIST-recommended
257 cryptographic algorithms and their individual components. Cryptographic algorithm validation is
258 a prerequisite of cryptographic module validation.

259 Cryptographic recommendations in this document are based on the time of publication of this
260 document and may be superseded by other publications in the future. Appendix F contains a list
261 of relevant FIPS, SPs, and Internet Engineering Task Force (IETF) standards related to IKE and
262 IPsec.

263 Approved algorithms and their options for IKE and IPsec as of this writing are listed in Table 1:

264   **Table 1: Approved Algorithms and Options**

Option	Recommended	Legacy	Expected
IKE			
Version	IKEv2	IKEv1	
IKEv2 exchanges	All	-	
IKEv1 exchanges	Main Mode, Quick Mode	Aggressive Mode	
Encryption	AES-GCM, AES-CTR, AES-CBC, AES-CCM (128, 192, 256-bit keys)	TDEA	
Integrity/Pseudo Random Function (PRF)	HMAC-SHA-256, HMAC-SHA-384, HMAC-SHA-512	HMAC-SHA-1	HMAC-SHA-3
Diffie-Hellman (DH) group	DH 14 to DH 21 RFC [64] and RFC 5114 [65]		DH 31 and DH 32, RFC 8031 [72]
Peer authentication	RSA, DSA, and ECDSA with 128-bit security strength (for example, RSA with 3072-bit or larger key)	RSA, DSA, and ECDSA with less than 112 bits of security strength	
Lifetime	24 hours		
IPsec			
Mode	tunnel mode, transport mode		
Protocol	ESP, IPComp	AH	
Version	IPsec-v3	IPsec-v2	
Encryption	AES-GCM, AES-CTR, AES-CBC, AES-CCM, (128, 192, 256-bit keys)		
Integrity	HMAC-SHA-256, HMAC-SHA-384, HMAC-SHA-512, AES-GMAC		HMAC-SHA-3
Perfect Forward Secrecy (PFS)	Same or stronger DH as initial IKE DH		

Option	Recommended	Legacy	Expected
Lifetime	8 hours		

265

266 Some of the cryptographic requirements will change at the end of 2020, see SP 800-131A [47]
267 for details. Therefore, Federal agencies who want to provide IPsec VPN services after 2020 must
268 ensure that their systems are upgradeable to the new NIST-approved algorithms and key lengths
269 before the end of 2020, and that their IPsec VPN vendors guarantee that such upgrades will be
270 available early enough for testing and deployment in the field.

271 The strongest possible cryptographic algorithms and key lengths that are NIST-approved should
272 be used for authentication, encryption, and integrity protection unless they are incompatible with
273 interoperability, performance, and export constraints.

274 In addition to providing specific recommendations related to configuring cryptography for IPsec,
275 this guide presents a phased approach to IPsec planning and implementation that can help in
276 achieving successful IPsec deployments. The five phases of the approach are as follows:

277 1. **Identify Needs**—Identify the need to protect network communications and determine
278 how that need can best be met.

279 2. **Design the Solution**—Make design decisions in four areas: architectural considerations,
280 authentication methods, cryptography policy, and packet filters. The placement of an
281 IPsec gateway has potential security, functionality, and performance implications. An
282 authentication solution should be selected based primarily on maintenance, scalability,
283 and security. Packet filters should apply appropriate protections to traffic and not protect
284 other types of traffic for performance or functionality reasons.

285 3. **Implement and Test a Prototype**—Test a prototype of the designed solution in a lab or
286 test environment to identify any potential issues. Testing should evaluate several factors,
287 including connectivity, protection, authentication, application compatibility,
288 management, logging, performance, the security of the implementation, and component
289 interoperability.

290 4. **Deploy the Solution**—Gradually deploy IPsec throughout the enterprise. Existing
291 network infrastructure, applications, and users should be moved incrementally over time
292 to the new IPsec solution. This provides administrators an opportunity to evaluate the
293 impact of the IPsec solution and resolve issues prior to enterprise-wide deployment.

294 5. **Manage the Solution**—Maintain the IPsec components and resolve operational issues;
295 repeat the planning and implementation process when significant changes need to be
296 incorporated into the solution.

297 As part of implementing IPsec, organizations should also implement additional technical,
298 operational, and management controls that support and complement IPsec implementations.
299 Examples include establishing control over all entry and exit points for the protected networks,
300 ensuring the security of all IPsec endpoints, and incorporating IPsec considerations into
301 organizational policies.

Table of Contents

475

476   **List of Tables**

479

480 **1   Introduction**

481 **1.1   Purpose and Scope**

482 This publication seeks to assist organizations in mitigating the risks associated with the
483 transmission of sensitive information across networks by providing practical guidance on
484 implementing security services based on Internet Protocol Security (IPsec). This document
485 presents information that is independent of particular hardware platforms, operating systems, and
486 applications, other than providing real-world examples to illustrate particular concepts.
487 Specifically, the document includes a discussion of the need for network layer security services,
488 then focuses on how IPsec provides them and how organizations can implement IPsec. The
489 document uses a case-based approach to show how IPsec can be used to provide security for
490 different scenarios. It also describes alternatives to IPsec and discusses the circumstances under
491 which each alternative may be appropriate.

492 **1.2   Document Structure**

493 The remainder of this document is organized into the following sections and appendices:

494   • Section 2 discusses the need for network layer security, introduces the concept of virtual
495   private networking (VPN), and defines the primary VPN architectures for IPsec.
496   • Section 3 explains the Internet Key Exchange (IKE) protocol.
497   • Section 4 covers the fundamentals of IPsec protocols, focusing on Encapsulating Security
498   Payload (ESP).
499   • Section 5 describes the interactions between the IKE and IPsec subsystems.
500   • Section 6 provides information on troubleshooting common situations with IPsec VPNs.
501   • Section 7 points out issues to be considered during IPsec planning and implementation.
502   • Section 8 discusses several alternatives to IPsec and describes when each method may be
503   appropriate.
504   • Section 9 presents several IPsec planning and implementation case studies that show how
505   IPsec could be used in various scenarios.
506   • Section 10 briefly discusses future directions for IPsec.
507   • Appendix A defines the required configuration parameters for IKE and IPsec.
508   • Appendix B discusses the needs for IPsec-related policy and provides examples of
509   common IPsec policy considerations.
510   • Appendix C contains configuration files referenced by the case studies in Section 9.
511   • Appendices D and E contain a glossary and acronym list, respectively.
512   • Appendix F lists the references.

513

514 **2   Network Layer Security**

515 This section provides a general introduction to *network layer security*—protecting network
516 communications at the layer that is responsible for routing packets across networks. It first
517 introduces the Internet Protocol (IP) model and its layers, then discusses the need to use security
518 controls at each layer to protect communications. It provides a brief introduction to IPsec,
519 primarily focused on the types of protection IPsec can provide for communications. This section
520 also provides a brief introduction to VPN services and explains what types of protection a VPN
521 can provide. It introduces different VPN architectures and discusses the features and common
522 uses of each one.[1]

523 **2.1   The Need for Network Layer Security**

524 *IP networking* (sometimes called TCP/IP, although it encompasses more than just TCP, the
525 Transmission Control Protocol) is the standard used throughout the world to provide network
526 communications. IP communications are roughly composed of four layers that work together.
527 When a user wants to transfer data across networks, the data is passed from the highest layer
528 through intermediate layers to the lowest layer, with each layer adding additional information.[2]
529 The lowest layer sends the accumulated data through the physical network; the data is then
530 passed up through the layers to its destination. Essentially, the data produced by a layer is
531 encapsulated in a larger container by the layer below it. The four IP layers, from highest to
532 lowest, are shown in Figure 1.

> **Application Layer.** This layer sends and receives data for particular applications, such as Domain Name System (DNS), web traffic via Hypertext Transfer Protocol (HTTP) and HTTP Secure (HTTPS), and email via Simple Mail Transfer Protocol (SMTP) and the Internet Message Access Protocol (IMAP).
>
> **Transport Layer.** This layer provides connection-oriented or connectionless services for transporting application layer services between networks. The transport layer can optionally assure the reliability of communications. The Transmission Control Protocol (TCP), which provides reliable connection-oriented communications, and the User Datagram Protocol (UDP), which provides unreliable connectionless communications, are commonly used transport layer protocols.

[1] This document discusses only the most common VPN scenarios and uses of IPsec.
[2] At each layer, the logical units are typically composed of a header and a payload. The payload consists of the information passed down from the previous layer, while the header contains layer-specific information such as addresses. At the application layer, the payload is the actual application data.

> **Network Layer.** This layer routes packets across networks. The Internet Protocol (IP) is the fundamental network layer protocol for TCP/IP. Other commonly used protocols at the network layer are the Internet Control Message Protocol (ICMP) and the Internet Group Management Protocol (IGMP).

> **Data Link Layer.** This layer handles communications between the physical network components. The best-known data link layer protocols are Ethernet and the various WiFi standards such as the Institute of Electrical and Electronics Engineers (IEEE) 802.11.

533   **Figure 1: IP Model**

534 Security controls exist for network communications at each layer of the IP model. As previously
535 explained, data is passed from the highest to the lowest layer, with each layer adding more
536 information. Because of this, a security control at a higher layer cannot provide full protection
537 for lower layers, because the lower layers perform functions of which the higher layers are not
538 aware. The following items discuss the security controls that are available at each layer:

539   • **Application Layer.** Separate controls must be established for each application. For
540   example, if an application needs to protect sensitive data sent across networks, the
541   application may need to be modified to provide this protection. While this provides a
542   high degree of control and flexibility over the application's security, it may require a
543   large resource investment to add and configure controls properly for each application.
544
545   Designing a cryptographically sound application protocol is very difficult, and
546   implementing it properly is even more challenging, so creating new application layer
547   security controls is likely to create vulnerabilities. Also, some applications, particularly
548   commercial off-the-shelf (COTS) software, may not be capable of providing such
549   protection.
550
551   While application layer controls can protect application data, they cannot protect
552   communication metadata, such as source and destination IP addresses, because this
553   information exists at a lower layer. Whenever possible, application layer controls for
554   protecting network communications should be standards-based solutions that have been
555   in use for some time. One example is Secure/Multipurpose Internet Mail Extensions
556   (S/MIME) [14], which is commonly used to encrypt email messages. Another example is
557   the Secure Shell (SSH) [15] protocol that encrypts remote login sessions.
558
559   • **Transport Layer.** Controls at this layer can be used to protect the data in a single
560   communication session between two hosts, often called a *netflow*. Because IP
561   information is added at the network layer, transport layer controls cannot protect it. In the
562   past there have been many protocols that protect different netflows, but the current best
563   practice is to use Transport Layer Security (TLS) [16] to protect TCP streams, and
564   Datagram Transport Layer Security (DTLS) [17] to protect UDP datagrams.
565

3

566   The use of DTLS or TLS typically requires each application to support DTLS or TLS;
567   however, unlike application layer controls, which typically involve extensive
568   customization of the application, transport layer controls such as DTLS and TLS are less
569   intrusive because they simply protect network communications and do not need to
570   understand the application's functions or characteristics. Although using DTLS or TLS
571   may require modifying some applications, these protocols are well-tested and are a
572   relatively low-risk option compared to adding protection at the application layer instead.
573
574   Alternatively, an application could use a TLS proxy instead of building native support for
575   DTLS or TLS. The transport layer can only provide transport security, not data origin
576   security. For example, a TLS-based connection between two email servers protects the
577   transport from eavesdroppers but does not protect the message content transmitted within
578   that TLS connection from manipulation by one of the two email servers. DTLS and TLS
579   are sometimes deployed as a generic VPN solution protecting all IP traffic instead of only
580   protecting a netflow. Such VPNs, commonly called SSL-based VPNs, work on the
581   network layer but use an application at the transport layer.
582
583   • **Network Layer.** Controls at this layer apply to all applications and are not application-
584   specific. For example, all network communications between two hosts or networks can be
585   protected at this layer without modifying any applications on the clients or the servers. In
586   many environments, network layer controls such as IPsec provide a much better solution
587   than transport or application layer controls because of the difficulties in adding controls
588   to individual applications. Network layer controls also provide a way for network
589   administrators to enforce certain security policies.
590
591   Another advantage of network layer controls is that since IP information (e.g., IP
592   addresses) is added at this layer, the controls can protect both the data within the packets
593   and the IP information for each packet. However, network layer controls provide less
594   control and flexibility for protecting specific applications than transport and application
595   layer controls.
596
597   • **Data Link Layer.** Data link layer controls are applied to all communications on a
598   specific physical link, such as a dedicated circuit between two buildings or a WiFi
599   network. Data link layer controls for dedicated circuits are most often provided by
600   specialized hardware devices known as *data link encryptors*; data link layer controls for
601   WiFi networks are usually provided through WiFi chipset firmware. Because the data
602   link layer is below the network layer, controls at this layer can protect both data and IP
603   information.
604
605   Compared to controls at the other layers, data link layer controls are relatively simple,
606   which makes them easier to implement; also, they support other network layer protocols
607   besides IP. Because data link layer controls are specific to a particular physical link or
608   local WiFi signal, they are poorly suited to protecting connections to remote endpoints,
609   such as establishing a VPN over the Internet.
610

611   An Internet-based connection is typically composed of several physical links chained
612   together; protecting such a connection with data link layer controls would involve many
613   parties and different protocols for each part of the physical chain. It is easier to consider
614   the internet as a whole to be untrustworthy and use controls at the network, transport, or
615   application layer. Data link layer protocols have been used for many years primarily to
616   provide additional protection for specific physical links that should not be trusted.

617   Because network layer security controls can provide protection for many applications at once
618   without modifying them, these controls have been used frequently for securing communications,
619   particularly over shared networks such as the Internet. Network layer security controls provide a
620   single solution for protecting all data from all applications, as well as protecting IP address,
621   protocol, and port information. However, in many cases, controls at another layer are better
622   suited to providing protection than network layer controls. For example, if only one or two
623   applications need protection, a network layer control may be overkill. An application is often not
624   aware of the (lack of) protection offered by the network or data link layer. Controls at each layer
625   offer advantages and features that controls at other layers do not. Information on data link,
626   transport, and application layer alternatives to network layer controls is provided in Section 8.

627 ## 2.2   The IPsec Protocol

628   IPsec has emerged as the most commonly used network layer security control for protecting
629   communications. IPsec is a framework of open standards for ensuring private communications
630   over IP networks. The Internet Key Exchange (IKE) protocol is used to securely negotiate IPsec
631   parameters and encryption keys. IKE is described in Section 3.

632   The IPsec Working Group at the Internet Engineering Task Force (IETF) is responsible for
633   maintaining and publishing the standards for IKE and IPsec. Documents produced by IETF
634   Working Groups are defined in two types of documents: Request for Comment (RFC), which are
635   completed specifications; and Internet-Drafts, which are working documents that may become
636   RFCs. IKEv2 is specified in [18]. The Encapsulating Security Protocol (ESP), the core IPsec
637   security protocol, is specified in [19]. Algorithm implementation and usage guidelines are
638   specified in [20] for IKEv2 and in [21] for IPsec. Various extensions to IKEv2 have their own
639   RFC specifications. The IKE and IPsec protocols originated at the IETF almost three decades
640   ago. Some of their history, such as the difference between IPsec-v2 and IPsec-v3, has been
641   documented in the IPsec roadmap document [22].

642   Depending on how IPsec is implemented and configured, it can provide any combination of the
643   following types of protection:

644   • **Confidentiality**. IPsec ensures that data cannot be read by unauthorized parties. This is
645   accomplished by encrypting and decrypting data using a cryptographic algorithm and a
646   secret key—a value known only to the two parties exchanging data. The data can only be
647   decrypted by someone who has the secret key. While it is possible to use IPsec without
648   encryption, it is not recommended.

649   • **Integrity**. IPsec determines if data has been changed (intentionally or unintentionally)
650   during transit. The integrity of data can be assured by generating a message
651   authentication code (MAC) value, which is a cryptographic checksum (hash) of the data
652   made with a mutually agreed secret key (different from the encryption secret key). If the
653   data is altered and the MAC's verification will fail.

654   • **Confidentiality and Integrity.** Both types of checks can be combined into one
655   Authenticated Encryption with Associated Data (AEAD) algorithm. This combines
656   symmetric encryption and cryptographic checksums into one process. Both parties still
657   need to have the same secret key and additional data.

658   • **Peer Authentication.** Each IPsec endpoint confirms the identity of the other IPsec
659   endpoint with which it wishes to communicate, ensuring that the network traffic and data
660   is only transmitted to the expected and authorized endpoint.

661   • **Replay Protection.** The same data will not be accepted multiple times, and data is not
662   accepted grossly out of order. This prevents attackers from copying and retransmitting
663   valid IPsec encrypted data for malicious purposes. IPsec (like UDP) does not ensure that
664   data is delivered in the exact order in which it was sent. The receiver has a Replay
665   Window where it will store out of order received messages before decrypting and
666   delivering these messages to the operating system in the right order.

667   • **Traffic Analysis Protection.** When IPsec's tunnel mode is used (see Section 4.1.1), a
668   person monitoring network traffic does not know which parties are communicating, how
669   often communications are occurring, or how much data is being exchanged. While the
670   number and size of the encrypted packets being exchanged can be counted, the traffic
671   flow confidentiality (TFC) capabilities of ESP can pad all packets to a single length
672   (usually the maximum transmission unit [MTU]), and dummy packets can be sent to
673   further obfuscate the timing of the actual communication.

674   • **Access Control.** IPsec endpoints can perform filtering to ensure that only authorized
675   IPsec users can access particular network resources. IPsec endpoints can also allow or
676   block certain types of network traffic, such as allowing Web server access but denying
677   file sharing. This is called *policy-based IPsec*. *Routing-based IPsec* accepts all traffic at
678   the IPsec policy layer, but both endpoints filter valid traffic by setting routes into a
679   specific IPsec interface. In other words, the routing table acts as the policy filter.

680   Policy-based IPsec is more secure than routing-based IPsec, as the security of the policy
681   works independently from the security of the remote endpoint. Policy-based IPsec is not
682   vulnerable to accidental or malicious routing table changes, and it prevents leaking
683   packets to the local network, since local packets do not use the routing table. IPsec-based
684   access control works independently from other access control mechanisms, such as
685   firewall services or other mandatory access control mechanisms.

686   • **Perfect Forward Secrecy (PFS).** IPsec endpoints create session keys that are changed
687   frequently, typically once an hour. Afterwards, the endpoints wipe the old session keys
688   from volatile memory, and no entities are left with a copy of these private decryption
689   keys. Since expired keys are not saved, any encrypted traffic monitored and stored cannot

690   be decrypted at a later time by compromising an IPsec endpoint and obtaining the
691   encryption/decryption keys belonging to past IPsec sessions.

692   Normally, new keys are generated based on the generated shared secret of the original
693   key exchange using a key derivation function (KDF). To guarantee that new key material
694   has no relationship to the old key exchange, fresh session keys can, optionally, be
695   generated by performing a new Diffie-Hellman (DH) key exchange instead of reusing the
696   old key exchange's generated shared secret to generate new session keys. This method of
697   using a fresh key exchange provides *perfect forward secrecy (PFS)*.

698   • **Mobility.** The outer IP address of an endpoint can change without causing an interruption
699   of the encrypted data flow. Since the application is communicating using the inner
700   (encrypted) IP address, it does not matter that the outer IP address changes. This allows a
701   device to switch from WiFi to Ethernet to mobile data without application interruption.

2.3   Virtual Private Networking (VPN)

703   The most common use of IPsec implementations is providing VPN services. A *VPN* is a virtual
704   network, built on top of existing physical networks, that can provide a secure communications
705   mechanism for data and IP information transmitted between networks or between different nodes
706   on the same network. Because a VPN can be used over existing networks, such as the Internet, it
707   can facilitate the secure transfer of sensitive data across public networks. This is often less
708   expensive than alternatives such as dedicated private telecommunication links between
709   organizations or branch offices. Since dedicated private communication lines are often multi-
710   tenant solutions themselves, such as those partitioned via Multi-Protocol Label Switching
711   (MPLS) [23] and run by third-party telecommunication companies, even those dedicated links
712   are now usually protected by an IPsec VPN. Remote access VPNs provide flexible solutions,
713   such as securing communications between remote workers and the organization's servers. A
714   VPN can be established within a single network to protect particularly sensitive communications
715   from other parties on the same network, or even deploy a mesh of IPsec connections between all
716   nodes in a single network so that no unencrypted data ever appears on the network. Section 2.4
717   discusses these different deployment models.

718   Below are further discussions of the cryptographic security services provided by IPsec for VPNs.

2.3.1   Confidentiality

720   VPNs use symmetric cryptography to encrypt and decrypt their command and data channels.
721   Symmetric cryptography is generally more efficient and requires less processing power than
722   asymmetric cryptography, which is why symmetric encryption is typically used to encrypt the
723   bulk of the data being sent over a VPN. NIST-approved algorithms that implement symmetric
724   encryption include Advanced Encryption Standard (AES) and Triple Data Encryption Standard

725   (3DES)[3]. One of the NIST-approved symmetric encryption algorithms is AES-Galois Counter
726   Mode (AES-GCM); see Table 1 for the other NIST-approved symmetric encryption algorithms.

2.3.2   Integrity

728   Integrity is provided by a message authentication algorithm. The algorithm takes input data and a
729   secret integrity key and produces a message authentication code (MAC). The data and MAC are
730   sent across the network. The receiver calculates the MAC on the received data using the same
731   secret integrity key (which has been previously established between the sender and receiver). If
732   there is any change in the message or/and its MAC, a verification of the MAC will fail, and the
733   message can be discarded. Common algorithms that implement integrity protection are:

734   • The keyed-hash message authentication code (HMAC) algorithm specified in FIPS 198
735   [24], which uses a hash function from FIPS 180 [25] (i.e., Secure Hash Algorithm
736   (SHA): SHA-1 or the SHA-2 family of hash functions)[4]
737   • A mode of AES, as specified in FIPS 197 [26]. Included modes are AES-Cipher Block
738   Chaining (AES-XCBC),[5] AES-Cipher-Based Message Authentication Code (AES-
739   CMAC) [27], and AES-Galois Message Authentication Code (AES-GMAC) [28]

2.3.3   Establishment of Shared Secret Keys

741   VPNs typically use the DH key exchange algorithm to create a confidential communication
742   channel to calculate a shared key between the two endpoints that an eavesdropper cannot obtain
743   or compute. DH key exchanges can be based on finite field cryptography ("classic" or "modular"
744   DH) or on elliptic curve (ECDH). After performing the DH key exchange and calculating the
745   shared key, the endpoints still need to authenticate to each other to ensure that the confidential
746   communication channel is set up with the expected party, and not somebody else.

2.3.4   Peer Authentication

748   A digital signature algorithm is used for peer authentication. It uses two separate keys: a public
749   key and a private key. The private key is used to digitally sign the data, and the public key is
750   used to verify the digital signature. These keys are often referred to as *public/private key pairs*.
751   When an individual's private key is used to digitally sign data, only that same individual's
752   corresponding public key can be used to verify the digital signature. Common algorithms that are
753   used to generate and verify digital signatures include RSA, the Digital Signature Algorithm
754   (DSA), and the Elliptic Curve Digital Signature Algorithm (ECDSA).[6] NIST-approved digital
755   signature algorithms are specified in [29].

---

[3]   Triple DES is deprecated and is expected to be disallowed in the near future.
[4]   The term HMAC-SHA-2 is used to describe three members of the HMAC-SHA-2 family, HMAC-SHA256, HMAC-
      SHA384 and HMAC-SHA512
[5]   While commonly deployed on Internet of Things (IoT) devices, AES-XCBC is not a NIST-approved integrity algorithm.
[6]   NIST-approved algorithms must also be used for digital signatures. See https://csrc.nist.gov/projects/cryptographic-
      algorithm-validation-program for information on such algorithms.

756   VPNs usually use asymmetric cryptography for identity authentication. This can be in the form
757   of raw public/private key pair or X.509 certificate-based public/private key pair. A VPN entity is
758   authenticated by proving it has possession of the private key of a known public/private key pair
759   as well as the secret key computed by the parties during the DH key exchange. This binds the
760   private communication channel (i.e., the VPN) to the expected identities. The public key can
761   verify this proof without having a copy of the private key. Thus, as long as both parties each
762   have the other's public key and their own private key, they can establish an authenticated private
763   channel through which they can communicate.

764   A less secure method of identity authentication is using a preshared key (PSK). Parties
765   authenticate each other's identity based on the fact that no one else has possession of this shared
766   key, which must be established out-of-band.[7] A VPN entity's identity is authenticated by proving
767   that it has possession of the PSK as well as the secret key computed by the parties during the DH
768   key exchange. This binds the private communication channel to the expected identities. The
769   main disadvantage of VPNs using PSKs for authentication is that all parties that know the PSK
770   can impersonate every other party in the group. PSKs are also vulnerable to online and offline
771   dictionary attacks. That means that PSKs must be highly random (providing at least 112 bits of
772   security strength) and must not be based on simple words or phrases, otherwise an attacker
773   observing the key exchange can attempt to use an offline brute force attack to find the PSK by
774   calculating the authentication payload based on dictionary words and comparing the generated
775   authentication payloads to the observed authentication payload. Unfortunately, experience has
776   shown that administrators often use weak PSKs that are vulnerable to dictionary attacks.

777   **2.3.5   Deployment Risks**

778   VPNs do not remove all risk from networking, particularly for communications that occur over
779   public networks. One potential problem is the strength of the implementation. For example,
780   flaws in an encryption algorithm or the software implementing the algorithm could allow
781   attackers to decrypt intercepted traffic, and random number generators that do not produce
782   sufficiently random values could provide additional attack possibilities. Another issue is
783   encryption key disclosure; an attacker who discovers a symmetric key could decrypt previously
784   recorded or current traffic. An attacker obtaining the private key of a public/private key pair (or
785   PSK) used for identity authentication could potentially pose as a legitimate user.

786   Another area of risk involves availability. A common model for information assurance is based
787   on the concepts of confidentiality, integrity, and availability. Although VPNs are designed to
788   support confidentiality and integrity, they generally do not improve availability, the ability for
789   authorized users to access systems as needed. In fact, many VPN implementations actually tend
790   to decrease availability somewhat because they add more components, complexity, and services
791   to the existing network infrastructure.

---

[7]   *Out-of-band* refers to using a separate communications mechanism to transfer information. For example, the VPN cannot be
used to exchange the keys securely because the keys are required to provide the necessary protection.

792   Risks are highly dependent upon the chosen VPN architecture and the details of the
793   implementation. Section 2.4 describes the primary VPN architectures.

794   **2.4   Primary IPsec-Based VPN Architectures**

795   There are four primary architectures for IPsec-based VPNs:

796   • Gateway-to-gateway
797   • Remote access
798   • Host-to-host
799   • Mesh

800   **2.4.1   Gateway-to-Gateway**

801   IPsec-based VPNs are often used to provide secure network communications between two
802   networks. This is typically done by deploying a VPN gateway onto each network and
803   establishing a VPN connection between the two gateways. Traffic between the two networks that
804   needs to be secured passes within the established VPN connection between the two VPN
805   gateways. The VPN gateway may be a dedicated device that only performs VPN functions, or it
806   may be part of another network device, such as a firewall or router. Figure 2 shows an example
807   of an IPsec network architecture that uses the gateway-to-gateway model to provide a protected
808   connection between the two networks.

809

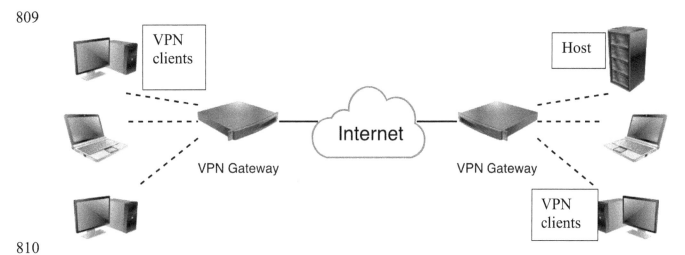

810

Figure 2: Gateway-to-Gateway VPN Architecture Example

811 This model is relatively simple to understand. To facilitate VPN connections, one of the VPN
812 gateways issues a request to the other to establish an IPsec connection. The two VPN gateways
813 exchange information with each other and create an IPsec connection. Routing on each network
814 is configured so that as hosts on one network need to communicate with hosts on the other
815 network, their network traffic is automatically routed through the IPsec connection, protecting it
816 appropriately. A single IPsec connection establishing a tunnel between the gateways can support
817 all communications between the two networks, or multiple IPsec connections can each protect
818 different types or classes of traffic. The gateways connect to each other using IPv4 or IPv6
819 protocols. When using tunnel mode, the IP address family of the outer ESP packets transmitted
820 between the gateways does not need to be the same as the IP address family of the encrypted IP
821 packets. For example, an IPsec connection between the hosts on IPv6 addresses 2001:db8:1:2::45
822 and 2001:db8:1:2::23 could be used to transport IPv4 traffic from 192.0.2.0/24 to
823 198.51.100.0/24. These types of IPsec connections are often called 6in4 or 4in6 to denote the
824 inner and outer IP families.

825 Figure 2 illustrates a gateway-to-gateway VPN that does not provide full protection for data
826 throughout its transit. In fact, the gateway-to-gateway architecture only protects data between the
827 two gateways, as denoted by the solid line. The dashed lines indicate that communications
828 between VPN clients and their local gateway, and between the remote gateway and destination
829 hosts (e.g., servers) are not protected by the gateway-to-gateway architecture. The other VPN
830 models provide protection for more of the transit path. The gateway-to-gateway architecture is
831 most often used when connecting two secured networks, such as linking a branch office to
832 headquarters over the Internet. The gateway-to-gateway architecture is the easiest to implement
833 in terms of user and host management. Gateway-to-gateway VPNs are typically transparent to
834 users; the use of a gateway-to-gateway VPN connection is not noticeable to them. Also, the
835 users' systems and the target hosts (e.g., servers) do not need to have any VPN client software
836 installed, nor should they require any reconfiguration, to be able to use the VPN.

837 If the gateway-to-gateway VPN connects two different organizations, it is possible that some
838 special DNS configuration is required if machines in one network need to be able to reach

839   machines in the other network by DNS name. If machines are found by their IP address, no
840   special DNS handling is required.

841   **2.4.2   Remote Access**

842   An increasingly common VPN architecture is the remote access architecture. The organization
843   deploys a VPN gateway onto its network; each remote access user then establishes a VPN
844   connection between their device (host) and the VPN gateway. As with the gateway-to-gateway
845   architecture, the VPN gateway may be a dedicated device or part of another network device.
846   Figure 3 shows an example of an IPsec remote access architecture that provides a protected
847   connection for the remote user.

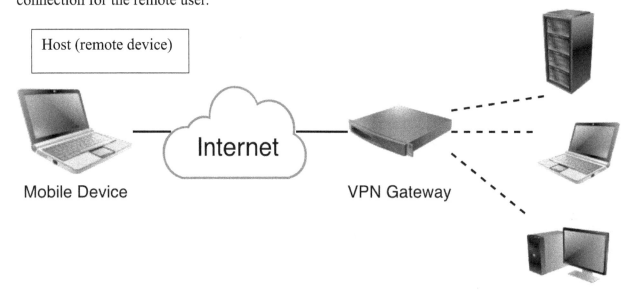

848

Figure 3: Remote Access VPN Architecture Example

849   In this model, IPsec connections are created as needed for each individual mobile device, which
850   have been configured to act as IPsec clients with the organization's IPsec gateway. When a
851   remote user wishes to use computing resources through the VPN, the host initiates
852   communications with the VPN gateway. The user is typically asked by the VPN gateway to
853   authenticate his identity before the connection can be established. The VPN gateway can perform
854   the authentication itself or consult a dedicated authentication server. The client (the remote
855   device in Figure 3) and gateway exchange information, and the IPsec connection is established.
856   The user can now use the organization's computing resources, and the network traffic between
857   the user's host (the remote device in Figure 3) and the VPN gateway will be protected by the
858   IPsec connection.

859   Some organizations do not want to receive all the internet traffic generated by a remote host. If
860   that host is browsing the internet, that traffic will not go through the VPN connection. Only
861   traffic for the organization itself will be sent over the VPN connection. This is called a *split-*
862   *tunnel VPN.* Other organizations do not trust the remote hosts to directly communicate with the
863   internet while being connected via a VPN connection to the organizational computer resources,
864   since that Internet connection could be used to attack or infiltrate the VPN connection. If an

865   organization normally has a strict firewall preventing unauthorized access by the hosts in the
866   local network, it would not want a remote host to bypass this security when it is connecting from
867   a remote location. In that case, a remote host will send all its traffic via the VPN connection to
868   the VPN gateway; this allows IPsec protection to be applied to this traffic as well. Traffic
869   received and decrypted by the VPN gateway that is not meant for the local organization can be
870   sent further to the organization's firewall for inspection, and then sent onwards through the
871   organization's internet connection. Reply traffic similarly will flow back via the organization's
872   firewall to the VPN gateway and will then be sent via the VPN connection to the remote host.

873   As shown in Figure 3, the remote access VPN does not provide full protection for data
874   throughout its transit. The dashed lines indicate that communications between the gateway and
875   the destination hosts (e.g., servers) on the right side of the figure are not protected. The remote
876   access VPN architecture is most often used when connecting hosts on unsecured networks to
877   resources on secured networks, such as linking traveling employees around the world to
878   headquarters over the Internet. The remote access VPN is somewhat complex to implement and
879   maintain in terms of user and host management (the VPN gateway (or a designated device) must
880   manage credentials of all of the remote machines (hosts) and their authorized users and all of
881   these might change often.) Remote access VPNs are typically not transparent to users because
882   they must authenticate before using the VPN. Also, the user's device needs to have a VPN
883   connection configured. Some devices do not allow more than one VPN connection to be active at
884   a time.

885   Remote access users can find themselves on networks that, intentionally or not, cause VPN
886   connections to fail. Some unintentional failures can be worked around by always having the
887   latest software and IPsec VPN features supported.[8] Standard IKE runs over the UDP protocol,
888   and ESP can also use UDP. Some networks block all UDP packets, causing IKE and ESP-over-
889   UDP traffic to be dropped. As a method of last resort, IPsec communication can be tunneled over
890   TCP, which is a more universally accepted protocol. For added insurance, TLS can be used in
891   conjunction with TCP to work around network failures with native IPsec packets.

892   Modern devices often have more than one network interface, and the user can switch between
893   different network interfaces automatically. For instance, when a mobile device loses a WiFi
894   connection, it can automatically fall back to a mobile network (LTE/5G) provider. IPsec
895   provides mobility support to ensure that the VPN connection keeps working without interruption
896   when switching between such networks.

897   **2.4.3 Host-to-Host**

898   The host-to-host VPN architecture is used for a variety of reasons. For security reasons, some
899   hosts may only accept connections protected by a VPN. This makes it more secure against
900   unauthenticated access attempts. For example, if the web server software on the host is

---

[8]   A common unintentional breaking of IPsec happens when a network does not handle IP fragmentation correctly. This can
       cause the setup of the IPsec connection to fail. Modern implementations of IPsec support their own IKE fragmentation that
       ensures the network layer never needs to fragment IKE packets.

901   vulnerable to a specific attack, it is only exposed to those who also have VPN credentials to
902   contact the host. Another common issue is the presence of attackers performing port scans or
903   dictionary attacks against the login method (for example, SSH). With a VPN, these ports are not
904   accessible to attackers.

905   In this case, the organization configures the server to provide VPN services, and the system
906   administrators' machines (or some users' machine) to act as VPN clients. The system
907   administrators use the VPN client when needed to establish protected connections to the remote
908   server. Figure 4 shows an example of an IPsec network architecture that uses the host-to-host
909   architecture to provide a protected connection to a server for an administrator (or just a user).The
910   point of a host-to-host VPN connection is that the traffic is protected all the way from one end to
911   the other of the connection.

912   In this model, IPsec connections are created as needed for each individual VPN user. Users'
913   hosts have been configured to act as IPsec clients with a remote host that is server. When a user
914   wishes to use resources on the server, the user's host initiates IPsec communications with the
915   server. The server acts as an IPsec server that requests the user to authenticate before the
916   connection can be established. The user's host and the server exchange information, and if the
917   authentication is successful, the IPsec connection is established. The user can now access the
918   server, and the network traffic between the user's host and the server will be protected by the
919   IPsec connection.

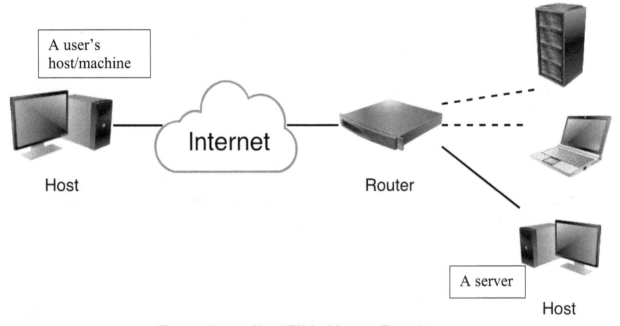

Figure 4: Host-to-Host VPN Architecture Example

920   As shown in Figure 4, the host-to-host VPN provides protection for data throughout its transit.
921   This can be a problem because network-based firewalls, intrusion detection systems, and other
922   network devices cannot be deployed to inspect the traffic in transit, which effectively

923   circumvents certain layers of security.[9] The host-to-host VPN is most often used when a small
924   number of trusted users need to use or administer a remote system that requires the use of
925   insecure protocols (e.g., a legacy system) and which can be updated to provide VPN services.

926   Host-to-host VPNs can be resource-intensive to implement and maintain in terms of
927   configuration management. Host-to-host VPNs are not transparent to users because they must
928   authenticate the user before using the VPN. Also, all end user systems and servers that will
929   participate in VPNs need to have VPN software installed and/or configured. However, the host-
930   to-host architecture can be deployed in a more automated way that requires no end user
931   interaction to establish a VPN.

932   A special case of host-to-host VPNs is a large-scale host-to-host IPsec deployment. This is
933   typically used when one wants to encrypt all connections within a network, cloud, or datacenter.
934   Whenever one node in such a network wishes to communicate with another node in the network,
935   it first establishes an IPsec connection. This is also called *mesh encryption*. Usually, these IPsec
936   connections are packet triggered. An application sends a packet to a remote host. The kernel of
937   the host on which the application runs receives the packet from the application and determines
938   that it does not have an IPsec connection to that remote host, so it triggers the setup of an IPsec
939   connection. Once the IPsec connection is established, the packet is encrypted and sent to the
940   remote host. This way, no unencrypted packet is ever sent over the network. Hosts authenticate
941   each other using X.509 certificates or Domain Name System Security Extensions (DNSSEC).
942   These types of authentication are based on a shared trust anchor, an X.509 certificate authority
943   (CA) or a DNSSEC zone key. This allows hosts to be added to a network without the need to
944   reconfigure all other hosts to learn about the newly deployed host.

945   One advantage of this type of IPsec architecture is that every host is responsible for its own
946   protection; no large expensive IPsec gateways are required, which also means there is no single
947   point of failure added to the network architecture. Hosts in a network can be configured to insist
948   on IPsec, or to attempt IPsec but to allow cleartext communication if that fails. This architecture
949   can be combined with the gateway-to-gateway architecture, where hosts within one network can
950   initiate IPsec to hosts in the network, extending the network mesh encryption to both networks.
951   The two networks are connected by a gateway-to-gateway architecture so the internet can still be
952   used to connect these two networks, at the cost of packets being encrypted twice—once by the
953   host-to-host deployment and once by the gateway-to-gateway deployment.

954   **2.4.3.1 SDN-Based VPN Encryption**

955   *Software Defined Networking* (SDN) is an architecture of dynamic cloud networking. An *SDN*
956   *network* (sometimes called a *Software Defined Wide Area Network*, or *SDWAN*) is a network
957   with a Security Controller and compute nodes. All the nodes (hosts) are configured by the
958   Security Controller, usually via the Network Configuration Protocol (NETCONF) [30]. For
959   nodes within a network, or for nodes between two different networks, the node consults its local

---

9   Device placement can also be an issue in remote access and gateway-to-gateway architectures, but in those architectures, it
     is usually possible to move devices or deploy additional devices to inspect decrypted data. This is not possible with a host-
     to-host architecture.

960   Security Controller. If the nodes have enough resources to set up IPsec, the Security Controllers
961   can relay the authentication and connection parameters to their respective nodes, and the two
962   nodes can then negotiate the IPsec VPN connection.

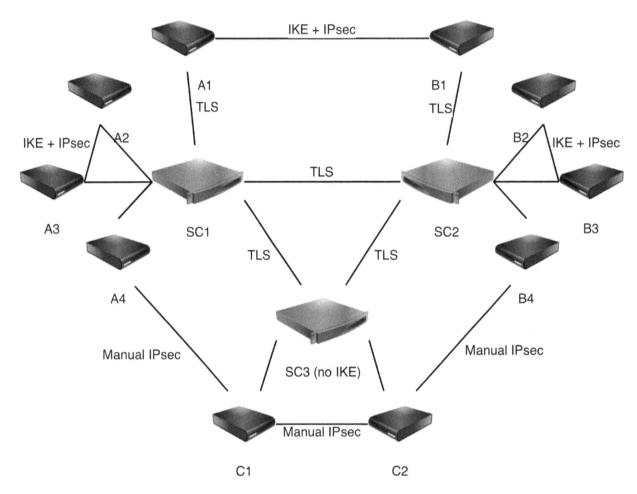

963

964   **Figure 5: SDWAN Architecture Example**

965   This is shown in Figure 5 for communication between the nodes A1 and B1 (at the top of the
966   figure). Host A1 contacts its Security Controller SC1. SC1 and SC2 (host B1's Security
967   Controller) negotiate the IKE and IPsec parameters and convey them to their respective hosts
968   (A1 or B1, as appropriate). Host A1 can now initiate an IKE session with B1 and an IPsec
969   connection is established between A1 and B1. The IPsec secret key material is only known by
970   the A1 and B1 nodes and not by the Security Controller. The hosts could optionally transfer
971   these secret keys to their Security Controller to facilitate monitoring via decryption by the
972   Security Controller or another dedicated monitoring device that takes its configuration from the
973   Security Controller.

974   If the hosts do not have enough resources to negotiate IPsec with many other nodes, each
975   Security Controller can negotiate an IPsec connection on behalf of one of their hosts, and then
976   give the keying material and security policies for the IPsec connection to that host. The two hosts

977   receive the exact IPsec policies and the same encryption keys from their Security Controllers to
978   install in their IPsec subsystems (key exchange is performed by the 2 corresponding Security
979   Controllers). This latter method is called an *IKEless IPsec connection*. It is not the preferred
980   method since, in this case, the Security Controllers are aware of all the secret keys used by their
981   hosts, and the Security Controllers (or whoever manages to get control of one of them) can
982   decrypt all the host-to-host IPsec protected traffic or masquerade as one of the hosts under its
983   control.

984   A third method for configuring hosts by a Security Controller is for the hosts to give their key-
985   exchange public keys to the Security Controller. When two devices establish an IPsec
986   connection, the Security Controller distributes each device's key-exchange public key and a
987   nonce to the other device. Each of the two devices uses the public and nonce from the other
988   device along with own private key to generate a secret shared key which is then used for an IPsec
989   connection. The Security Controller does not know the private keys or the shared key of the
990   IPsec devices. Therefore, the Security Controllers cannot decrypt any host-to-host
991   communication and cannot masquerade as one of the hosts.[10]

992   **2.4.3.2 Anonymous IPsec VPN**

993   The hardest part of rolling out an IPsec deployment is the authentication mechanisms, which
994   depend on the prior deployment of a CA or other identity verifier. If a network only needs to
995   protect itself against passive attackers—that is, attackers that can eavesdrop but not send their
996   own malicious packets—then anonymous IPsec can be used. Therefore, anonymous IPsec
997   connections are typically host-to-host connections and not gateway-based connections because
998   an IPsec gateway typically requires authentication of the connecting host and authenticates itself
999   to that host. A variant of this is server-only authenticated IPsec. This works similarly to regular
1000 HTTPS connections where a client connects to the server and the server has to authenticate itself
1001 to the client, but the client remains anonymous. Any client authentication then happens at the
1002 application layer, and not at the network layer.

1003 The advantage of anonymous IPsec is that it can be rolled out quickly. Once in place and
1004 protecting against passive attackers, the configuration can be slowly migrated to an authenticated
1005 IPsec deployment that also protects against active attacks.

1006 Due to its security risk, anonymous IPsec VPNs are discouraged by NIST.

1007 **2.5 Summary**

1008 Section 2 describes the IP model and its layers—application, transport, network, and data link—
1009 and explains how security controls at each layer provide different types of protection for IP
1010 communications. IPsec, a network layer security control, can provide several types of protection
1011 for data, depending on its configuration. The section describes VPNs and highlights the VPN
1012 architectures. IPsec is a framework of open standards for ensuring private communications over
1013 IP networks that is the standard used for network layer security control. It can provide several

---

[10] This is currently specified in an IETF draft document, draft-carrel-ipsecme-controller-ike [31].

1014   types of protection, including maintaining confidentiality and integrity, preventing packet replay
1015   attacks and traffic analysis, and can incorporate access restrictions.

1016   • IKE is the protocol that is used to negotiate, update, and maintain IPsec connections.
1017   • A VPN is a virtual network built on top of existing networks that can provide a secure
1018   communications mechanism for data and IP information transmitted between networks.
1019   • VPNs can be used to secure communication between individual hosts (host-to-host) or
1020   between multiple networks (gateway-to-gateway), or to provide secure remote access for
1021   mobile devices to a home or enterprise network. Hosts within a network can build a mesh
1022   of IPsec connections between all nodes or can use a Security Controller to assist them
1023   with building up VPN connections to other nodes.
1024   • Although VPNs can reduce the risks of operating over an insecure network, they cannot
1025   eliminate it. For example, a VPN implementation may have flaws in algorithms or
1026   software that attackers can exploit. Also, VPN implementations often have at least a
1027   slightly negative impact on availability, because they add components and services to
1028   existing network infrastructures.
1029

1030 **3   Internet Key Exchange (IKE)**

1031   When two hosts want to set up an IPsec connection with each other, they need to negotiate the
1032   parameters of the IPsec connection, such as the source and destination IP addresses that are
1033   allowed, the encryption algorithms to use, and the cryptographic key material to use for the
1034   encryption and decryption of packets. The hosts also need to authenticate each other. All of this
1035   is done using the Internet Key Exchange (IKE) protocol. The version of the IKE protocol
1036   described in this section is IKE version 2 (IKEv2) and is specified in RFC 7296[11] [18]. The
1037   differences between IKEv1 and IKEv2 are described at the end of this section.

1038   Typically, IKE runs as a privileged process, while IPsec usually runs as part of the operating
1039   system kernel. The IKE process is responsible for configuring the kernel for IPsec. The kernel is
1040   responsible for the actual packet encryption and decryption operations. The IKE process can
1041   insert a policy into the kernel that will instruct the kernel to warn the IKE process when an
1042   unencrypted packet matching certain source and destination IP addresses and/or other criteria is
1043   about to be transmitted. If the peers can mutually authenticate each other, and agree on other
1044   policy details, then the IKE process can negotiate an IPsec tunnel that covers this packet. This is
1045   used for creating IPsec tunnels on demand.

1046   **3.1   Overview of IKE**

1047   The IKE protocol can be considered the command channel. The IPsec protocol is the data
1048   channel; it encrypts and decrypts the IP packets and verifies that the source and destination IP
1049   address conform to the negotiated policies. The IKE protocol command channel itself also needs
1050   to be encrypted to ensure the privacy of the parameters of the IPsec connection. In other words,
1051   first the IKE encrypted connection is established, and then one or more IPsec connections are
1052   established through the protected IKE command channel.[12] An IKE's connection establishment
1053   is called an *IKE Security Association* (IKE SA) [18].[13] An IPsec connection is called an *IPsec SA*
1054   or *Child SA*.[14] Both IKEv2 SAs and IPsec SAs are identified by their Security Parameters Index
1055   (SPI) numbers; for IKEv1, other fields are used as the SA identifier until the IPsec SPIs are
1056   established.

1057   The IKE protocol consists of UDP messages on port 500 and 4500. As shown in Figure 6, each
1058   IKE packet consists of a fixed IKE header (the first five lines of the figure) followed by the
1059   variable-length IKE data.

---

[11]   The base protocol is defined in [18], but many IKE extensions have their own RFCs.
[12]   The IKEv2 protocol has been optimized to do some of this in parallel. As a result, the first IKE connection and the first
       IPsec connection are established at the same time.
[13]   An IKE SA is also called a Parent SA. In IKEv1, these were called ISAKMP SA or "Phase 1".
[14]   In IKEv1, these were called "Phase 2".

Byte 1		Byte 2		Byte 3	Byte 4
IKE SA Initiator's SPI					
IKE SA Responder's SPI					
Next Payload		Major IKE Version	Minor IKE Version	Exchange Type	Flags
Message ID					
Length of total message (IKE header plus data)					
IKE DATA					

1060

Figure 6: The IKEv2 Packet Format

1061 The initiator of an IKE exchange generates a four-byte Initiator SPI. The responder generates the
1062 four-byte Responder SPI. In the first IKE packet sent by the Initiator, the Responder SPI is
1063 0x00000000. The SPI numbers uniquely identify an established IKE SA. Each endpoint selects
1064 the IKE decryption key for an encrypted IKE message based on the SPI numbers.

1065 An IKE session consists of IKE packet *exchanges*. Each exchange consists of a single request
1066 packet and a single reply packet. If there is any packet loss, it is the initiator's responsibility to
1067 retransmit its request.[15] Each exchange packet has a message ID, which starts at zero and is
1068 incremented for each message exchange. The message ID allows detecting retransmitted packets
1069 and handling out-of-order IKE packets. There is a distinct message ID for messages started at
1070 each IKE peer.

1071 The IKEv2 protocol uses two exchanges to establish an IKE SA and an associated IPsec SA. The
1072 IKE SA is then used to send and receive further configuration and management commands. The
1073 first exchange is called IKE_SA_INIT, and the second exchange is called IKE_AUTH. Together
1074 these two exchanges are referred to as the *initial exchanges*. Once these two exchanges are
1075 completed, both the initiator and the responder have established the IKE SA and one IPsec SA.
1076 Once the IKE SA is established, other additional exchange types are used to establish additional
1077 IPsec SAs, rekey the existing IKE SA or IPsec SAs, make configuration changes, perform a
1078 liveness detection of peers, and terminate IKE or IPsec SAs.

1079 The following sections describe the IKE exchanges in detail and explain how they work together
1080 to establish IPsec connections.

1081 **3.2   IKE Exchange Types**

1082 The exchange type for additional IPsec SA messages is called CREATE_CHILD_SA. Another
1083 common exchange type is the INFORMATIONAL exchange, which is used for notification
1084 messages such as IPsec SA deletions, rekeying, liveness (dead peer detection), and mobility
1085 updates. Each exchange can relay additional information about supported features or algorithms
1086 using Notify payloads.

---

[15]   In IKEv1, either party could retransmit, which led to race conditions and amplification attacks.

3.2.1   The IKE_SA_INIT Exchange

1087

1088   The IKE_SA_INIT exchange sends the cryptographic IKE proposals for setting up the encrypted
1089   IKE SA. Each proposal consists of a list of components needed to establish an IKE SA. These
1090   components are called *transforms*. For IKEv2, four types of transforms are required: encryption
1091   (AEAD algorithms or encryption algorithms), integrity (none for AEAD[16], or a MAC otherwise),
1092   (Elliptic Curve) Diffie-Hellman, and Pseudo Random Function (PRF). The IKE_SA_INIT
1093   exchange also includes data that will be used to generate a shared secret that is used to derive
1094   symmetric keys to protect later traffic between the two peers, such as the sender's (EC)DH
1095   public value (carried in the Key Exchange [KE] payload), a random nonce (in the nonce
1096   payload), and both IPsec SPIs (in the IKE Header). The initiator can propose multiple alternative
1097   transform combinations, and the responder picks out its preferred proposal with preferred
1098   transforms and returns a single proposal with those transforms and its own KE and nonce
1099   payloads and a responder SPI.

1100   The initiator needs to know or guess the cryptographic policy that is accepted by the responder.
1101   The initiator sends a list of transforms that represents its policy. For the initiator's most preferred
1102   (EC)DH Key Exchange algorithm, it will include the corresponding KE payload (e.g., a EC
1103   public key). If it turns out that the responder does not allow this (EC)DH algorithm, the
1104   responder will reply with an INVALID_KE notification that contains the responder's preferred
1105   value based on the list that the initiator sent. The initiator can use this to create a new
1106   IKE_SA_INIT packet with a proper KE payload that is acceptable to both initiator and responder
1107   policies.

1108   Since an (EC)DH computation is CPU intensive, a malicious entity could send many spoofed
1109   IKE_SA_INIT messages, causing the responder to perform multiple (EC)DH calculations,
1110   resulting in a denial of service attack. When a responder deems it is under attack, it may respond
1111   to an IKE_SA_INIT message with a special COOKIE payload, instead of the regular payloads.
1112   The initiator has generated this COOKIE value so it can determine that it has recently generated
1113   this COOKIE for a client that is still using the same IP address as when it was given this
1114   COOKIE payload. The initiator must resend its IKE_SA_INIT message and include the given
1115   COOKIE. This assures the responder that the initiator is a participant in the IKE exchange and
1116   not simply sending malicious packets using a forged (spoofed) IP address.

1117   The IKE_SA_INIT exchange is also used to detect the presence of network address translation
1118   (NAT) devices. If NAT is detected, the IKE negotiation will move to port 4500, and the IPsec
1119   connection will be configured to use UDP or TCP encapsulation to avoid problems with the
1120   NAT device rewriting the IP address of the IPsec packets. Often, NAT routers also drop all IP
1121   protocols except UDP and TCP, so by encapsulating the IPsec (ESP) packets into UDP or TCP,
1122   the packets will not be dropped by the NAT router. The endpoint behind the NAT device will
1123   also send one-byte KEEPALIVE packets, typically at 20 second intervals, to ensure that the
1124   NAT device will keep the port mapping open that is used by the endpoint behind NAT. This is

---

[16]   AEAD algorithms combine encryption and integrity using a single private key. For the IKEv2 protocol, AEAD algorithms
       are listed as encryption algorithms. The (separate) integrity algorithm for AEAD is either not included or the special value
       for None is used.

1125   especially important with deployments of Carrier Grade NAT (CGN) that are typically deployed
1126   on mobile data networks (LTE/5G). The KEEPALIVE packets serve no purpose beyond passing
1127   the NAT device and are discarded by any endpoint IPsec stack that receives them.

1128   After the IKE_SA_INIT exchange has completed, both endpoints have performed the (EC)DH
1129   key exchange and have generated the secret value called the SKEYSEED. All encryption and
1130   authentication keys will be derived from this value using the negotiated PRF transform.[17] From
1131   here on, all further packets are encrypted. However, both the initiator and the responder still need
1132   to authenticate each other's identity.

3.2.2   The IKE_AUTH Exchange

1134   The peers still need to verify each other's identities and prove that the initial unencrypted IKE
1135   SA messages were not modified in transit. The IKE_AUTH exchange contains the payloads
1136   needed for the receiver to authenticate the sender and its previous IKE_SA_INIT exchange. The
1137   IKE_AUTH exchange also contains payloads to negotiate the first IPsec SA, such as the
1138   proposals and transforms to negotiate the cryptographic parameters, the source/destination
1139   packet policies for the IPsec SA in the form of traffic selectors for the initiator (TSi) and
1140   responder (TSr), and other options such as the mode of the IPsec SA and Configuration Payload
1141   requests for obtaining an IP address and a DNS nameserver IP address.

1142   Since authentication can involve X.509 certificates and intermediary CA certificates, this packet
1143   can end up being larger than the network MTU. To work around networks that do not handle IP
1144   fragmentation properly, the IKE protocol itself supports fragmentation to prevent fragmentation
1145   at the network layer. Typically, only the IKE_AUTH packets trigger IKE fragmentation.

1146   Typical authentication methods are X.509 certificates, raw public keys (e.g., RSA or ECDSA),
1147   or PSKs. IKE supports the Extensible Authentication Protocol (EAP). If EAP authentication is
1148   required, more than one IKE_AUTH exchange might be required to complete the authentication.
1149   The authentication method can be different between the two endpoints, although they often use
1150   the same method. One example of using different authentication methods by each party is a
1151   remote access VPN where the server is authenticated using its X.509 certificate, but clients are
1152   authenticated via EAP-TLS.[18]

1153   Once the IKE_SA_INIT and IKE_AUTH exchanges have successfully completed, the two hosts
1154   have set up an IKE SA and an IPsec SA. Any further communication will be sent using the
1155   encrypted and authenticated IKE SA.

---

[17] Usually, the integrity algorithm and the PRF negotiated are the same algorithm. When using an AEAD cipher that does not
      require an integrity algorithm, the PRF negotiated is obviously a different algorithm—usually a hash function from the
      SHA-2 family.
[18] Since IPsec is usually a system service, using a certificate on the client would require administrative privileges on the client.
      If EAP credentials are used on the client instead, they could be stored in the non-administrative user's own profile.

1156   **3.2.2.1   Traffic Selectors**

1157   The IKE_AUTH exchange negotiates the IPsec SA network parameters, such as source and
1158   destination IP address, address family, source and destination ports, and protocol, using traffic
1159   selectors. A traffic selector consists of:

1160   • The traffic selector type (e.g., IPv4 or IPv6 type)
1161   • The IP address range (start address and end address)
1162   • The IP protocol number (0 means all protocols)
1163   • The port range (start and end port, 0-65535 means all ports)[19]

1164   Additional traffic selector components are possible, too, such as Network Label or Security
1165   Context.

1166   Traffic selectors are negotiated in sets of two. A set of two traffic selectors denotes the policy for
1167   the source and destination traffic of one (inbound or outbound) IPsec SA. The IKE_AUTH
1168   request contains at least the TSi and TSr. The TSi describes the sending and receiving address of
1169   the initiator, and the TSr describes the sending and receiving address of the responder.

1170   IKEv2 allows the concept of narrowing, where the responder picks a subset of the TSi/TSr that
1171   the initiator requested. This facilitates setting up a number of smaller-range IPsec SAs instead of
1172   one large network-to-network IPsec SA. This can enhance parallel processing. It is also used for
1173   the initiator obtaining an IP address from the responder where the initiator requests every address
1174   on the internet (by requesting 0.0.0.0/0) and is narrowed down by the responder to one IP
1175   address (for example, 192.0.2.1/32).

1176   An additional traffic selector pair can be included that contains the actual source, destination, and
1177   protocol values from the packet that triggered the IKE session at the initiator. This assists the
1178   responder in narrowing traffic selectors to a range that includes the traffic that the initiator wants
1179   to send to the responder.

1180   **3.2.2.2   Configuration Payloads**

1181   Optionally, during IKE_AUTH, the hosts can also exchange Configuration Payloads (CPs). The
1182   initiator can request a number of configuration options, and the responder can respond with
1183   appropriate values. The main CPs are:

1184   • Internal IPv4 and IPv6 address and netmask
1185   • Internal IPv4 and IPv6 DNS server to use as generic DNS resolver
1186   • Internal IPv4 or IPv6 subnet
1187   • Internal IPv4 or IPv6 Dynamic Host Configuration Protocol (DHCP) relay address
1188   • Internal DNS domains for domains that must be resolved via the VPN
1189   • Internal DNSSEC trust anchors to use for internal DNSSEC-signed domains

---

[19]   For protocols without ports, 0 is used. For protocols with no ports but types, such as ICMP, the value is used to denote type
       ranges.

1190   • Application version

1191   All these CPs enable the remote access VPN client to find and use resources on the remote
1192   network. And by obtaining an IP address on that remote network, other hosts on that network can
1193   potentially reach the remote VPN clients as if they were present locally. CPs are not used and are
1194   ignored on gateway-to-gateway and host-to-host IPsec deployments.

1195   CPs are the successor to the IKEv1 non-standard XAUTH and ModeCFG payloads.

3.2.3 The CREATE_CHILD_SA Exchange

1197   The CREATE_CHILD_SA exchange is used for three separate tasks:

1198   • Create an additional IPsec SA
1199   • Rekey an IPsec SA
1200   • Rekey the IKE SA

1201   Creating an additional IPsec SA uses similar IPsec payloads as those used to create the initial
1202   IPsec SA in the IKE_AUTH exchange. Either endpoint can initiate a CREATE_CHILD_SA
1203   exchange. Lifetimes for IKE and IPsec SAs are not negotiated. Each peer is responsible for
1204   rekeying the relevant SAs before the lifetime of their local policy is exceeded.

1205   *Rekeying* is the process of creating fresh cryptographic keys for an IKE SA or IPsec SA. IKE and
1206   IPsec keys are ephemeral and only stored in volatile memory for the duration of the session.
1207   Once an SA is rekeyed, the old cryptographic keys are wiped from memory. In the event of a
1208   compromise of one of the IPsec hosts, only the current session keys are still in memory and
1209   previously recorded sessions cannot be decrypted. IKE SA and IPsec SA session keys typically
1210   have a lifetime of one to eight hours. A rekey request can be for one of the IPsec SAs or for the
1211   IKE SA. A new IPsec SA is negotiated and installed. The outbound IPsec SA is used
1212   immediately. Once traffic is received on the new inbound IPsec SA, the old IPsec SAs are
1213   deleted. This ensures that rekeying does not lead to any traffic flow interruptions or leaking of
1214   unencrypted packets. Once an IKE rekey is complete, the associated IPsec SAs of the old IKE
1215   SA are transferred to the new IKE SA. The old IKE SA is then deleted.

3.2.4 The INFORMATIONAL Exchange

1217   The purpose of the IKE INFORMATIONAL exchange is to provide the endpoints with a way to
1218   send each other status and error messages. Some commonly used informational messages are:

1219   • Delete one or more IPsec SAs
1220   • Delete this IKE SA
1221   • Liveness probe (aka Dead Peer Detection (DPD))
1222   • Mobility IP address updates for Mobile IKE (MOBIKE)

1223   Either endpoint can initiate an informational exchange. The other endpoint is obliged to return an
1224   answer to prevent the initiator (of the informational exchange) from retransmitting. A delete

1225 message denotes the SPI of the IPsec SAs or IKE SA to be deleted. Deleting the IKE SA will
1226 also cause all of its IPsec SAs to be deleted.

1227 An endpoint that has not received any IPsec traffic in a while might want to verify if the remote
1228 endpoint is still alive. To do so, it can send an informational exchange message (i.e., a probe
1229 message) containing zero payloads.[20] An endpoint receiving such an informational message must
1230 respond with an empty informational message. If these probes are not answered for a configured
1231 time period, the IKE SA and IPsec SA are terminated.

1232 A mobile device that is switching its connection (e.g., from LTE/5G to WiFi) needs to send an
1233 informational message with a notification to its remote endpoint. The remote endpoint uses both
1234 the content of the informational message, as well as the IP addresses observed from the IKE
1235 packet itself, as an indication for which IP address to use as the updated IP address for the
1236 mobile endpoint. Successful decryption of the packet (with properly incremented Message ID to
1237 prevent replays) verifies the new IP address to use. This process is called Mobile IKE
1238 (MOBIKE) and is specified in [32].

3.3   IKE Authentication Models

1240 Different deployments require different authentication methods. Usually, hosts authenticate each
1241 other using the same authentication method. But sometimes a client host authenticates a server
1242 host differently from the method used by the server to authenticate the client.

3.3.1   Certificate-Based Authentication

1244 This method, also called *machine certificate authentication*, is most often used for deploying
1245 IPsec within an organization when it involves a large number of devices. The organization can
1246 set up a new internal X.509 certificate deployment or reuse an existing X.509 certificate-based
1247 solution. Setting up a new host does not require any changes to the already deployed hosts.
1248 Certificate Revocation Lists (CRLs) and the Online Certificate Store Protocol (OCSP) can be
1249 used to revoke a particular certificate. Remote access VPN clients are often authenticated using
1250 X.509 certificates. Cloud (mesh) encryption also often uses certificate-based authentication.

1251 A host that requires the other end to authenticate itself using certificates can send a CERTREQ
1252 payload (during IKE_SA_INIT or IKE_AUTH). Both parties then exchange their certificates in
1253 CERT payloads during the IKE_AUTH exchange. Intermediate CAs can also be sent as part of
1254 the CERT payload.[21]

1255 Since certificate-based authentication requires certificates generated by CAs that may not be
1256 trusted by the organizations verifying the certificates, this method is not always a usable solution
1257 to connect two different organizations, as one (or both) of the organizations would need to trust

---

[20] There will be one encrypted payload containing zero payloads. These probes are sometimes combined with other features, in
      which case other payloads may be present within the encrypted payload.
[21] Some implementations have (wrongly) implemented sending multiple intermediate CA chains using PKCS#7. This has
      caused some interoperability issues. It is best to avoid intermediate CAs when possible.

1258   an external CA party not under their own control. For US government organizations, the Federal
1259   Bridge CA can be used as a mutually trusted CA.

1260   ### 3.3.2   Extensible Authentication Protocol (EAP)

1261   EAP is a framework for adding arbitrary authentication methods in a standardized way to any
1262   protocol. It uses a model of a client, a server, and a backend authentication, authorization, and
1263   accounting (AAA) server. The client initiates an EAP authentication to the server. The server
1264   forwards these messages to and from the AAA server. The AAA server will let the server and
1265   client know that the client and server have successfully authenticated each other. AAA protocols
1266   with EAP support include RADIUS [33] and Diameter [34].

1267   The most common EAP method used with IKEv2 is EAP-Transport Layer Security (EAP-TLS),
1268   although EAP-Microsoft Challenge Handshake Authentication Protocol version 2 (EAP-
1269   MSCHAPv2) is used as well. EAP-TLS uses certificates issued to users, instead of certificates
1270   issued to hosts. Some devices, such as mobile phones, often do not make such a distinction.
1271   However, laptops generally have non-privileged users that cannot modify the operating system's
1272   machine certificate store. These users cannot install a machine certificate but can install a
1273   certificate for themselves for use with EAP-TLS.

1274   Usually, Clients use EAP to authenticate themselves to the server, but the server is authenticated
1275   by the clients using regular certificate-based authentication.

1276   ### 3.3.3   Raw Public Key Authentication

1277   Authentication using the raw public key of the other entity in a communication (there are no
1278   certificates which bind the public key with the other entity's identity) is mostly used for Internet
1279   of Things (IoT) devices or when authentication of the public keys is done via publication in
1280   DNSSEC.[22] IoT devices often do not have the memory, storage, or CPU capacity to perform
1281   X.509 certificate validation. These devices often have a hard-coded public key of the other end
1282   in firmware for authenticating its signatures.

1283   When public keys are stored in DNS, and the DNS is secured against tampering or spoofing
1284   using DNSSEC, there is no more need to use X.509 certificates. Certificates provide trust via the
1285   entity that signs the certificate, but in this case the DNS itself containing the public key is already
1286   signed. The trust anchor is not a CA, but a DNSSEC trust key responsible for that part of the
1287   DNS hierarchy. And instead of certificates stating the validity period of the public key, raw
1288   public keys in DNS are valid as long as these are still published in the DNS. DNSSEC prevents
1289   replaying of old DNS data by adding signature lifetimes to DNS records. This type of
1290   deployment is most commonly used within a single administrative network, similar to machine-
1291   based certificate authentication.

---

[22]   DNSSEC is a system of digital signatures to authenticate DNS content. The DNSSEC core specifications are defined in
       IETF RFCs 4033, 4034, and 4035.

1292 **3.3.4 Pre-shared Secret Key (PSK) Authentication**

1293 PSK-based authentication is often deployed because it is the easiest to configure. Each end of the
1294 communication has the identity of the other end and their pre-shared key. It does not require
1295 generating public keys or certificates or running an EAP infrastructure. It is most commonly
1296 used for gateway-to-gateway deployments, as it does not involve adding a third-party trust
1297 anchor to the VPN gateway device.

1298 Some deployments use a PSK shared with all remote access VPN clients. Once the PSK has been
1299 obtained by an attacker, it can be used to impersonate the remote access VPN server. Even if the
1300 clients are using one-time passwords (OTPs), a man-in-the-middle attacker can obtain an OTP
1301 and log in as the remote user to the real remote access VPN. Therefore, group PSKs are strongly
1302 discouraged.

1303 PSKs are often derived from dictionary words and are less than 32 characters long. Such insecure
1304 deployments are vulnerable to offline dictionary attacks.[23] PSKs must have a high entropy value.
1305 A good PSK is pseudo-randomly created and has at least 128 bits of entropy.

1306 **3.3.5 NULL Authentication**

1307 NULL authentication is a special kind of authentication. It really means that no authentication is
1308 required. There are two common use cases for this.

1309 The first use case is to deploy IPsec to a large number of nodes where the goal is to only protect
1310 against passive attacks. It does not protect against attackers that can perform a man-in-the-middle
1311 attack. An advantage is that no authentication system, such as certificates, EAP, or DNSSEC
1312 needs to be deployed. For small-scale deployments this method should never be used, and strong
1313 PSKs should be used instead. Sometimes a NULL authentication deployment is gradually
1314 upgraded to an authenticated deployment.

1315 The second use case only uses NULL authentication for the initiator. The responder still
1316 authenticates itself to the client using another authentication method, such as by a machine
1317 certificate. This creates a situation that is similar to HTTPS-based web sites: the client remains
1318 anonymous, but the server is authenticated. This is the method used for internet-based
1319 opportunistic IPsec, where two IPsec hosts attempt to establish an IPsec connection without a
1320 pre-existing configuration or knowledge of each other. This usually involves authentication
1321 based on DNSSEC or a widely acknowledged CA such as Let's Encrypt.[24] The advantage of this
1322 type of deployment is that only the servers need to have an identity for authentication. The
1323 clients (usually laptops and phones) do not need to have any kind of identity and can remain
1324 anonymous, at least at the network layer. Similar to HTTPS, the application layer might require
1325 the client to authenticate before it is allowed to access a particular resource.

---

[23] Technically, the attacker needs to man-in-the-middle the VPN client for one IKE_INIT and IKE_AUTH exchange; then the
attacker can go offline for the dictionary attack,

[24] Let's Encrypt is a non-profit CA that has automated the deployment of free SSL/TLS certificates used to secure website
communication, but their certificates can be used for IKE/IPsec as well. https://www.letsencrypt.org

1326 NIST does not recommend the use of NULL authenticated-based IPsec. Any deployment of
1327 NULL authenticated IPsec must be categorized as being identical to plaintext unprotected
1328 network traffic.

1329 **3.4   Network Address Translation (NAT)**

1330 During the IKE_SA_INIT exchange, both endpoints exchange information about what they
1331 believe their IP address is.[25] The other end will confirm if that matches the source address of the
1332 packet they received. If the endpoints detect that a NAT is present, they will move further IKE
1333 communication from port 500 to port 4500. The change of UDP port was originally done to
1334 prevent bad interaction with NAT devices that tried to support "IPsec passthrough". This feature
1335 caused more harm than good, and by moving to a new port, the IPsec passthrough modifications
1336 performed by NAT devices were avoided.

1337 These days, no NAT devices perform IPsec passthrough. Once an IPsec SA has been negotiated,
1338 the hosts will also enable UDP or TCP encapsulation of ESP packets to facilitate traversing the
1339 NAT over a single port. This avoids two problems. The first problem is that NAT devices
1340 commonly only support UDP and TCP, meaning that IPsec (ESP) packets would not be dropped
1341 by some NAT devices. The second problem is that the NAT device needs to keep a port mapping
1342 between the internal device's ports used and how these ports are mapped onto the NAT device's
1343 public facing ports. It is easiest if one device behind the NAT device only needs one port
1344 mapping for IKE and IPsec (ESP) traffic. The host behind NAT will also send one-byte
1345 keepalive packets to ensure that the NAT device does not expire its NAT port mapping if the
1346 VPN does not produce any traffic for some time. Otherwise, if the remote IPsec host starts
1347 sending traffic towards the NAT device, the NAT device would no longer remember which
1348 internal device to forward that traffic to, and the IPsec connection would no longer function.

1349 Some cloud providers issue an ephemeral or semi-static public IP address to some virtual
1350 machines inside their cloud. The virtual machines are deployed with only an internal [35] IP
1351 address. The cloud infrastructure uses NAT to translate the public IP address to the virtual
1352 machine's private IP address. This NAT will also trigger the NAT traversal mechanism of IKE.
1353 This poses another problem. If the IPsec tunnel is configured with the public IP address as the
1354 tunnel endpoint, the virtual machine cannot create packets with its public IP address as the
1355 source address, since this public IP address is not configured on the machine itself. Packets
1356 received after decryption are dropped because the operating system is not looking for packets
1357 with the public IP address. A common workaround is for such virtual machines to configure the
1358 public IP address on one of their network interfaces.

1359 **3.5   IKE Fragmentation**

1360 IKE packets can be larger than the common ethernet MTU of 1500 bytes. If these packets are
1361 sent over the network, they will most likely be fragmented. Too often, those fragments will be
1362 dropped by a firewall and the host will fail to receive the fragments for reassembly. This problem

---

[25] Technically, they exchange SHA-1 hashes of their IP addresses so as to add some level of privacy regarding the pre-NAT IP
      addresses used.

1363   is avoided by using IKE fragmentation, which fragments the packets at the application layer
1364   instead of the network layer.

1365   IKEv2 fragmentation is specified in RFC 7383 [36]. The main difference with the IKEv1
1366   vendor-specific implementations is that IKEv2 fragments are encrypted. This makes it harder for
1367   an attacker to interfere. Note that while the fragments are encrypted, the fragments are not (yet)
1368   authenticated because the IKE exchange has not yet completed. Once all fragments have been
1369   received, the original IKE packet can be reconstructed and processed as if it was received in one
1370   packet.

1371   IKEv2 fragmentation is supported for every exchange type except IKE_SA_INIT. Typically,
1372   only the IKE_AUTH exchange requires fragmentation, since that exchange carries the big X.509
1373   certificates.

3.6   Mobile IKE (MOBIKE)

1375   It is common these days that devices, such as mobile phones and laptops, have multiple network
1376   interfaces. This allows those devices to switch to cheaper and/or faster networks when available.
1377   Phones may use the local WiFi network at the office or at home and mobile networks (5G/LTE)
1378   at other locations. Switching also happens when an existing network connection suddenly
1379   degrades. Switching networks changes the source IP address used by the device. VPN traffic is
1380   still sent to the old, no longer used IP address until the device establishes a new IPsec
1381   connection.

1382   MOBIKE [32] addresses this issue. It assumes that an internal IP address is assigned by the VPN
1383   on the device using CPs. This internal IP address will remain with this device, regardless of the
1384   outer IP address used by the device. Once a device switches between its network interfaces, it
1385   will send an INFORMATIONAL exchange packet with an UPDATE_SA_ADDRESS
1386   notification. This packet will be sent using the new IP address. The VPN server will be able to
1387   recognize the IPsec SA based on the SPI numbers, despite the fact that it is suddenly coming
1388   from a different IP address. Once decrypted and authenticated, the VPN server will notice the
1389   UPDATE_SA_ADDRESS payload and change the endpoint IP address (and port if
1390   encapsulation is used due to NAT). It will reply with a confirmation message. At this point, all
1391   IPsec SA traffic is sent and received using the client's new IP address. Since the VPN client's
1392   applications are only using the obtained VPN IP address for communication to the remote access
1393   network, and this IP address does not change when the device itself changes its network interface
1394   and outer IP address, all existing connections remain intact. The applications are not even aware
1395   that the network interfaces have switched.

1396   A device that wakes up from battery saving mode will generally send a MOBIKE update
1397   whether or not its IP address changed. This ensures any NAT state updates that have happened
1398   since the device went to sleep are reported back to the VPN server. For example, the NAT device
1399   might have terminated the unused NAT port mapping between the device and the VPN server.
1400   The MOBIKE packet will create a new fresh NAT port mapping entry, and the VPN server will
1401   immediately be able to update the client's IP address and port number and activate the updated
1402   VPN connection.

1403   MOBIKE allows for more complicated setups with multiple IP addresses. While MOBIKE can
1404   be used as a failover mechanism for the gateway-to-gateway architecture, care should be taken
1405   with such a deployment. If one of the endpoints is compromised, its state could be copied onto a
1406   machine on the other side of the world, and a MOBIKE update message could be sent to redirect
1407   all traffic to the rogue location. The most secure option is to disable MOBIKE unless the IPsec
1408   configuration is for a remote access VPN client.

1409   ## 3.7   Post-Quantum Preshared Keys (PPKs)

1410   It is unclear when a quantum computer will become available. Sufficiently large quantum
1411   computers will be able to break the finite field (classic) DH and ECDH key exchanges within the
1412   timeframe in which it would be expected that IPsec traffic should remain confidential. That is,
1413   the key exchange could be broken in weeks or months, while the expectation of confidentiality
1414   would be in the timeframe of decades. Adversaries could store today's encrypted
1415   communications for later decryption using quantum computers. This problem is not unique to
1416   IKE. Other encryption protocols, such as TLS, suffer from the same problem. It is expected that
1417   in the near future, quantum-resistant algorithms will be standardized and deployed for IKE, TLS,
1418   and other protocols. Until then, some deployments of IKE and IPsec might use PPKs to
1419   strengthen the current algorithms against potential future attacks using quantum computers.

1420   With the exception of IKEv1 using a very strong PSKs, all IKEv1 and IKEv2 configurations are
1421   vulnerable to quantum computers. IKEv2 supports Postquantum Preshared Keys (PPKs) [37] as
1422   a countermeasure. For the purpose of defending against quantum computers, the PPK works
1423   similarly to the PSK in IKEv1 in that the PPK is mixed into the key derivation process in
1424   addition to the DH values. The PPK must be a cryptographically strong random key and is
1425   exchanged out of band. PPKs are identified by a static or ephemeral PPK Identity. This can be
1426   used to protect the identity of the connecting clients and facilitates the use of OTPs as the source
1427   of the PPK.

1428   IKEv2 allows the gradual migration of a network from not using PPK to using PPK. First, some
1429   hosts are configured with PPK, and when two hosts both support PPK and have each other's
1430   PPK ID for which they find a matching PPK, the hosts will use the PPK as an additional input to
1431   create the KEYMAT and SKEYSEED that are used as input to the PRFs that generate the keying
1432   material for the IKE and IPsec SAs. Once all hosts support PPK, their configurations can be
1433   updated to mandate PPK.

1434   While this protects the IPsec SAs since their key material derivation depends on the PPK, the
1435   initial IKE SA DH process is not protected by the PPK and can still be broken by a quantum
1436   computer. This will lead to a loss of privacy of the IKE identities and other information
1437   exchanged during the initial IKE Exchange, such as the traffic selectors used for the first IPsec
1438   SA. This can be prevented if the IKE implementation allows setting up a childless IKE SA
1439   (without IPsec) and then immediately rekeying the IKE SA. This rekeyed IKE SA is protected by
1440   the PPK, and IPsec SAs can then be set up using this new IKE SA without exposing any
1441   information to adversaries with quantum computers.

1442   PPKs shall have at least of 128 bits of entropy.

1443   **3.8   IKE Redirect**

1444   The IKE Redirect [38] notify payload allows an IPsec server to send a redirection request to
1445   connecting or connected VPN clients. This can be used to reduce the load of overloaded IPsec
1446   servers or to take a server out of use (for instance, to update its operating system). Clients being
1447   redirected MUST use the same credentials they were originally using before being redirected. A
1448   redirection message includes an IP address or DNS name of the forwarding VPN that the VPN
1449   client will need to initiate a connection with .

1450   Redirected messages sent in IKE_AUTH are only processed after both ends have authenticated
1451   each other. This allows a server to only send specific clients to another server, for instance all
1452   clients of a certain customer in a multi-tenant deployment or some individual power users
1453   generating a lot of traffic. But it still requires that the (overloaded) server performs full IKE
1454   exchanges to all connecting clients, only to redirect them to different server hosts.

1455   Redirected messages sent in IKE_SA_INIT are not authenticated. Clients that accept such
1456   redirected messages should take necessary precautions to prevent denial of service attacks. The
1457   advantage for the host performing the redirection is that it can redirect clients without performing
1458   a full IKE exchange.[26] The disadvantage is that redirections in IKE_SA_INIT cannot select the
1459   specific clients for redirection by their IDs, since the client ID has not yet been transmitted to the
1460   server.

1461   Redirected messages can be used to provide a redundant set of servers for the gateway-to-
1462   gateway deployment. A failing server can redirect clients to the other (backup) server. In such an
1463   architecture, it is recommended that redirect messages be limited for each endpoint based on
1464   preconfigured IP addresses.

1465   **3.9   Differences Between IKEv2 and the Obsolete IKEv1**

1466   The IKEv2 protocol builds on the lessons learned with IKEv1. IKEv2 is simpler, faster, and
1467   more secure. IKEv2 has some important new features over IKEv1, such as mobility support
1468   (MOBIKE), support for newer cryptographic algorithms, anti-distributed denial of service
1469   (DDoS) support, and server redirection support. It is recommended that existing IKEv1
1470   installations be upgraded to IKEv2.

1471   For those familiar with IKEv1, the main differences between IKEv1 and IKEv2 are:

1472   • IKEv1 was designed to be a far more general-purpose key exchange protocol, but many
1473   extraneous features ended up not being used at all. IKEv2 no longer has these features.
1474   • Some IKEv1 protocol extensions are now part of the IKEv2 core specification, such as
1475   IKE fragmentation[27], NAT Traversal, and Liveness Detection—formerly called Dead
1476   Peer Detection (DPD). This means that these features are always available in IKEv2.

---

[26]   Most importantly, it can skip the DH calculation, which is the most expensive operation of an IKE exchange.
[27]   Technically, IKE fragmentation is a separate RFC, but it is implemented by most vendors.

1477
1478
1479
- IKEv1 has a large number of exchange types to choose from (Main Mode, Aggressive Mode, Revised Mode, etc.) With IKEv2, there is no choice of exchange methods, so this no longer needs to be explicitly configured.

1480
- The IKEv2 exchange has anti-DDoS protection using cookies.

1481
1482
1483
1484
- When an IKEv1 endpoint uses the wrong PSK to encrypt a message, the other endpoint is unable to decrypt the encrypted message. For the endpoint receiving this erroneous message, it has no way to distinguish this error from other problems such as packet corruption.

1485
1486
1487
- In IKEv1, both endpoints are responsible for retransmissions, leading to conflicting retransmits and denial of service vectors. In IKEv2, only the exchange initiator is responsible for retransmission.

1488
1489
1490
1491
- In IKEv1, the IKE SA can expire while the IPsec SA is still active. This could lead to strange scenarios with DPD. In IKEv2, every IPsec SA has an IKE SA. If the IKE SA expires, all IPsec SAs are torn down as well. This guarantees that every IPsec SA has a functional control channel, which was not the case with IKEv1.

1492
1493
1494
1495
1496
1497
- In IKEv1, rekeying always requires a reauthentication of the two end points. Some proprietary extensions allow rekeying without reauthentication. Reauthentication is not always desirable, especially with the use of OTPs or hardware tokens requiring the use of a PIN or fingerprint for activation by the user (such as a VPN client), as it would require human interaction to keep the IPsec connection alive. In IKEv2, rekeying and reauthentication are separate processes with their own lifetimes.

1498
1499
1500
1501
- In IKEv1, transport mode and compression are negotiated, and a mismatched configuration would lead to a fatal IKE error. In IKEv2, the initiator can request these, but if the responder does not confirm those requests, the IPsec SA is established in tunnel mode (or without compression).

1502
1503
1504
1505
1506
1507
1508
1509
1510
1511
1512
- In IKEv1, the IKE SA and IPsec SA can use different DH groups during key establishment (i.e., the DH group used to establish the IKE SA can be different than the DH group used to establish the IPsec SA). This is possible because the IKE and IPsec parameters are negotiated in 2 different message exchanges, taking place at different times. In IKEv2, there is only one exchange of parameters, and the first IPsec SA is established using the IKE SA DH group. Subsequent IPsec SAs can perform an additional DH exchange, thus ensuring the property of PFS; that exchange can use a different group. However, when configuring multiple IPsec SAs, there is no guarantee which one will be brought up first, either through an operator or by on-demand tunnel establishments. Therefore, in IKEv2 the DH group selected should be the same for the IKE SA and the IPsec SAs.

1513
1514
1515
1516
- In IKEv1, ESP encapsulation can only happen in UDP. IKEv2 can also use TCP and TLS encapsulation on any port. The TCP/TLS encapsulation cannot be negotiated and must be configured manually or via configuration provisioning. TCP port 4500 is often the default used. This might require firewall-rule updates.

1517
1518
1519
1520
- When migrating from IKEv1 to IKEv2, an upgrade of the algorithms used is strongly recommended. 3DES, MD5, SHA-1 and DH Group 2 and 5 should not be used. Instead, AES-XCBC with HMAC-SHA-2 or AES-GCM with either DH group 14 or an ECDH group (19, 20, or 21) should be used.

- IKEv2 Traffic Selector negotiations allow narrowing. This helps with creating multiple parallel IPsec SAs per traffic flow, which generally improves performance as hardware (i.e., central processing units [CPUs] and network interface cards [NICs]) can then handle multiple parallel streams at once.
- In IKEv1 it is not always possible to detect different groups of clients early enough to select the right authentication mechanism or the right PSK. This complicates multi-tenant VPNs. In IKEv2, the initiator can optionally send the expected ID of the peer in the IDr payload. This allows the responder (i.e., the server) to always select the proper tenant group.
- IKEv1 with PSK has the side effect of offering quantum computing resistance. In IKEv2 this is no longer the case, but a separate RFC [37] specifies how to use PPKs to gain the same protection in IKEv2.

3.10 Manual Keying

While it is possible to hard-code the IPsec information using out-of-band communication—called *manual keying*—this MUST NOT be used. The IKE protocol handles a number of other security properties, none of which are enforced when using manual keying. Encryption keys would never be refreshed when a fixed key is manually input and used, so any compromise would allow an attacker to decrypt all previously monitored traffic under the fixed key. Some values, such as nonces, counters, and IVs, must never be used more than once, otherwise the encryption may become vulnerable (weaken).

The only time that manual keying might be acceptable is if another trusted entity, such as a Security Controller in the SDWAN paradigm, assumes these responsibilities. Another example is the 3GPP protocol, which negotiates the IPsec parameters between a cell tower and handset using a non-IKE protocol.

Administrators sometimes mistakenly believe that manual keying is easier to set up than automated keying via IKE. However, manual keying is much harder to set up than IKE.

Manual keying is typically only used for software testing and IPsec benchmark tests.

This recommendation discourages the use of manual keying.

3.11 IKE Summary

- IPsec uses IKE to create security associations, which are sets of values that define the security of IPsec-protected connections. The first IPsec SA is created in conjunction with the IKE SA during the initial exchanges.
- The IKE SA is used to securely communicate IPsec configuration, status, and management information, such as setting up additional IPsec SAs, rekey events, deletions, and other notifications.
- IKEv2 is faster, more versatile, and uses more modern cryptography compared to IKEv1. IKEv1 should not be used for new deployments, and existing deployments using IKEv1 should be converted to IKEv2 when possible.

1559 **4   The IPsec Protocols**

1560   IPsec is a collection of protocols that assist in protecting communications over networks.[28] This
1561   section focuses on the primary component of IPsec, the Encapsulating Security Payload (ESP),
1562   which protects the confidentiality and integrity of data packets. The section also briefly covers
1563   the other IPsec components, the IP Payload Compression Protocol (IPComp) and the
1564   Authentication Header (AH) protocol. All the parameters and cryptographic keys needed by the
1565   IPsec protocols are negotiated using the IKE protocol as described in Section 3.

1566   **4.1   Encapsulating Security Payload (ESP)**

1567   ESP is the core IPsec security protocol. It has largely been unchanged since its second version,
1568   published in 1998. The current version (IPsec-v3) was specified in RFC 4303 in 2005 [19]. It
1569   contains only a few updates to the IPsec-v2 specification in RFC 2406 [39]. Since all the changes
1570   to ESP are either backwards compatible or are new features that would need to be negotiated via
1571   IKE before these are enabled for ESP, there are no compatibility issues between IPsec
1572   implementations receiving and sending ESP packets. Regardless, practically all current
1573   implementations support IPsec-v3. Features only available in IPsec-v3 are:

1574   • Support for AEAD algorithms
1575   • Extended Sequence Numbers (ESNs)
1576   • Enhanced policy support (via Security Policy Database [SPD]/Security Association
1577   Database [SAD])
1578   • Padding support
1579   • Dummy packet support

1580   The use of padding and the capability of sending dummy messages increase traffic flow
1581   confidentiality (TFC) by making it harder for an eavesdropper who cannot decrypt the packets to
1582   deduce anything from the encrypted packet sizes or timings.

1583   ESP provides encryption and integrity protection. The outer header is not fully protected,
1584   allowing for routers that forward ESP packets to still modify certain flags, such as Quality of
1585   Service (QoS) and Time to Live (TTL) values.

1586   ESP's encryption functionality can be disabled through the selection of the Null ESP encryption
1587   algorithm or the AES-GMAC AEAD algorithm. AES-GMAC is a variant of the AES-GCM
1588   algorithm that provides integrity protection without encryption. ESP can be used to provide
1589   either encryption and integrity protection; or only integrity protection. AH deployments should
1590   be migrated to these ESP algorithms. ESP supports AEAD and classic (non-AEAD) encryption
1591   with integrity methods.

---

[28]   RFC 4301 provides an overview of IPsec [40].

1592   **4.1.1   Tunnel Mode and Transport Mode**

1593   ESP has two modes: transport and tunnel. In *tunnel mode*, (see Figure 7), a new packet is
1594   constructed that contains the (original) IP packet being sent through the tunnel by 1) placing an
1595   ESP header and trailer around the original IP header and its payload, 2) encrypting the original
1596   header, payload and ESP trailer, 3) computing an integrity check value (ICV) over the ESP
1597   header and the encrypted data, 4) placing the ICV at the end of the packet being constructed, and
1598   5) adding a new IP header to the beginning of the packet. The ICV computation does not include
1599   the new IP header.

1600   The new IP header lists the endpoints of the ESP tunnel (such as two IPsec gateways) as the
1601   source and destination of the packet, and contains as its payload the entire, now encrypted,
1602   original packet. Because of this, tunnel mode can be used with all VPN architectures described in
1603   Section 2.4. As shown in Figure 7, tunnel mode can encrypt and protect the integrity of both the
1604   data and the original IP header for each packet. Encrypting the original IP header and its payload
1605   protects their confidentiality; encrypting the original IP header conceals the nature of the
1606   communications, such as the actual source or destination of the packet, protocol, and ports used
1607   that would indicate which application is likely being used. The ICV is used to detect any changes
1608   to the data over which the ICV is computed.

New IP Header	ESP Header	Original IP Header	Original IP data containing Transport and Application Protocol Headers and Data (optional TFC padding)	ESP Trailer (ESP padding, Next Header)	ESP Integrity Check Value - ICV (variable)

Encrypted

Authenticated (Integrity Protection)

1609   **Figure 7: ESP Tunnel Mode Packet**

1610   ESP tunnel mode is used for gateway to gateway deployments, remote access VPNs, and various
1611   network virtualization deployments. It is also required when the IPsec connection needs to
1612   traverse a NAT, which rewrites the outer IP address.

1613   For host-to-host deployments within data centers, local networks, and virtual machines where no
1614   NAT is deployed, ESP transport mode is often used. In *transport mode* (see Figure 8), ESP uses
1615   the original IP header instead of creating a new one. The ESP payload and trailer are encrypted,
1616   and an ICV is computed over the ESP header and the encrypted data. Integrity protection is not
1617   provided for the IP header. The overhead of the transport mode is less than for the tunnel mode
1618   because it does not have to create an entire new IP header.

1619   Transport mode is incompatible with NAT. For example, in each TCP packet, the TCP checksum
1620   is calculated on both the TCP and IP fields, including the source and destination addresses in the
1621   IP header. If NAT is being used, one or both of the IP addresses are altered, so NAT needs to
1622   recalculate the TCP checksum. If ESP is encrypting packets, the TCP header is encrypted; NAT
1623   cannot recalculate the checksum, so NAT fails. This is not an issue in tunnel mode; because the
1624   entire TCP packet is hidden, NAT will not attempt to recalculate the TCP checksum of the inner
1625   encrypted packet, only of the outer IP address which is not part of the ESP encryption. However,

1626   tunnel mode and NAT have other potential compatibility issues.[29] Section 7.2.1 provides
1627   guidance on overcoming NAT-related issues.

IP Header	ESP Header	Transport and Application Protocol Headers and Data	ESP Trailer (ESP padding, Next Header)	ESP Integrity Check Value- ICV (variable)
		Encrypted		
	Authenticated (Integrity Protection)			

1628   **Figure 8: ESP Transport Mode Packet**

1629   ### 4.1.2   Encryption with Separate Integrity Protection

1630   ESP uses symmetric cryptography to provide encryption for IPsec packets. Accordingly, both
1631   endpoints of an IPsec connection protected by ESP encryption must use the same key to encrypt
1632   and decrypt the packets. When an endpoint encrypts data, it divides the data into small blocks
1633   (for the AES algorithm, blocks of 128 bits each), and then performs multiple sets of
1634   cryptographic operations (known as rounds) using the data blocks and key. Encryption
1635   algorithms that work in this way are known as *block cipher algorithms*. When the other endpoint
1636   receives the encrypted data, it performs decryption using the same key and a similar process, but
1637   with the steps reversed and the cryptographic operations altered.

1638   After encryption has been performed, the first step for providing integrity protection is to create a
1639   MAC on a message using a MAC algorithm and a secret key shared by the two endpoints. The
1640   MAC is added to the packet, and the packet is sent to the recipient. The recipient can then
1641   regenerate the MAC using the shared key and confirm that the two MACs match, thus
1642   determining whether the data has been modified. IPsec mostly uses a keyed-hash message
1643   authentication code (HMAC) algorithm [41] for integrity protection, which uses approved hash
1644   functions. Examples of HMAC are HMAC-SHA-256 and HMAC-SHA-1. Another common
1645   non-HMAC integrity algorithm is AES Cipher Block Chaining MAC (AES-XCBC-MAC-96)
1646   [42].[30]

1647   ### 4.1.3   AEAD Encryption with Built-In Integrity

1648   Encryption with separate integrity protection (as described in Section 4.1.2) requires two
1649   separate cryptographic processes over the data using two different secret keys. AEAD combines
1650   these two processes. This significantly increases performance. It also provides more constant-
1651   time processing when errors occur, resulting in a more robust error handling process that is less
1652   susceptible to timing attacks. The reverse process produces either the plaintext data or an error
1653   indication. For IKEv2 and ESP, AES-GCM is specified in [43] as an AEAD algorithm. Due to

---

[29]   One possible issue is the inability to perform incoming source address validation to confirm that the source address is the
       same as that under which the IKE SA was negotiated. Other possible issues include packet fragmentation, NAT mapping
       timeouts, and multiple clients behind the same NAT device.

[30]   Federal agencies are required to use NIST-approved algorithms and FIPS-validated cryptographic modules. HMAC with a
       hash function from the SHA-2 family is NIST-approved, but AES-XCBC-MAC-96 is not.

1654   the way that IKEv1 handles the separation of encryption from data integrity protection in IKE
1655   packets, AEAD algorithms cannot be used in IKEv1. IKEv1 can, however, still negotiate AEAD
1656   algorithms for ESP.

1657   The nonce used by an AEAD algorithm must be unique for every encryption operation with the
1658   same secret key but does not need to be unpredictable.[31] The nonce in IKE is built using an
1659   implicit part (the salt) and an explicit part (the initialization vector, or IV). The implicit part is
1660   based on the keying material calculated from the DH key exchange and negotiated PRF,
1661   similarly to how secret encryption keys are generated. This value is never transmitted and binds
1662   the encryption to the DH channel. The explicit part is transmitted and usually based on an
1663   increasing, and thus unique, counter. Reuse of the IV with the same secret key compromises the
1664   security of the data. Thus, these algorithms must be used in conjunction with IKE, and cannot be
1665   used with static or manual keys. An SA must be terminated before the counter reaches its
1666   maximum possible value.

1667   **4.1.4   Common ESP Algorithms**

1668   Examples of common algorithms used by ESP are AES-GCM [44] and AES-Cipher Block
1669   Chaining (AES-CBC) [45] with a SHA-2-HMAC. Most algorithms have limitations on the
1670   amount of data that can be safely encrypted with a single key, and requirements for auxiliary
1671   parameters.

1672   The Triple DES (3DES) encryption algorithm is no longer recommended. It is much slower than
1673   AES-GCM and AES-CBC, and it requires more frequent rekeying to avoid birthday attacks due
1674   to its smaller block size of 64 bits. The HMAC-MD5 and HMAC-SHA-1 integrity algorithms are
1675   also no longer NIST-approved.

1676   For the latest cryptographic recommendations, see NIST SP 800-131A [47] and FIPS 140 [13].

1677   **4.1.5   ESP Packet Fields**

1678   ESP adds a header and a trailer around each packet's payload. As shown in Figure 9, each ESP
1679   header is composed of two fields:

1680   • **SPI.** Each IPsec SA (inbound and outbound) contains an SPI value, which acts as a
1681   unique identifier for the IPsec SA. The endpoints use these SPI values, along with the
1682   destination IP address and (optionally) the IPsec protocol type (in this case, ESP) to
1683   determine which SA is being used, and which decryption key should be used.
1684   • **(Extended) Sequence Number.** Each packet is assigned a sequential sequence number,
1685   and only packets within a sliding window of sequence numbers are accepted. This
1686   provides protection against replay attacks because duplicate packets will use the same

---

[31]   The terms nonce and IV have not seen consistently use between NIST and IETF publications. In general, what is required is
       the use of a guaranteed unique non-secret value. Note that the IV needed for the AEAD algorithm is separate from the
       integrity check value (ICV) used in each packet to ensure that two identical plaintext payloads encrypt to different encrypted
       payloads (and thus cannot be detected as identical).

1687   sequence number. This also helps to thwart denial of service attacks because old packets
1688   that are replayed will have sequence numbers outside the window and will be dropped
1689   immediately without performing any more processing. Originally (in IPsec-v2) the
1690   sequence numbers for IPsec packets were defined as a 32-bit number. Current hardware
1691   can transmit 100 gigabits per second (Gbps), or about 150 million packets per second,
1692   meaning that the 32-bit sequence number space would be exhausted in 30 seconds. It
1693   would be impractical to rekey an IPsec SA every 30 seconds, so IPsec-v3 [19] introduced
1694   Extended Sequence Numbers (ESNs). If negotiated with IKE, the IPsec SA is installed
1695   with 64-bit sequence numbers. The ESP wire format is unchanged, however, and only the
1696   lower 32 bits of the Sequence Number are transmitted in the ESP packet. Each endpoint
1697   keeps track of the higher 32-bit value and performs all integrity calculations based on the
1698   entire 64-bit sequence number.[32]

1699   The next part of the packet is the payload. It is composed of the encrypted payload data and the
1700   IV, which is not encrypted. This is helpful in deterring traffic analysis. The IV is used during
1701   encryption. Its value is different in every packet, so if two packets have the same content, the
1702   inclusion of the IV will cause the encryption of the two packets to have different results. This
1703   makes ESP less susceptible to cryptanalysis.

1704   To obfuscate the length and frequency of information sent over IPsec, the protocol allows for
1705   sending dummy data called *traffic flow confidentiality (TFC) padding*. TFC padding can be
1706   added to the unencrypted data before encryption, or it can be injected as a whole new packet with
1707   only padding being encrypted to a certain size between real encrypted data transmissions. An
1708   observer cannot tell if TFC is enabled, and more importantly, can no longer make any reasonable
1709   assumptions based on packet size or frequency. One common deployment of TFC is to pad all
1710   packets to the maximum MTU value, resulting in all ESP packets sent being the exact same
1711   length. This would increase the amount of encrypted data sent, so on links where transmission
1712   costs depend on the amount of data sent (e.g., LTE/5G), there is a cost associated with using
1713   TFC.

1714   The third part of the packet is the ESP trailer, which contains at least two fields and may
1715   optionally include one more:

1716   • **ESP Padding.** An ESP packet may optionally contain padding, which is additional bytes
1717   of data that make the packet larger and are discarded by the packet's recipient. Because
1718   ESP uses block ciphers for encryption, padding may be needed so that the encrypted data
1719   is an integral multiple of the block size. Padding may also be needed to ensure that the
1720   ESP trailer ends on a multiple of four bytes.
1721   • **ESP Padding Length.** This number indicates the length of the padding in bytes. The
1722   Padding Length field is mandatory.

---

[32]   It is assumed that an application would notice a packet loss of 2^{32} packets, which would lead the hosts to use a different
        high-order 32-bit value and fail the integrity check of the packet. [48] does specify a method of coping with such an unusual
        situation.

1723   • **Next Header.** In tunnel mode, the outer (original) IP header is followed by an inner
1724   (new) IP header; thus, the next payload is an IP packet, so the Next Header value is set to
1725   four, indicating IP-in-IP (one IP packet tunneled in another IP packet). In transport mode,
1726   the payload is usually a transport layer protocol, often TCP (protocol number 6) or UDP
1727   (protocol number 17). Every ESP trailer contains a Next Header value.
1728   • **Integrity Check Value (ICV).** This is used to verify the integrity of the encrypted data.
1729   For AES-GCM and AES-Counter with CBC-MAC (AES-CCM), it consists of an 8, 12,
1730   or 16-byte Authentication Tag. The 16-byte ICV value is recommended by NIST and by
1731   RFC 8247 [20]. The recipient of the packet can recalculate the ICV value to confirm that
1732   the portions of the packet other than the outermost IP header have not been altered in
1733   transit.

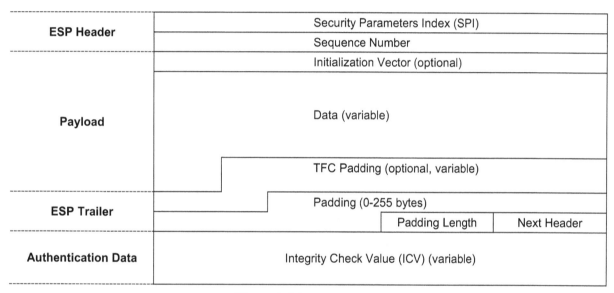

1734   **Figure 9: ESP Packet Fields**

1735   ### 4.1.6 How ESP Works

1736   Reviewing and analyzing actual ESP packets can provide a better understanding of how ESP
1737   works. Figure 10 shows the bytes that compose an actual ESP packet and their ASCII
1738   representations. The ESP packet only contains four sections (ignoring the link layer): IP header,
1739   ESP header, encrypted data (payload and ESP trailer), and (optionally) authentication
1740   information. By examining the encrypted data, it is not possible to determine if this packet was
1741   generated in transport mode or tunnel mode. However, because the IP header is unencrypted, the
1742   IP protocol field in the header does reveal which IPsec protocol the payload uses (in this case,
1743   ESP). As shown in Figure 7 and Figure 8, the unencrypted fields in both modes (tunnel and
1744   transport) are the same.

5 0.078396 193.1.2.45 193.1.2.23 ESP 154 ESP (SPI=0xa6f554a4)

```
▶ Frame 5: 154 bytes on wire (1232 bits), 154 bytes captured (1232 bits)
▼ Ethernet II, Src: 0e:85:75:ef:71:df (0e:85:75:ef:71:df), Dst: 52:72:63:54:21:4c (52:72:63:54:21:4c)
    ▶ Destination: 52:72:63:54:21:4c (52:72:63:54:21:4c)
    ▶ Source: 0e:85:75:ef:71:df (0e:85:75:ef:71:df)
      Type: IPv4 (0x0800)
▼ Internet Protocol Version 4, Src: 193.1.2.45, Dst: 193.1.2.23
      0100 .... = Version: 4
      .... 0101 = Header Length: 20 bytes (5)
    ▶ Differentiated Services Field: 0x00 (DSCP: CS0, ECN: Not-ECT)
      Total Length: 140
      Identification: 0xb00a (45066)
    ▶ Flags: 0x4000, Don't fragment
      Time to live: 64
      Protocol: Encap Security Payload (50)
      Header checksum: 0x03ef [validation disabled]
      [Header checksum status: Unverified]
      Source: 193.1.2.45
      Destination: 193.1.2.23
▼ Encapsulating Security Payload
      ESP SPI: 0xa6f554a4 (2801095844)
      ESP Sequence: 1
```

```
0000  52 72 63 54 21 4c 0e 85  75 ef 71 df 08 00 45 00   RrcT!L.. u.q...E.
0010  00 8c b0 0a 40 00 40 32  03 ef c1 01 02 2d c1 01   ....@.@2 .....-..
0020  02 17 a6 f5 54 a4 00 00  00 01 98 07 e2 1a fb 3d   ...T.. ........=
0030  a9 51 21 42 4c 71 1e 6f  a5 67 24 02 d6 71 8d 9a   .Q!BLq.o .g$..q..
0040  14 bc 6e 8c eb 55 3c e3  4a f7 29 fe 2b a5 16 b2   ..n..U<. J.).+..
0050  e1 1a dc f8 51 a1 5c a4  b4 e8 3f da a4 73 75 23   ....Q.\. ..?..su#
0060  89 78 b7 85 4b 45 de 18  b6 dd d2 91 56 ac 5b dc   .x..KE.. ....V.[.
0070  f5 43 61 7e d5 17 f5 c2  d8 6c e7 67 55 24 68 15   .Ca~.... .l.gU$h.
0080  35 1c 78 c2 0a 54 24 9d  ed 5f 50 f4 e0 14 cb 7a   5.x..T$. ._P....z
0090  ac e9 de a9 25 8c 5f ba  71 42                     ....%._. qB
```

Figure 10: ESP Packet Capture Using Wireshark, Showing Sequence Number 1

Although it is difficult to tell from Figure 10, the ESP header fields are not encrypted. Figure 11 shows a network traffic capture, made with the tcpdump tool, of encrypted traffic generated by the ping command, followed by an IKE session, followed by another ping that is now protected by ESP. Each direction uses its own negotiated SPI value for its packets, which corresponds to an ESP connection being composed of two one-way connections, each with its own SPI. Both hosts initially set the sequence number to 1, and both incremented the number to 2 for their second packets. The tcpdump tool labels IKE packets as "isakmp", a legacy name from the IKEv1 protocol.

```
13:45:34.118804 IP 203.0.113.1 > 198.51.100.1: ICMP echo request, id 27083, seq 2, length
64
13:45:34.118850 IP 198.51.100.1 > 203.0.113.1: ICMP echo reply, id 27083, seq 2, length 64
13:45:39.469941 IP 203.0.113.1.isakmp > 198.51.100.1.isakmp: isakmp: parent_sa
ikev2_init[I]
13:45:39.472043 IP 198.51.100.1.isakmp > 203.0.113.1.isakmp: isakmp: parent_sa
ikev2_init[R]
13:45:39.481690 IP 203.0.113.1.isakmp > 198.51.100.1.isakmp: isakmp: child_sa
ikev2_auth[I]
13:45:39.525826 IP 198.51.100.1.isakmp > 203.0.113.1.isakmp: isakmp: child_sa
ikev2_auth[R]
13:45:39.587728 IP 203.0.113.1 > 198.51.100.1: ESP(spi=0xc55ed62b,seq=0x1), length 120
13:45:39.587773 IP 198.51.100.1 > 203.0.113.1: ESP(spi=0xf6fc7c09,seq=0x1), length 120
13:45:40.646761 IP 203.0.113.1 > 198.51.100.1: ESP(spi=0xc55ed62b,seq=0x2), length 120
13:45:40.646800 IP 198.51.100.1 > 203.0.113.1: ESP(spi=0xf6fc7c09,seq=0x2), length 120
```

Figure 11: tcpdump Capture of ping, IKE, and ESP Packets

4.2   ESP Encapsulation

ESP packets cannot traverse a NAT device in all circumstances. If an IPsec connection uses transport mode, changing the IP address on the packets will invalidate the integrity checks imposed by IPsec. The NAT device cannot rewrite the ICV because it does not have access to the keying material needed to do so. For all intents and purposes, the NAT device is a malicious actor that IPsec protects against.

The ESP protocol has no ports. If multiple clients send ESP from behind the same NAT router, it would be difficult to track the ESP packets to the respective clients, as they would all have the same destination IP—that of the NAT device. And while SPI numbers are uniquely generated for each IPsec host, there is no guarantee that two hosts behind the same NAT will not end up picking the same SPI number for an IPsec SA. Furthermore, often NAT routers do not understand or translate anything other than the UDP and TCP protocols, causing ESP packets to be dropped by the NAT device.

4.2.1   UDP Encapsulation of ESP

To overcome these issues, ESP can be encapsulated in UDP (ESPinUDP). The NAT device can rewrite the IP address of the outer UDP packet and track multiple clients by the UDP port number. For historical reasons,[33] when IKE detects a NAT during the negotiation, it switches the IKE negotiation from UDP port 500 to UDP port 4500. It uses a regular UDP packet header, followed by a four-byte header with all zeroes (Non-ESP Marker) following the UDP header. Then the IKE header follows.

ESPinUDP also uses port 4500 to ensure that the NAT device only has one NAT mapping for all traffic (ESP and IKE). Following the regular UDP packet header, the ESP header follows. The first four bytes of the ESP header is the SPI number, which cannot be 0. Thus, an implementation receiving a packet on port 4500 can determine whether the packet is an ESPinUDP packet or an

---

[33] Some NAT devices tried to be helpful by looking at the SPI and rewriting or multiplexing these. It just made things break more. The solution was to avoid UDP port 500 completely to avoid any NAT "helper" algorithms. IKEv2 even allows skipping UDP port 500 altogether and using UDP port 4500 for all IKE messages.

1796   IKE packet, depending on whether or not it sees the SPI number of the non-ESP marker.
1797   Usually, the kernel receiving an ESPinUDP packet will just strip the UDP header away without
1798   bothering with the UDP checksum (which not all NAT routers properly recalculate) and process
1799   the remaining ESP data as if it was received as an ESP packet without encapsulation. If the
1800   kernel detects an IKE packet, it will send this packet to the IKE process for processing by the
1801   IKE daemon.

1802   Starting with IKEv2, even if no NAT was detected, endpoints need to support receiving ESP and
1803   ESPinUDP packets on all their IPsec SAs. Each endpoint may decide when to use encapsulation
1804   and when not to. IKEv2 also allows initiating a new IKE_SA_INIT on UDP port 4500,
1805   bypassing UDP port 500 completely.

1806   **4.2.2   TCP Encapsulation of ESP**

1807   Implementations supporting TCP encapsulation [49], where ESP packets are wrapped into a TCP
1808   stream, can also choose to use TCP. This provides a much-needed method to prevent IPsec from
1809   being easily filtered and blocked. Lacking TCP encapsulation was one of the reasons why SSL
1810   VPNs came into existence, as these could not be easily blocked by blocking the IPsec protocols
1811   (UDP port 500 and 4500 and protocol ESP). TCP encapsulation ports cannot be negotiated, as
1812   this would require that the negotiations start on the well-known port susceptible to blocking.
1813   Therefore, the TCP port has to be preconfigured manually or via the IPsec client provisioning
1814   system.

1815   The ESP in TCP encapsulation uses an ASCII prefix tag of "IKETCP" so that an additional layer
1816   can be used, such as TLS. In that case, encrypted packets are encapsulated using a TCP
1817   connection that uses TLS. The packet processor can read the prefix and detect the start of an
1818   IKE/ESP stream, in which case it can send this traffic to the proper handler. Since restrictive
1819   networks often still (have to) allow access to HTTPS websites, using TLS on port 443 to protect
1820   (or really, hide) the TCP stream containing the encapsulated ESP packets will yield the best
1821   results. However, networks are often only misconfigured to drop all UDP traffic. Moving to ESP
1822   encapsulation on TCP port 4500 without TLS framing will usually be enough to be able to
1823   establish IPsec connections.

1824   Implementations are encouraged to regularly try to go back to UDP encapsulation. TCP
1825   encapsulation means there are possibly two TCP layers involved in a packet: the TCP connection
1826   being encrypted and the TCP connection carrying the ESP packet. These two TCP layers will
1827   both independently determine retransmissions. Especially when there is packet loss, these two
1828   TCP streams will badly interfere with each other.

1829   **4.3   IP Payload Compression Protocol (IPComp)**

1830   ESP can be deployed with IPComp. Before a packet is encrypted, the packet will be considered
1831   for compression. If the packet is very small already, such as an ICMP message, no compression
1832   is done, and the packet is encrypted as is; otherwise, the packet is compressed. However, various
1833   compression algorithms do not guarantee that an attempted compression does not end up being
1834   larger than the original. If this turns out to be the case, the original packet is encrypted without

1835　compression. If the compressed result is smaller, the compressed packet is encrypted. On the
1836　receiving end the packet is decrypted, and if it was compressed, it will be decompressed.

1837　However, applications that send large amounts of data usually already compress their data. At
1838　that point, attempting to compress already compressed data will not yield smaller packets, and a
1839　host only ends up wasting CPU cycles at the IPsec layer attempting futile compression. As such,
1840　IPsec level compression has not seen widespread use. This might change in the near future with
1841　the emergence of IoT devices and other battery-powered devices that use mobile data (LTE/5G).
1842　These devices save battery power by transmitting fewer bytes, even if that reduction requires
1843　more CPU power for compression.

4.4　Authentication Header (AH)

1845　As with ESP, AH can be used in tunnel mode and transport mode. It only offers integrity
1846　algorithms and provides no confidentiality. The ESP protocol can use null encryption (ESP
1847　algorithm number 12) with an integrity algorithm such as HMAC-SHA-2[34] to accomplish the
1848　same as AH. Alternatively, ESP can use an AEAD algorithm such as AES-GMAC (ESP
1849　algorithm number 21) to offer integrity without confidentiality to replace AH.

1850　| The use of AH is discouraged in this publication. The IETF has specified that AH is an optional
1851　| IPsec protocol, which means it is not mandatory to implement and might not be available with all
1852　| IPsec implementations. It is recommended that null encryption with the ESP protocol be used
1853　| instead of the AH protocol when encryption is not desired.

1854　Some implementations support the legacy IPsec-v2 ESP without authentication in combination
1855　with AH. This is usually referred to as *AH+ESP*. This combined mode (ESP for encryption and
1856　AH for integrity) is no longer recommended [20], as it provides no advantage over regular ESP
1857　with authentication. Regular ESP with authentication also reduces the MTU compared to
1858　AH+ESP, due to the additional overhead of an AH header plus an ESP header versus just an ESP
1859　header with authentication.

1860　NIST discourages the use of AH.

4.5　Summary

1862　This section has described the IPsec protocols ESP, IPComp, and AH. The following
1863　summarizes the key points from the section:

1864　• The IKE protocol is used to manage IPsec security associations.
1865　• ESP is the main IPsec protocol and provides integrity protection for all packet headers
1866　and data, with the exception of a few IP header fields that routinely change unpredictably
1867　in transit. Since those header fields can change as the packet travels from sender to
1868　receiver, they cannot be included in the integrity check calculation; if they were, that

---

[34]　HMAC-SHA-2 is used throughout the document to mean HMAC using a hash function from the SHA-2 family of hash
functions specified in FIPS 180 [25].

1869 value would then be different for the sender and the receiver. ESP also provides
1870 confidentiality protection through the use of encryption, encrypting the data. It does not
1871 encrypt the headers, since the header fields are used to correctly process and deliver the
1872 data as it traverses the Internet.
1873 •
1874 • ESP can be used in transport mode and tunnel mode.
1875   o In tunnel mode, ESP provides encryption and integrity protection for an
1876   encapsulated IP packet, as well as integrity protection for the ESP header of the
1877   outer (constructed) IP packet.
1878   o In transport mode, ESP provides encryption and integrity protection for the
1879   payload of the IP packet, as well as integrity protection for the ESP header.
1880   Transport mode is not compatible with NAT. Transport mode can only be used
1881   for host-to-host deployments. It is commonly used for large scale host-to-host
1882   mesh deployments within an administrative domain without NAT.
1883 • ESP in tunnel mode is the most commonly used IPsec mode because it can encrypt the
1884   entire original IP packet, which conceals the true source and destination of the packet.
1885   ESP in tunnel mode is a requirement for gateway-to-gateway communications. ESP in
1886   tunnel mode can be encapsulated in UDP and TCP, making it compatible with NAT.
1887 • ESP can add padding to packets and send dummy packets, further complicating attempts
1888   to perform traffic analysis.
1889 • ESP can use IPComp but rarely does because the gains made from data compression
1890   depend strongly on the type of traffic sent. Applications sending a lot of data typically
1891   compress their data before providing it to the lower layers for transmission. Applying
1892   IPComp to already compressed data would waste CPU power.
1893 • AH has been obsoleted and should not be implemented or deployed. If encryption is
1894   undesirable, ESP with null encryption (ESP-NULL or AES-GMAC) should be used
1895   instead of AH.
1896

1897 **5   Deployment of IPsec Using IKE**

1898 This section describes the interactions between the IKE and IPsec subsystems. The interaction
1899 depends on the implementation. This section describes the standard protocols used to
1900 communicate between IKE and IPsec. However, some devices have their own proprietary
1901 method of communication. In general, the concepts explained in this section will apply to those
1902 proprietary implementations as well.

1903 The IKE protocol is usually implemented as an application running on the operating system,
1904 whereas the IPsec protocol is generally implemented in the kernel of the operating system. Some
1905 devices implement the IPsec subsystem in userland, but for the remainder of this chapter it is
1906 assumed that IPsec is implemented in the kernel.

1907 The communication between IKE and IPsec is usually implemented using the PF_KEYv2 [50] or
1908 NETLINK [51] protocol. Linux uses NETLINK with the XFRM application programming
1909 interface (API), whereas BSD-based systems use PF_KEYv2.[35]

1910 This section puts IKE and IPsec components together to illustrate how IPsec sessions are set up
1911 and executed. Each example includes the use of IKE to establish SAs.

1912 **5.1   IPsec States and Policies**

1913 Each IPsec SA has a state and a policy. While each state must have a policy, not all policies need
1914 to have a state. For example, on-demand IPsec connections have a policy that allows the kernel
1915 to detect that an outgoing packet should trigger an IKE negotiation. Once the IKE SA has been
1916 established and an IPsec SA has been negotiated, the IKE daemon will install an IPsec state with
1917 corresponding policies. During the negotiation, the kernel can drop the packet, cache the packet
1918 for later transmission, or let the packet go out unencrypted. Usually UDP packets are dropped,
1919 since their unreliable nature requires that applications sending these packets need to know when
1920 to transmit their packets anyway. TCP packets are usually cached because TCP retransmissions
1921 are usually very slow, and it would make the on-demand tunnel very slow if the first TCP packet
1922 is always lost. Leaking packets in cleartext is only done when the network considers the IPsec
1923 protection optional instead of mandatory.

1924 Once an IPsec SA has been established between two hosts, all traffic that falls within the IPsec
1925 SA policy MUST be IPsec-protected. If for some reason unencrypted traffic is received, it is
1926 assumed to have been forged, and the traffic will be dropped.

1927 **5.1.1   The Security Association Database (SAD)**

1928 The kernel maintains a state for each IPsec SA. An IPsec connection between two hosts consists
1929 of a pair of IPsec SAs, one for inbound and one for outbound traffic. These IPsec states are

---

[35] Linux uses the "ip xfrm" command, FreeBSD uses the "setkey" command, and OpenBSD uses the "ipsecctl" command.

45

1930 contained in the Security Association Database (SAD). Figure 12 shows an example of an IPsec
1931 SA using an AEAD algorithm.

1932
1933
1934
1935
1936
1937
1938
1939
1940
1941
1942
1943
1944
1945
1946
1947
1948
1949
1950
1951
1952
1953
1954
1955
1956
1957
1958
1959
1960
1961
1962

```
src 198.51.100.1 dst 203.0.113.1
    proto esp spi 0xba293cd3(3123264723) reqid 1(0x01) mode tunnel
    replay-window 32 seq 0x00000000 flag af-unspec (0x00100000)
    aead rfc4106(gcm(aes)) 0x2ee20e32be3017c1878b9ae514081ba1d[…] 128
    anti-replay context: seq 0x148a3, oseq 0x0, bitmap 0xffffffff
    lifetime config:
       limit: soft (INF)(bytes), hard (INF)(bytes)
       limit: soft (INF)(packets), hard (INF)(packets)
       expire add: soft 0(sec), hard 0(sec)
       expire use: soft 0(sec), hard 0(sec)
    lifetime current:
       102600783(bytes), 84090(packets)
       add 2019-01-06 21:57:45 use 2019-01-06 21:57:50
    stats:
       replay-window 0 replay 0 failed 0

src 203.0.113.1 dst 198.51.100.1
    proto esp spi 0x6273ec0a(1651764234) reqid 1(0x01) mode tunnel
    replay-window 32 seq 0x00000000 flag af-unspec (0x00100000)
    aead rfc4106(gcm(aes)) 0x0afaf19501d6d94174bb3036b84d59d78e[…] 128
    anti-replay context: seq 0x0, oseq 0x7829, bitmap 0x00000000
    lifetime config:
       limit: soft (INF)(bytes), hard (INF)(bytes)
       limit: soft (INF)(packets), hard (INF)(packets)
       expire add: soft 0(sec), hard 0(sec)
       expire use: soft 0(sec), hard 0(sec)
    lifetime current:
       2422796(bytes), 30761(packets)
       add 2019-01-06 21:57:45 use 2019-01-06 21:57:50
    stats:
       replay-window 0 replay 0 failed 0
```

1963   **Figure 12: Example of an ESP IPsec SA (Inbound and Outbound) Using an AEAD Algorithm on Linux**

1964 If a non-AEAD algorithm is used, such as AES-CBC with HMAC-SHA-1, the SA will contain
1965 the encryption and integrity keys separately. Figure 13 illustrates this. Note that this example
1966 uses FreeBSD, which calls the AES algorithm by its original candidate name, Rijndael.

```
1967   2001:db8:1:2::23 2001:db8:1:2::45
1968         esp mode=tunnel spi=1675186937(0x63d952f9) reqid=1(0x00000001)
1969         E: rijndael-cbc  1dd058ed 63905223 147979df 1865bfb3
1970         A: hmac-sha1  fde84c78 b2c90386 600927e3 1eb3dcf8 3163d053
1971         seq=0x00000000 replay=0 flags=0x00000000 state=mature
1972         created: Feb  2 17:29:42 2019   current: Feb  2 17:37:19 2019
1973         diff: 457(s)    hard: 3600(s)    soft: 2960(s)
1974         last:                            hard: 0(s)        soft: 0(s)
1975         current: 0(bytes)        hard: 0(bytes)  soft: 0(bytes)
1976         allocated: 0    hard: 0 soft: 0
1977         sadb_seq=1 pid=1404 refcnt=1
1978   2001:db8:1:2::45 2001:db8:1:2::23
1979         esp mode=tunnel spi=3301523791(0xc4c9414f) reqid=1(0x00000001)
1980         E: rijndael-cbc  d32b7287 8e0ef003 3a2bac01 4b14d0c7
1981         A: hmac-sha1  1a3b1fc7 091e76f5 860456f2 5342ceaa bc33a3d3
1982         seq=0x00000000 replay=4 flags=0x00000000 state=mature
1983         created: Feb  2 17:29:42 2019   current: Feb  2 17:37:19 2019
1984         diff: 457(s)    hard: 3600(s)    soft: 2611(s)
1985         last:                            hard: 0(s)        soft: 0(s)
1986         current: 0(bytes)        hard: 0(bytes)  soft: 0(bytes)
1987         allocated: 0    hard: 0 soft: 0
1988         sadb_seq=0 pid=1404 refcnt=1
```

1989   **Figure 13: Example of an ESP IPsec SA Using a Non-AEAD Algorithm on FreeBSD**

1990   The IPsec SA state information consists of:

1991   • The SPI that uniquely identifies the IPsec SA
1992   • The IP addresses of the local and remote host that send and receive IPsec packets
1993   • Cryptographic algorithms and their key material for encryption and integrity
1994   • A link to the associated Security Policy (sometimes called reqid)
1995   • The mode (tunnel or transport)
1996   • The encapsulation state (transport protocol, port numbers, and optional framing)
1997   • The current and maximum byte and packet counters allowed
1998   • The current and maximum timers for idleness and age allowed
1999   • Anti-replay context such as the current sequence number
2000   • A link to the IPComp state if present
2001   • Flags indicating various properties (TFC padding, etc.)

2002   The maximum counters and lifetimes have a soft and hard value. When the soft value is reached,
2003   the kernel will notify the IKE daemon so it can take preventative action. When the hard value is
2004   reached, the IPsec SA is deleted by the kernel, and the IKE daemon is notified. Each time a
2005   packet is encrypted or decrypted, this state is updated appropriately.

2006   **5.1.2   The Security Policy Database (SPD)**

2007   The kernel maintains a list of IPsec policies in the Security Policy Database (SPD). The policy
2008   describes the nature of the traffic that matches a policy rule, and links it to the state used to

2009 encrypt or decrypt the packet. Policies without states are used for on-demand IPsec connections.
2010 Figure 14 shows examples of two policies corresponding to the SAs in Figure 12.

```
2011  src 192.168.13.6/32 dst 0.0.0.0/0
2012      dir out priority 1040383 ptype main
2013      tmpl src 198.51.100.1 dst 203.0.113.1
2014          proto esp reqid 1 mode tunnel
2015
2016  src 0.0.0.0/0 dst 192.168.13.6/32
2017      dir in priority 1040383 ptype main
2018      tmpl src 203.0.113.1 dst 198.51.100.1
2019          proto esp reqid 1 mode tunnel
2020
```

2021   **Figure 14: Examples of Policies Corresponding to Figure 12 on Linux**

2022 The IPsec Security Policy information consists of:

2023 • The IP addresses of the IPsec gateways
2024 • The source IP addresses allowed in classless inter-domain routing (CIDR) format
2025 • The destination IP addresses in CIDR format
2026 • The transport protocol covered (0 for all)
2027 • The source and destination port ranges (0 for all)[36]
2028 • A link to the associated SA state
2029 • Direction (inbound, outbound, or forward[37])
2030 • Priority of the policy compared to other policy rules
2031 • IPsec protocol (ESP, AH, IPComp)
2032 • Mode (transport or tunnel)
2033 • IPComp information

2034 Using the SPD and SAD, packets are processed for encryption and decryption, and all the
2035 security policies are applied. If a policy violation is detected, the packet is dropped—for
2036 example, when an encrypted packet is decrypted into a packet with a source address that is not
2037 allowed by the Security Policy of the SA.[38] A policy can also point to a non-IPsec SA target.
2038 Commonly implemented targets are PASS (never encrypt with IPsec), DROP, REJECT (DROP
2039 and send an ICMP message), and HOLD (cache the packet until an IPsec SA has been
2040 established).

2041 Looking at the SAD and SPD entries of the previous figures, it can be seen that the host with IP
2042 address 198.51.100.1 is allowed to send ESP packets to the host with IP 203.0.113.1. The
2043 encrypted IP packet included can only have the source IP address 192.168.13.6 but can have any
2044 destination IP address. It is using AES-GCM as the AEAD encryption algorithm. In other words,

---

[36] For protocols without ports but with types, such as ICMP, the types are encoded as port numbers.
[37] Not all IPsec implementations have a forward policy. Think of it as a firewall within the IPsec subsystem.
[38] The SAD and SPD can be seen using the "ip xfrm" command on Linux. On BSD systems, the "setkey" tool can be used.

2045   there is a VPN client running on 198.51.100.1 that started a VPN connection to the VPN server
2046   on 203.0.113.1 and received the internal IP address 192.168.13.6.

2047   The IP address family of the IPsec host does not need to match the IP address family of the
2048   included encrypted IP packets. Figure 15 shows policies for two IPsec gateways using IPv6
2049   addresses that are used to connect two IPv4 subnets with each other.

```
src 192.0.0.0/24 dst 192.0.2.0/24
    dir out priority 1042407 ptype main
    tmpl src 2001:db8:1:2::45 dst 2001:db8:1:2::23
        proto esp reqid 16389 mode tunnel

src 192.0.2.0/24 dst 192.0.0.0/24
    dir in priority 1042407 ptype main
    tmpl src 2001:db8:1:2::23 dst 2001:db8:1:2::45
        proto esp reqid 16389 mode tunnel
```

Figure 15: Example of IPsec Policies for a Gateway Architecture Connecting IPv4 Subnets using IPv6 on Linux

2062   The output of the commands to inspect the current SAD and SPD differs per vendor. Figure 16
2063   shows the SAD and SPD entries for an IPv6 in IPv4 IPsec connection in tunnel mode using the
2064   `ipsecctl` command on OpenBSD.

```
FLOWS:
flow esp in from 2001:db8:0:1::/64 to 2001:db8:0:2::/64
  peer 203.0.113.1 srcid FQDN/east dstid FQDN/west type use
flow esp out from 2001:db8:0:2::/64 to 2001:db8:0:1::/64
  peer 203.0.113.1 srcid FQDN/east dstid FQDN/west type require

SAD:
esp tunnel from 198.51.100.1 to 203.0.113.1 spi 0x03f86d3a
 auth hmac-sha2-256 enc aes-256
esp tunnel from 203.0.113.1 to 198.51.100.1 spi 0x4df47d50
 auth hmac-sha2-256 enc aes-256
```

Figure 16: Example of IPsec States and Policies Connecting IPv6 Subnets using IPv4 on OpenBSD (line breaks added)

5.1.3 SAD Message Types

2079   Regardless of the implementation, the following types of messages are sent between the IKE and
2080   IPsec subsystems:

- IKE to IPsec:
  - Add, update, or remove an IPsec SA State
  - Add, update, or remove an IPsec SA Policy
  - Get IPsec SA information (byte counters, idleness)
  - Request a list of supported IPsec cryptographic algorithms

2086   • IPsec to IKE:
2087   o   Packet notification (with source/destination packet header information)
2088   o   Invalid SPI notification (IPsec packet received without matching SA with SPI)
2089   o   IPsec SA deleted (due to max life or max counter)
2090

5.2   Example of Establishing an IPsec Connection Using IKE

2092 In this example, the goal is to establish an IPsec connection that provides encryption and
2093 integrity protection services between endpoints A and B. The IPsec architecture is gateway-to-
2094 gateway; endpoint A uses gateway A on network A, and endpoint B uses gateway B on network
2095 B. If an IKE SA is not already in place, a packet will trigger the establishment of an IKE SA. In
2096 IKEv2, this is accompanied by the establishment of an IPsec SA as well:

2097 1. Endpoint A creates and sends a regular (non-IPsec) packet that has a destination address
2098   of endpoint B.

2099 2. Network A routes the packet to gateway A.

2100 3. Gateway A matches the packet's characteristics against those in its SPD. It determines
2101   that the packet should be protected by encryption and integrity protection through ESP.
2102   Because the SPD entry does not have a pointer to the SAD, it knows that no IPsec SA is
2103   currently established.

2104 4. Gateway A initiates an IKE SA negotiation with Gateway B. At the end of the
2105   negotiation, the IKE SA has been established, along with all the parameters and keying
2106   material required for the IPsec SA.

2107 5. The parameters specify that ESP tunnel mode will be used and that it will provide
2108   encryption and integrity protection. A pair of unidirectional IPsec SAs is created for the
2109   ESP tunnel and added to the SAD. The IPsec SAs are attached to the SPD entries. Each
2110   SA provides protection only for traffic going in one direction.

2111 6. Gateway A can finish processing the packet sent by endpoint A in step 1.

2112 7. Gateway A modifies the packet so that it is protected in accordance with the SA
2113   parameters. It creates a new IP header that uses gateway A's IP address as the source IP
2114   address, and gateway B's IP address as the destination IP address. It sets the IP protocol
2115   to ESP and fills in the SPI number. It encrypts the original IP packet and includes this as
2116   the payload for this packet based on the encryption key of the SAD entry. It calculates
2117   and adds the integrity ICV to the ESP payload data based on the integrity key (or AEAD
2118   encryption key) of the SAD entry. Gateway A then sends the packet to Gateway B.

2119 8. Meanwhile, Gateway B has also installed the IPsec SAs along with the SPD rules.

2120 9. Gateway B receives the packet and uses the value in the unencrypted SPI field from the
2121   ESP header to determine which SA should be applied to the packet. After looking up the
2122   SA parameters (including the secret key(s) needed for integrity protection and
2123   decryption), gateway B decrypts and validates the packet. This includes removing the
2124   additional IP packet header, checking the integrity of the encrypted data, optionally

2125   performing a replay check, and decrypting the original payload. Gateway B checks the
2126   SPD entry associated with the SAD entry to ensure that the decrypted IP packet complies
2127   to any source or destination restrictions, then sends the packet to its actual destination,
2128   endpoint B.

2129   If endpoint B wishes to reply to the packet, steps 6 to 9 of this process are repeated, except the
2130   parties are switched. Endpoint B would send a packet to endpoint A; routing would direct it to
2131   gateway B. Gateway B would modify the packet appropriately and send it to gateway A.
2132   Gateway A would process and validate the packet to restore the original IP address, then send the
2133   packet to endpoint A.

2134   Assuming that the IPsec connection between the gateways is sustained, eventually the IKE or
2135   IPsec SAs will approach one of the SA lifetime thresholds (maximum time or maximum bytes
2136   transmitted) as determined by the local policy on the respective gateways. The gateway with the
2137   shortest lifetime determines first that the maximum SA lifetime is approaching and initiates the
2138   rekeying process using the existing IKE SA. If the IPsec SA is being rekeyed, both ends install
2139   the new inbound and outbound IPsec SA before removing the old inbound and outbound IPsec
2140   SA. Once valid encrypted traffic is received on the new inbound IPsec SA, the old inbound IPsec
2141   SA will be deleted. This ensures that there is no interruption of the traffic flow during IPsec SA
2142   rekeying. If the IKE SA is being rekeyed, both ends replace the IKE SA, and all IPsec SAs
2143   belonging to the old IKE SA are attached to the new IKE SA.

2144   5.3   Procurement Considerations for IPsec Products

2145   IPsec VPN products vary in functionality, including protocol and algorithm support. They also
2146   vary in breadth, depth, and completeness of features and security services. Management features
2147   such as status reporting, logging, and auditing should provide adequate capabilities for the
2148   organization to effectively operate and manage the IPsec VPN and to extract detailed usage
2149   information. In the case of mesh encryption, too much logging can also be a concern.
2150   Traditionally, the management of IPsec products from different vendors has been problematic.
2151   Some recommendations and considerations include the following:

2152   •   Ensure that the cryptographic and networking capacity can accommodate the expected
2153   number of hosts and throughput.

2154   •   The Simple Network Management Protocol (SNMP) only provides a rudimentary and
2155   outdated interface for IKE and IPsec management. The IETF is working on a replacement
2156   management protocol using the YANG [52] data model language with ZEROCONF[39],
2157   which should provide a non-proprietary management interface that can be used across all
2158   vendors.

2159   •   AEAD algorithms such as AES-GCM for IPsec (ESP) significantly improve the
2160   performance of any IPsec product.

---

[39]   A good history and summary of ZEROCONF can be found at http://www.zeroconf.org/.

2161   • The IPsec VPN high availability, scalability, and redirection features should support the
2162   organization's requirements for automatic failover, where a secondary IPsec server is
2163   used as a spare that will automatically take over the IPsec services of a failing IPsec
2164   primary server. Or alternatively, support a deployment scenario where two IPsec servers
2165   perform load balancing for one logical IPsec service. State and information sharing are
2166   recommended to keep the IPsec server deployment process transparent to the user.

2167   • IPsec VPN authentication should provide the necessary support for the organization's
2168   current and future authentication methods and leverage existing authentication databases.
2169   IPsec VPN authentication should also be tested to ensure interoperability with existing
2170   authentication methods. For remote access VPNs, support for EAP-TLS is an important
2171   consideration. For host-to-host and mesh encryption deployments, public key and
2172   certificate-based authentication is important.

2173   • IPsec support within virtual machines or containers is usually provided by the operating
2174   system or container technology. This may require a different management system from
2175   physical IPsec gateway products. IPsec hardware offload needs careful consideration to
2176   ensure that the hardware offload capability is available within the virtualization
2177   technology without a performance penalty. In multi-tenant virtualization deployments, it
2178   might not be appropriate to use the hardware acceleration support, and support to disable
2179   hardware support should be available.

2180   • Many IoT devices are severely resource constrained, requiring a very small footprint of
2181   supported algorithms and random-access memory (RAM) usage. These devices tend to
2182   not support certificate authentication, and usually support one or a few encryption and
2183   integrity algorithms, such as only AES-CCM. IPsec gateways that will be used to connect
2184   IoT devices should be selected carefully to ensure algorithm compatibility.

2185   • IPsec products should be evaluated to ensure that they provide the level of granularity
2186   needed for access controls. Access controls should be capable of applying permissions to
2187   users, groups, and resources, as well as integrating with endpoint security controls. These
2188   considerations vary depending on the architecture that the IPsec product will be used for.
2189   Remote access VPNs need granularity at the user or device level, whereas host-to-host
2190   deployments could require access controls based on the IP address before accepting a
2191   connection based on proof of identity to prevent exposure to denial of service attacks.

2192

2193 **6   Troubleshooting IPsec VPNs**

2194   This section provides information on troubleshooting IPsec VPNs.

2195   **6.1   IKE Policy Exceptions**

2196   A few IKE and IPsec interactions need some careful attention to prevent the two subsystems
2197   from interfering with each other. Usually these are handled by the IKE implementation. If an
2198   IPsec implementation insisted that all communication between two hosts be encrypted with
2199   IPsec, those two hosts would never be able to send non-IPsec packets, including IKE packets.
2200   And without allowing IKE packets, no IPsec SA can be negotiated and installed, and the two
2201   hosts would never be able to communicate. Similarly, if one host crashes and restarts, it needs to
2202   be able to send IKE packets that are not IPsec encrypted, yet the remote endpoint still has a
2203   policy that only allows encrypted traffic to be received.

2204   To work around this, IPsec implements a policy exception for UDP port 500 and 4500 packets
2205   and will skip processing these via the regular SPD processing. If the kernel does not override
2206   IKE packets for IPsec processing, the IKE daemon needs to have a policy specifically for the
2207   IKE ports used with the highest preference, higher than the IPsec SA processing policy
2208   preference. Besides UDP port 500 and 4500, if TCP is used, those ports also need to have such a
2209   policy exception. Practically all IKE daemons perform this task on startup.

2210   **6.2   IPv6 Neighbor Discovery Policy Exception**

2211   A more subtle requirement is the need to exclude IPv6 neighbor discovery. If two hosts in the
2212   same subnet have established an IPsec SA over IPv6, and one of these hosts crashes and reboots,
2213   that host will send an unencrypted neighbor host discovery ICMP packet in an attempt to find the
2214   other host on the local network. If the host that did not crash drops the unencrypted ICMP
2215   packet, the two hosts will not be able to set up a new IPsec SA. If the host that did not crash
2216   performs DPD, it might find out in a few minutes that it needs to renegotiate the IPsec SA,
2217   otherwise communication will be blocked until the IPsec SA rekey or expiry timer runs out. This
2218   could be an outage that lasts anywhere between one and eight hours. Unfortunately, not all IKE
2219   daemons and IPsec implementations install the IPv6 neighbor discovery policy exception. It is
2220   recommended to test this scenario when using a new IKE/IPsec implementation.[40]

2221   If a kernel receives a packet with an SPI for which it has no IPsec SA, it can send a message to
2222   the IKE process containing the IP address of the host that sent the IPsec packet. Such an IKE
2223   process may be able to recognize the peer based on its (static) IP address, and initiate a new IKE
2224   exchange to try and set up a new IPsec SA that replaces the obsoleted IPsec SA on the host that
2225   did not crash. Not all kernels implement this mechanism to inform the IKE process.

---

[40]   To emulate, rather than actually crash a host, it is enough to send the IKE daemon a KILL signal, preventing it from telling
       the other side that it is shutting down, and then restart the IKE service.

2226   ### 6.3   Debugging IKE Configurations

2227   The method for debugging IKE and IPsec configurations depends on the specific
2228   implementation. For new configurations that are not working properly, the first step should be
2229   for both endpoint administrators to verify the configuration options they believe they have
2230   agreed upon. A checklist with the most common options to check can be found in Appendix A.
2231   A mismatch between basic IKE or IPsec parameters is most often the cause for new IPsec
2232   configurations not establishing properly.

2233   Using a network monitoring tool such as tcpdump is not very useful because only information
2234   from the first IKE_SA_INIT exchange can be inspected, and it only contains the DH groups, so
2235   it is unlikely that a misconfiguration can be detected at this point. All further captured IKE
2236   packets are encrypted, so they will not provide any additional information to diagnose the
2237   problem. It will be more helpful to enable additional logging or debugging. Remember to disable
2238   these settings again after the problem is resolved, otherwise large amounts of logs will
2239   continuously be produced.

2240   If an administrator controls both endpoints that will be configured for IPsec, it is often the case
2241   that this administrator is sitting behind one of the gateways and is using a secure remote login
2242   tool, such as a web interface or SSH connection, to configure the remote endpoint. If a
2243   configuration mistake is made or a partial configuration is accidentally activated, the IPsec hosts
2244   will drop all non-IPsec traffic and lock out the administrator's remote session. To prevent this
2245   problem, use a third host to indirectly log in to the remote IPsec endpoint for configuration.

2246   ### 6.4   Common Configuration Mistakes

2247   The HMAC integrity algorithm may be implemented with three different hash functions: SHA-
2248   256, SHA-384, and SHA-512. Different implementations use a different hash function for the
2249   "SHA2" indication that does not specify a specific hash function.

2250   Care should be taken with sending DPD/liveness probes too often. If the remote client is a device
2251   that might enter sleep mode, it may not be able to respond to such probes. Another issue is when
2252   the device's link is congested while the IPsec connection is idle. This will trigger DPD/liveness
2253   probes that could be dropped due to traffic congestion. If repeatedly dropped, these packets will
2254   trigger a false positive warning about the remote IPsec endpoint connection being lost, causing
2255   the server to terminate the IKE and IPsec SA, resulting in more packets to re-establish the VPN
2256   on an already congested link. Do not set DPD/liveness probes to values under one minute, which
2257   matches the recommendation in [18].

2258   PFS and DH group negotiation issues can be tricky to diagnose. In IKEv2, the first IPsec SA is
2259   established with the IKE SA establishment, and it does not really use a separate DH key
2260   exchange for PFS (unlike IKEv1). Any mismatch in DH group will only become apparent during
2261   a rekey message exchange hours later.

2262   VPN gateways commonly are also used as NAT devices. If packets from the internal network are
2263   NAT'ed to the VPN server's public IP before being considered for IPsec protection, the source

2264   IP no longer matches the IPsec policy, and the packet will not be sent out via IPsec. Instead, it
2265   could leak onto the internet without encryption, or be caught by the firewall subsystem running
2266   on the VPN gateway.

2267   In an IPv4-based network, machines within the same subnet use the Address Resolution Protocol
2268   (ARP) to find the Ethernet address belonging to a local IP address. If remote access clients are
2269   being assigned IP addresses from the remote LAN, the VPN server needs to be configured to
2270   answer for all IP addresses that are reachable via the IPsec VPN, since those remote VPN clients
2271   do not receive the local network ARP requests. This service is often called *proxy ARP*. Some
2272   IPsec implementations detect this automatically. For IPv6, this process is handled via IPv6
2273   neighbor discovery, which would also need to be performed by the VPN server if the local IPv6
2274   range would be used for remote access clients.

2275   The responder authenticates the initiator first, and fully establishes the IPsec SA before the
2276   initiator receives the IKE_AUTH response packet. If the initiator determines that the responder
2277   failed to authenticate itself, it can only notify the responder of this by immediately deleting the
2278   IKE SA, as the responder believes this is a fully established IKE SA and IPsec SA. This
2279   sometimes confuses administrators when debugging a problem, because from the responder's
2280   point of view, this was a successful—but very short—IPsec connection.

2281   ## 6.5   Routing-Based VPNs Versus Policy-Based VPNs

2282   IPsec implementations need to inspect packet streams to determine when a packet should be
2283   encrypted and when it should be transmitted unencrypted. One method is to use the routing table.
2284   If a route is pointing to a specific IPsec device, the IPsec implementation processes the packet
2285   based on its SPD/SAD rules. However, using routes can be fragile. Another subsystem could
2286   change the routing to accidentally or maliciously bypass the IPsec device, thus bypassing all
2287   encryption policies.

2288   Another issue of routing-based policies is that administrators often use a single IPsec policy from
2289   all possible IPv4 addresses (0.0.0.0/0) to all possible IPv4 addresses (0.0.0.0/0). Once the tunnel
2290   is established, routing is used to determine which packets to send over the IPsec connection. If a
2291   remote branch extends its network to use another subnet, say, 192.0.2.0/24, the only change
2292   needed is for the local branch to add a route for that IP range into the IPsec device. Firewall rules
2293   to limit the subnets allowed are omitted to allow this easy type of deployment, but this introduces
2294   a security problem as well as a compatibility problem. If the routes into the IPsec devices on both
2295   ends do not match, traffic will be encrypted in one direction but not in the other. At best, the
2296   IPsec gateway expecting encrypted packets will drop the unencrypted packets, and network
2297   connectivity fails. Or worse, the IPsec gateway will mistakenly route the unencrypted (and
2298   possibly modified) packets onto its local network.

2299   Policy-based VPNs covering only specific subnets and not every address (0.0.0.0/0) are a better
2300   solution and recommended over routing-based VPNs, despite the additional management
2301   overhead required. Depending on the implementation, policy-based VPNs can be a bit harder to
2302   debug, since it might not be obvious to the administrator where in the IP stack a packet is taken
2303   to be processed by the IPsec subsystem. This can lead to unexpected issues in hub-spoke

2304   deployments. For example, if a host with LAN IP address 10.0.2.1 and public IP 192.0.2.1
2305   creates an IPsec tunnel to a remote host on IP 192.0.2.2 to cover traffic between 10.0.2.0/24 and
2306   10.0.0.0/8, such an IPsec gateway might lose access to its own LAN, since a packet with
2307   destination 10.0.2.13 will be sent over the IPsec tunnel because it falls within the destination
2308   IPsec policy range of 10.0.0.0/8. Routing-based VPNs do not have this issue, as LAN packets do
2309   not pass through the routing table and instead find the target host to send the packet to via ARP.

2310   One common implementation processes the packets for IPsec after the network monitoring hooks
2311   are consulted. This leads to debugging tools such as the tcpdump tool seeing the packet as
2312   leaving the host unencrypted, while in fact the packet is encrypted after it is shown to the
2313   network debugging tool.

2314   6.6   Firewall Settings

2315   The most common network issue when setting up IPsec is that a firewall on the VPN server or on
2316   the network is blocking the IKE ports, UDP 500 and 4500. If an IPsec connection works for
2317   simple ping commands, but not when an application is trying to use the IPsec connection, the
2318   cause is most likely due to broken path MTU discovery. While this problem is not directly
2319   related to IPsec, it is often triggered because of the extra overhead of the ESP header making
2320   each 1500-byte original packet larger than 1500 bytes after the ESP header is added. The ESP
2321   packets would fragment and, too often, some stateful router or firewall mistakenly drops these
2322   packets.

2323   If the ESP packet contains a TCP packet, it can also cause problems with the Maximum Segment
2324   Size (MSS). For TCP to work properly, it needs to be able to send ICMP packets (Packet too
2325   big), but ICMP is often blocked. Some IPsec policies might only allow TCP packets and prohibit
2326   ICMP packets. This also commonly manifests itself as an administrator who can log in over the
2327   IPsec connection using the SSH protocol, but as soon as they try to actually use this session, their
2328   screen freezes. Decreasing the MTU of the IPsec interface can work around this issue. For TCP,
2329   a common workaround is to use TCP MSS clamping to the path MTU or to a fixed value (e.g.,
2330   1380).

2331

2332
7   IPsec Planning and Implementation

2333 This section focuses on the planning and implementation of IPsec in an enterprise. As with any
2334 new technology deployment, IPsec planning and implementation should be addressed in a
2335 phased approach. A successful deployment of IPsec can be achieved by following a clear, step-
2336 by-step planning and implementation process. The use of a phased approach for deployment can
2337 minimize unforeseen issues and identify potential pitfalls early in the process. This model also
2338 allows for the incorporation of advances in new technology, as well as adapting IPsec to the
2339 ever-changing enterprise. This section explores each of the IPsec planning and implementation
2340 phases in depth, as follows:

2341   1. **Identify Needs.** The first phase of the process involves identifying the need to protect
2342   network communications, determining which computers, networks, and data are part of
2343   the communications, and identifying related requirements (e.g., minimum performance).
2344   This phase also involves determining how that need can best be met (e.g., IPsec, TLS,
2345   SSH) and deciding where and how the security should be implemented.

2346   2. **Design the Solution.** The second phase involves all facets of designing the IPsec
2347   solution. For simplicity, the design elements are grouped into four categories:
2348   architectural considerations, authentication methods, cryptography policy, and packet
2349   filters.

2350   3. **Implement and Test a Prototype.** The next phase involves implementing and testing a
2351   prototype of the designed solution in a lab or test environment. The primary goals of the
2352   testing are to evaluate the functionality, performance, scalability, and security of the
2353   solution, and to identify any issues with the components, such as interoperability issues.

2354   4. **Deploy the Solution.** Once the testing is completed and all issues are resolved, the next
2355   phase includes the gradual deployment of IPsec throughout the enterprise.

2356   5. **Manage the Solution.** After the IPsec solution has been deployed, it is managed
2357   throughout its lifecycle. Management includes maintenance of the IPsec components and
2358   support for operational issues. The lifecycle process is repeated when enhancements or
2359   significant changes need to be incorporated into the solution.

2360 Organizations should also implement other measures that support and complement IPsec
2361 implementations. These measures help to ensure that IPsec is implemented in an environment
2362 with the technical, management, and operational controls necessary to provide adequate security
2363 for the IPsec implementation. Examples of supporting measures are as follows:

2364   • Establish and maintain control over all entry and exit points for the protected network,
2365   which helps to ensure its integrity.

2366   • Ensure that all IPsec endpoints (gateways and hosts) are secured and maintained
2367   properly, which should reduce the risk of IPsec compromise or misuse.

2368   • Revise organizational policies as needed to incorporate appropriate usage of the IPsec
2369   solution. Policies should provide the foundation for the planning and implementation of

2370   IPsec. Appendix B contains an extensive discussion of IPsec-related policy
2371   considerations.

2372   **7.1   Identify Needs**

2373   The purpose of this phase is to identify the need to protect communications and determine how
2374   that need can best be met. The first step is to determine which communications need to be
2375   protected (e.g., all communications between two networks, certain applications involving a
2376   particular server). The next step is to determine what protection measures (e.g., providing
2377   confidentiality, assuring integrity, authenticating the source) are needed for each type of
2378   communication. It is also important to identify other general and application-specific
2379   requirements, such as performance, and to think about future needs. For example, if it is likely
2380   that other types of communications will need protection in a year, those needs should also be
2381   considered.

2382   After identifying all the relevant needs, the organization should consider the possible technical
2383   solutions and select the one that best meets the identified needs. Although IPsec is typically a
2384   reasonable choice, other protocols such as TLS or SSH may be equally good or better in some
2385   cases. See Section 8 for descriptions of such protocols and guidance on when a particular
2386   protocol may be a viable alternative to IPsec. In some cases, IPsec is the only option—for
2387   example, if a gateway-to-gateway VPN is being established with a business partner that has
2388   already purchased and deployed an IPsec gateway for the connection. Another possibility is that
2389   the solution may need to support a protocol that is only provided by IPsec.

2390   Assuming that IPsec is chosen as the solution's protocol, the Identify Needs phase should result
2391   in the following:

2392   • Identification of all communications that need to be protected (e.g., servers, client hosts,
2393   networks, applications, data), and the protection that each type of communication needs
2394   (preferably encryption, integrity protection, and peer authentication)

2395   • Selection of an IPsec architecture (e.g., gateway-to-gateway, remote access VPN, host-to-
2396   host, mesh encryption)

2397   • Specification of performance requirements (normal and peak loads).

2398   **7.2   Design the Solution**

2399   Once the needs have been identified, and it has been determined that IPsec is the best solution,
2400   the next phase is to design a solution that meets the needs. This involves four major components,
2401   which are described in more detail in Sections 7.2.1 through 7.2.5:

2402   • **Architecture.** Designing the architecture of the IPsec implementation includes host
2403   placement (for host-to-host architectures)[41] and gateway placement (for remote access

---

[41] In most cases, the hosts are already placed on the network; the architectural considerations are focused on identifying
       intermediate devices between the hosts, such as firewalls performing NAT.

2404 and gateway-to-gateway architectures), IPsec client software selection (for host-to-host
2405 and remote access architectures), and host address space management considerations (for
2406 host-to-host and remote access architectures).

2407 • **Cryptography for Authentication.** The IPsec implementation must have an
2408 authentication method selected, such as the use of a digital signature or PSK. Only NIST-
2409 approved methods and algorithms shall be used. See NIST SP 800-131A [47].

2410 • **Cryptography for Key Exchange, Confidentiality and Integrity.** The algorithms for
2411 DH key exchange, encryption, and integrity protection must be selected, as well as the
2412 key lengths for algorithms that support multiple key lengths. Only NIST-approved
2413 methods and algorithms shall be used. See NIST SP 800-131A [47].

2414 • **Packet Filter.** The packet filter determines which types of traffic should be permitted and
2415 which should be denied, and what protection and compression measures (if any) should
2416 be applied to each type of permitted traffic (e.g., ESP tunnel using AES for encryption
2417 and HMAC-SHA-256 for integrity protection; Lempel-Ziv-Stac (LZS) for compression).

2418 The decisions made regarding cryptography and packet filters are all documented in the IPsec
2419 policy. In its simplest form, an IPsec policy is a set of rules that govern the use of the IPsec
2420 protocol. It specifies the data to secure and the security method to use to secure that data. An
2421 IPsec policy determines the type of traffic that is allowed through IPsec endpoints, and generally
2422 consists of a packet filter and a set of security parameters for traffic that matches the packet
2423 filter. Those parameters include the authentication and encryption scheme and tunnel settings.
2424 When communications occur, each packet filter can result in the establishment of one or more
2425 IPsec SAs that enable protected communications satisfying the security policy for that packet
2426 filter.

2427 Other decisions should also be made during the design phase, such as setting IKE and IPsec SA
2428 lifetimes and identifying which DH group number is best. Besides meeting the organization's
2429 cryptographic requirements of NIST SP 800-131A [47] and FIPS 140 [13], design decisions
2430 should incorporate the organization's logging and data management strategies, incident response
2431 and recovery plans, resource replication and failover needs, and current and future network
2432 characteristics, such as the use of wireless, NAT, and IPv6. Section 7.2.6 covers these
2433 considerations and design decisions in more detail.

2434 ### 7.2.1 Architecture

2435 The architecture of the IPsec implementation refers to the selection of devices and software to
2436 provide IPsec services and the placement of IPsec endpoints within the existing network
2437 infrastructure. These two considerations are often closely tied together; for example, a decision
2438 could be made to use the existing Internet firewall as the IPsec gateway. This section will
2439 explore three particular aspects of IPsec architecture: gateway placement, IPsec client software
2440 for hosts, and host address space management.

2441   **7.2.1.1 Gateway Placement**

2442   Due to the layered defense strategy used to protect enterprise networks, IPsec gateway placement
2443   is often a challenging task. As described later in this section, the gateway's placement has
2444   security, functionality, and performance implications. Also, the gateway's placement may have
2445   an effect on other network devices, such as firewalls, routers, and switches. Incorporating an
2446   IPsec gateway into a network architecture requires strong overall knowledge of the network and
2447   security policy. The following are major factors to consider for IPsec gateway placement:

2448   • **Device Performance.** IPsec can be computationally intensive, primarily because of
2449   encryption and decryption. Providing IPsec services from another device (e.g., a firewall,
2450   router) may put too high of a load on the device during peak usage, causing service
2451   disruptions. A possible alternative is to offload the cryptographic operations to a
2452   specialized hardware device, such as a network card with built-in cryptographic
2453   functions. Organizations should also review their network architecture to determine if
2454   bottlenecks are likely to occur due to network devices (e.g., routers, firewalls) that cannot
2455   sustain the processing of peak volumes of network traffic that includes IPsec-
2456   encapsulated packets.[42] For remote access architectures, the choice of DH group is
2457   important because it is the most computationally demanding part of IKE.

2458   • **Traffic Examination.** If IPsec-encrypted traffic passes through a firewall, the firewall
2459   cannot determine what protocols the packets' payloads contain, so it cannot filter the
2460   traffic based on those protocols. Intrusion detection systems encounter the same issue;
2461   they cannot examine encrypted traffic for attacks. However, it is generally recommended
2462   to design the IPsec architecture so that a firewall and intrusion detection software can
2463   examine the unencrypted traffic. Organizations most commonly address this by using
2464   their Internet firewalls as VPN gateways or placing VPN gateway devices just outside
2465   their Internet firewalls. A full mesh encryption bypasses all network-based firewalls and
2466   intrusion detection systems because those systems can only accept or reject the encrypted
2467   stream without being able to inspect the data that has been encrypted. This could mean a
2468   reduction of security. This is discussed in greater detail in [54].

2469   • **Traffic Not Protected by IPsec.** Organizations should consider carefully the threats
2470   against network traffic after it has been processed by the receiving IPsec gateway and
2471   sent without IPsec protection across additional network segments. For example, an
2472   organization that wants to place its VPN gateway outside its Internet firewalls should
2473   ensure that the traffic passing between the IPsec gateway and the Internet firewalls has
2474   sufficient protection against breaches of confidentiality and integrity.

2475   • **Gateway Outages.** The architecture should take into consideration the effects of IPsec
2476   gateway outages, including planned maintenance outages and unplanned outages caused
2477   by failures or attacks. For example, if the IPsec gateway is placed inline near the Internet
2478   connection point, meaning that all network traffic passes through it, a gateway failure
2479   could cause a loss of all Internet connectivity for the organization. Also, larger IPsec

[42]   The network architecture review is also beneficial in identifying intermediate network devices that may need to be
        reconfigured to permit IPsec traffic to pass through.

2480   implementations may use a gateway management server; a server failure could severely
2481   impact the management of all gateways. Generally, if the network is designed to be
2482   redundant, the IPsec gateways and management servers should also be designed to be
2483   redundant.

2484   • **NAT.** NAT provides a mechanism to use private addresses on the internal network while
2485   using public addresses to connect to external networks. NAT can map each private
2486   address to a different public address, while the network address port translation (NAPT)
2487   variant of NAT can map many private addresses to a single public address, differentiating
2488   the original addresses by assigning different public address ports.[43] NAT is often used by
2489   enterprises, small offices, and residential users that do not want to pay for more IP
2490   addresses than necessary or wish to take advantage of the security benefits and flexibility
2491   of having private addresses assigned to internal hosts. Unfortunately, as described in
2492   Section 4, there are known incompatibilities between IPsec and NAT because NAT
2493   modifies the IP addresses in the packet, which directly violates the packet integrity
2494   assurance provided by IPsec. However, there are a few solutions to this issue, as follows:

2495   o **Perform NAT before applying IPsec.** This can be accomplished by arranging
2496   the devices in a particular order, or by using an IPsec gateway that also performs
2497   NAT. For example, the gateway can perform NAT first and then IPsec for
2498   outbound packets. This is sometimes required because an IPsec service provider
2499   with multiple customers cannot build tunnels to each customer using the same
2500   internal IP addresses, and thus requires their customers to use specific RFC 1918
2501   [35] IP addresses.

2502   o **Use UDP or TCP encapsulation of ESP packets.** Encapsulation requires tunnel
2503   mode. Encapsulation adds a UDP or TCP header to each packet, which provides
2504   an IP address and UDP/TCP port that can be used by NAT (including NAPT).
2505   This removes conflicts between IPsec and NAT in most environments.[44] IKE
2506   negotiates the use of encapsulation. During the IKE initial exchanges, both
2507   endpoints perform NAT discovery to determine if NAT services are running
2508   between the two IPsec endpoints. NAT discovery involves each endpoint sending
2509   a hash of its original source address(es) and port to the other endpoint, which
2510   compares the original values to the actual values to determine if NAT was
2511   applied. IKE then moves its communications from UDP port 500 to port 4500 in
2512   order to avoid inadvertent interference from NAT devices that perform
2513   proprietary alterations of IPsec-related activity. Detection of NAT and the use of
2514   encapsulation can also cause the host behind the NAT device to send keepalive
2515   packets to the other endpoint, which should keep the NAPT port-to-address
2516   mapping from being lost. Although all IKEv2 implementations must support UDP

---

[43]   Additional information on NAT and NAPT is available from [53].
[44]   In some cases, either the network architecture or the type of traffic may require additional measures to allow IPsec traffic to
       negotiate NAT successfully. For example, protocols such as Session Initiation Protocol (SIP) for Voice over IP (VoIP) and
       File Transfer Protocol (FTP) have IP addresses embedded in the application data. Handling such traffic correctly in NAT
       environments may require the use of application layer gateways (ALGs).

2517   encapsulation, TCP encapsulation is a recent addition that has not yet reached
2518   universal support in IPsec devices.

2519   **7.2.1.2 Third-Party IPsec Client Software for Hosts**

2520   In IPsec host-to-host and remote access architectures, each host must have an IPsec-compliant
2521   implementation installed and configured. Most operating systems on computers and mobile
2522   devices have built-in support for IPsec and only require configuration or an enterprise
2523   provisioning system that provides and installs the required configurations. However, some
2524   mobile devices or embedded devices do not have a built-in IPsec implementation. Also, some
2525   built-in clients might be lacking a feature required for a certain deployment or might not support
2526   an enterprise provisioning system. In such cases, a third-party client might need to be deployed
2527   instead. Third-party clients must be distributed and installed, then configured or provisioned.[45]

2528   Features that may be of interest when evaluating IPsec client software include support for the
2529   following:

2530   • IKEv2

2531   • IKEv1 (if communicating to legacy equipment)

2532   • IKEv2 fragmentation

2533   • IKEv2 encapsulation (UDP, TCP, or TCP-TLS)

2534   • IKEv2 PPK

2535   • Particular encryption, integrity protection, and compression algorithms

2536   • Particular authentication methods such as EAP-TLS, RSA, and ECDSA

2537   • Multiple simultaneous tunnels[46]

2538   • Authentication support for hardware tokens utilizing Open Authorization (OAuth), OTP,
2539   or Fast Identity Online (FIDO)

2540   • Flexible X.509 certificates and optional IPsec Extended Key Usage (EKU) restrictions

2541   • CRL and/or OCSP support

2542   • Certificate uniform resource indicator (URI) and raw keys for embedded clients

2543   • DNSSEC provisioning of enterprise trust anchors

2544   Another important IPsec client feature is the ability to allow or prevent split tunneling. Split
2545   tunneling occurs when an IPsec client on an external network is not configured to send all its

---

[45] Organizations deploying third-party clients should pay particular attention to mobile devices and application stores. On
      some mobile phone platforms, many questionable VPN implementations are being made available where the goal of the
      VPN service is to monitor and/or modify the user's traffic before it is protected by IPsec.
[46] In some cases, it may be desirable to permit a host to establish multiple tunnels simultaneously. For example, the host may
      perform two types of communications that each need different protective measures from IPsec.

2546   traffic to the organization's IPsec gateway. Requests with a destination on the organization's
2547   network are sent to the IPsec gateway, and all other requests are sent directly to their destination
2548   without going through the IPsec tunnel. The client host is effectively communicating directly and
2549   simultaneously with the organization's internal network and another network (typically the
2550   Internet). If the client host were compromised, a remote attacker could connect to the host
2551   surreptitiously and use its IPsec tunnel to gain unauthorized access to the organization's network.
2552   This would not be possible if the IPsec client software had been configured to prohibit split
2553   tunneling. However, any compromise of an IPsec client host is problematic, because an attacker
2554   could install utilities on the host that capture data, passwords, and other valuable information.

2555   Prohibiting split tunneling can limit the potential impact of a compromise by preventing the
2556   attacker from taking advantage of the IPsec connection to enter the organization's network; the
2557   attacker could only connect to the compromised system when it is not using IPsec. However,
2558   many hosts have multiple methods of connectivity, such as mobile data, wired LAN, and
2559   wireless LAN; if an attacker can connect to a network interface other than the one used for IPsec,
2560   it may be possible to use the IPsec tunnel even if split tunneling is prohibited. This can allow
2561   access to a more trusted network—the network protected by IPsec—from a less trusted network,
2562   such as an improperly secured wireless LAN. Accordingly, hosts should support being
2563   configured so that only the network interface used for IPsec is enabled when IPsec is in use.
2564   Some VPN clients can be configured to disable other network interfaces automatically. An
2565   alternative is to configure a personal firewall on the host so that it blocks unnecessary and
2566   unauthorized network traffic on all interfaces. Due to its security complications/risks, split
2567   tunneling is strongly discouraged.

2568   As described in Section 7.2.6, not allowing split tunneling is also helpful in preventing IPsec
2569   clients' hosts from being compromised. If a user mistakenly tries to connect to a malicious site,
2570   the traffic would be forced to go through the VPN where an enterprise firewall or proxy server
2571   could filter malicious traffic. Some organizations prefer split tunneling because it prevents non-
2572   enterprise traffic from reaching the enterprise. It also reduces the internet bandwidth capacity
2573   needed by the enterprise to support its remote VPN clients. There might also be legal reasons
2574   why an enterprise prefers not to handle traffic unrelated to its organization.

2575   There are other factors that may differentiate IPsec clients. For example, one client may provide
2576   substantially better performance than another client or consume less of the host's resources.
2577   Another consideration is the security of the client software itself, such as how frequently
2578   vulnerabilities are identified, and how quickly patches are available. Client interoperability with
2579   other IPsec implementations is also a key concern; some client implementations only
2580   interoperate with their own vendor's gateway implementation or with a limited number of other
2581   vendors' gateway implementations. It is critical to ensure that the selected client will interoperate
2582   with each gateway implementation it might encounter. Section 7.3.1 discusses this topic in more
2583   detail.

2584   Organizations should also carefully consider how clients can be provisioned with IPsec client
2585   software and configuration settings, including policies. Many clients offer different features that
2586   can make client deployment, configuration, and management easier. For example, an
2587   administrator might be able to set policy for clients remotely, instead of manually visiting each

2588   host. Some clients offer administrators the ability to lock out or disable certain configuration
2589   options or functionality so that users cannot inadvertently or intentionally circumvent the
2590   intended security. If administrators cannot distribute pre-configured IPsec clients or remotely
2591   control IPsec configuration settings, the administrators might need to manually configure each
2592   IPsec client or rely on users to follow instructions and configure the clients themselves. The
2593   latter approach is often challenging for non-technical users.

2594   **7.2.1.3 Host Address Space Management**

2595   In remote access VPN architectures where the hosts are outside the organization (e.g., mobile
2596   devices, remote workers), the VPN client will receive an additional IP address from the
2597   organization's address space assigned as a virtual IP address to each external IPsec host. In the
2598   latter case, the client then establishes an IPsec connection that uses its real IP address in the
2599   external packet headers (so the IPsec-encapsulated packets can be routed across public networks)
2600   and its virtual IP address in the internal packet headers (so the packets can be routed across the
2601   organization's internal networks and treated as internally generated).

2602   Virtual addresses can be assigned from an address pool that resides on the VPN server. The VPN
2603   server can also use the DHCP Relay protocol or use an AAA service such as RADIUS or
2604   Diameter to obtain an IP address. A local pool can provide an easier indication that the IP
2605   address accessing a local resource is originating from a VPN client or is a client connecting from
2606   a certain region.

2607   It is important to ensure that any addresses the IPsec gateway manages are excluded from the
2608   ranges that other internal DHCP servers can assign to avoid address conflicts. Some vendors
2609   provide internal address assignment and authentication using proprietary functionality. This may
2610   present compatibility issues depending on the products being used.

2611   When deploying a remote access VPN in a data center or cloud where the only service offered is
2612   the VPN server without any other local resources, non-routable IP addresses such as those
2613   defined in RFC 1918 [35] can be used for the address pool of virtual IPs for the VPN clients. The
2614   VPN server then uses NAT to translate these IP addresses to its own public IP address. One
2615   potential issue with such a deployment is that some websites limit the number of users or
2616   connections coming from a single IP address. If dozens or hundreds of website users appear to
2617   all come from the one VPN server public IP address, the website might block the IP address
2618   because it assumes it is a malicious entity that obtained the credentials of many users. Using
2619   multiple public IP addresses on such a VPN server deployment could mitigate this problem.

2620   **7.2.2 IKE Authentication**

2621   The endpoints of a host-to-host and gateway-to-gateway IPsec architecture typically use the
2622   same authentication method to validate each other. Validation for remote access VPNs tend to
2623   use different mechanisms to authenticate each other, where the server is authenticated using a
2624   machine certificate and clients are authenticated using EAP-TLS.

2625   IPsec implementations typically support a number of authentication methods. The most common
2626   methods are certificate-based digital signatures or raw public keys, EAP, and PSK. When using
2627   IKEv1, a group PSK combined with a username and password is also common. This section
2628   discusses the primary advantages and disadvantages of these methods.

2629   PSKs should only be used for gateway-to-gateway scenarios that cross an administrative domain
2630   and only when based on generating strong and sufficiently long random PSKs with at least 112
2631   bits of entropy. Using a public-key key pair (with or without certificates) based on RSA, DSA or
2632   ECDSA is preferred over using PSKs, but if the implementations that need to interoperate do not
2633   share the same public key-based authentication method, PSKs are an appropriate alternative.
2634   Within an administrative domain, PSKs should not be used. For remote access VPN scenarios,
2635   EAP-TLS or machine certificate authentication should be used.

2636   **7.2.2.1 PSKs**

2637   To use PSKs, the IPsec administrator needs to create a strong random secret key or password
2638   string that is then configured in both IPsec devices (the end points) of an IPsec connection.[47]
2639   PSKs are the simplest authentication method to implement, but also by far the least secure.
2640   Administrators need to find IPsec products that provide key management capabilities for PSKs
2641   or implement their own key management mechanisms, such as generating, storing, deploying,
2642   auditing, and destroying keys; proper key management can be quite resource-intensive. Although
2643   it is easiest to create a single key that all endpoints share, this causes problems when a host
2644   should no longer have access—the key then needs to be changed on all other hosts. PSKs should
2645   also be updated periodically to reduce the potential impact of a compromised key. Another issue
2646   is that the key must be kept secret and transferred over secure channels. Individuals with access
2647   to an endpoint are almost always able to gain access to the PSK.[48] Depending on the key type,
2648   this could grant access from one, some, or all IP addresses. (A group shared key can only be used
2649   from addresses in a certain range, while a wildcard shared key can be used from any IP address.)
2650   Also, using the same key for a group of endpoints reduces accountability, as anyone within the
2651   group can impersonate another member of the group.

2652   Because of scalability and security concerns, PSK authentication is generally an acceptable
2653   solution only for small-scale implementations with known IP addresses or small IP address
2654   ranges. The use of a single PSK for a group of hosts is strongly discouraged for all but the most
2655   highly-controlled environments, such as a group of secure routers. PSKs are also generally not
2656   recommended for remote access clients that have dynamic IP addresses, because the keys cannot
2657   be restricted to a particular IP address or small range of IP addresses. PSKs are also frequently
2658   used during initial IPsec testing and implementation because of their simplicity. After the IPsec
2659   implementation is operating properly, the authentication method can then be changed.

---

[47]   Because PSKs are often long strings of random characters, manually typing them in to the endpoints can cause problems
from typos.

[48]   Some vendors protect stored PSKs using obfuscation, but since unattended access to these secrets is needed when booting
up the system, this obfuscation is usually trivially broken.

2660   **7.2.2.2   Certificate-based digital signatures**

2661   Certificates are typically used in machine certificate and EAP-TLS based authentication. The
2662   certificate owner produces a digital signature of the IKE exchange that proves its possession of
2663   the certificate's private key and authenticates the IKE session.

2664   A certificate identifies each device, and each device is configured to use certificates. User-
2665   specific certificates may be used instead of device-specific certificates, but some remote access
2666   VPN configurations do not allow a single user to log onto multiple devices simultaneously, so it
2667   is always better to generate a certificate per device rather than per user.

2668   Two IPsec endpoints will trust each other if a CA they both trust has signed their certificates.[49]
2669   The certificates must be securely stored in the local certificate store on the IPsec hosts and
2670   gateways or on a secure hardware token. Using a certificate-based method allows much of the
2671   key administration to be offloaded to a central certificate server, but still requires IPsec
2672   administrators to perform some key management activities, such as provisioning hosts with
2673   credentials, either through IPsec vendor-provided features or IPsec administrator-created
2674   capabilities. Many organizations implement a public key infrastructure (PKI) for managing
2675   certificates for IPsec VPNs and other applications such as secure email and Web access.[50]
2676   Certificates can be issued to limit their use using EKU attributes. Some IPsec hosts insist on
2677   IPsec-specific EKUs, while others accept the TLS-based EKUs (serverAuth or clientAuth) and
2678   some ignore all EKUs. The IETF PKI standard for IKE EKUs is specified in RFC 4945 [55]. A
2679   certificate issued for secure email might not be usable for IPsec on some of the VPN gateways
2680   deployed in an organization. Issuing certificates per device instead of per user avoids this issue
2681   and has the additional advantage that if a device is lost or stolen, not all of the user's VPN access
2682   will need to be revoked.

2683   Although the certificate authentication method scales well to large implementations and provides
2684   a much stronger security solution than PSKs, it does have some disadvantages. While certificates
2685   can be revoked and transmitted to the VPN servers via CRLs [57] in bulk, or on demand via
2686   OCSP) [58], typically these mechanisms provide no option for temporarily disabling a
2687   certificate. Additional complications can occur when the connection to the OCSP server itself is
2688   down, or worse, requires an IPsec tunnel to be negotiated that needs to use that OCSP server.
2689   Non-standard solutions using an AAA server or a Pluggable Authentication Module (pam
2690   authentication) are usually added for such use cases.

2691   Another potential problem with the certificate authentication method involves packet
2692   fragmentation. Packets in an IKE negotiation are typically relatively small and do not need to be
2693   fragmented. By adding certificates to the negotiation, packets may become so large that they
2694   need to be fragmented, which is not supported by some IPsec implementations.

---

[49]   This describes the most common CA model; other models, such as the Federal Bridge CA, function somewhat differently.
[50]   PKI implementations require a considerable investment in time and resources. It is outside the scope of this document to
        discuss a PKI in detail. See NIST SP 800-32, *Introduction to Public Key Technology and the Federal PKI Infrastructure*, for
        more information [56].

2695 **7.2.2.3 Raw public key digital signatures**

2696 Raw public key digital signatures work the same as certificate-based digital signatures, except
2697 instead of trusting a certificate (directly or indirectly via a CA), the trust is placed in the public
2698 key itself. Keys are usually represented in base64 format or using just the SubjectPublicKeyInfo
2699 (SPKI) part of a certificate.

2700 Public keys can be distributed to the endpoints via trusted provisioning software or can be
2701 fetched on demand from DNSSEC or a directory service (e.g., Lightweight Directory Access
2702 Protocol [LDAP]) based on the ID presented during the IKE exchange. Instead of specifying the
2703 validity period in a certificate, these publishing services can simply remove the key when it is no
2704 longer needed. The public key for a particular ID specified in IKE resides in the DNS or
2705 directory service under that ID name. Revocation is accomplished by removing the public key
2706 from the publishing service's database.

2707 For resource-constrained embedded devices that authenticate using a single hard-coded public
2708 key, a certificate by itself can be too large to be contained or operated on and serves no purpose
2709 since certificate validation is not performed.

2710 One disadvantage of raw public keys is that there are not as many tools that support these,
2711 because most IKE implementations have been written to be used with certificates or PSKs.

2712 **7.2.2.4 EAP**

2713 EAP support is included in IKEv2. Both older and newer EAP methods are supported. EAP can
2714 be used as the only authentication method, or as a second authentication method. Often, different
2715 authentication methods are used: the server is authenticated using certificate-based
2716 authentication, and the client (typically a laptop or mobile device) is authenticated using an EAP
2717 method. EAP authentication allows additional types of authentications to be used, such as a
2718 username with a password (EAP-MSCHAPv2), a user (not host) certificate (EAP-TLS), or an
2719 EAP method supporting two-factor authentication. EAP authentication is mostly used for laptops
2720 and mobile phones.

2721 **7.2.3 Cryptography for Confidentiality Protection, Integrity Protection and Key**
2722 **Exchange**

2723 Setting the cryptographic policy for confidentiality and integrity protection and key exchange
2724 involves choosing encryption and integrity protection algorithms, key lengths,[51] DH groups for
2725 key exchange, and IKE and ESP lifetimes. For up-to-date policies and advice on these settings,
2726 see NIST SP 800-131A [47] and FIPS 140 [13] as well as the recommendations of the IETF for
2727 IKE [20] and ESP [59]. Note that these documents will be updated over time or be obsoleted for
2728 newer publications.

---

[51] Only FIPS-validated implementations of NIST-approved algorithms shall be used.

2729   The IKE protocol sends just a few packets per hour, so it makes sense to be extra cautious and
2730   pick strong algorithms with large enough keys, and specifically a strong DH group. Approved
2731   DH groups are identified in NIST SP 800-56A [62]. The bulk of the CPU power of an IPsec host
2732   will be spent on IPsec, not IKE. In IKE, the most CPU-intensive operation is the DH calculation.
2733   When an IPsec host has hundreds or thousands of IKE (re)connections, choosing the right DH
2734   group becomes very important.

2735   It is recommended to use strong key sizes for IKE. The performance impact of larger key sizes is
2736   minimal because IKE traffic is negligible compared to IPsec traffic. For IPsec (ESP), the key
2737   size can have a significant impact on performance. In general, use larger key sizes for IPsec if
2738   performance is not an issue. For ESP, the choice of algorithms for confidentiality and integrity
2739   protection should also take performance into account. Using an AEAD algorithm such as AES-
2740   GCM that can provide both confidentiality and integrity protection in a single operation will give
2741   better performance than using non-AEAD algorithms that require separate operations (e.g., AES-
2742   CBC for encryption and HMAC for integrity protection). It is important to estimate the
2743   processing resources that the cryptographic computations will require during peak usage.

2744   It is uncommon to use 192-bit AES keys, and this key length is optional in [20]. It is worth
2745   mentioning as well that in the future, an adversary with a quantum computer may be able to
2746   reduce the key strength of an AES key by a factor of two, in which case a 256-bit AES key may
2747   effectively provide around 128 bits of security in the quantum computer world (note that this
2748   level of security strength is a magnitude stronger than the current level of 128 bits for classical
2749   security).

2750   AES-GCM (an AEAD algorithm) is often offloaded to hardware, making it significantly faster
2751   than AES-CBC (a non-AEAD algorithm). The CPU is typically the hardware component most
2752   affected by cryptographic operations. In some cases, a hardware-based cryptographic engine
2753   with customized CPUs, also known as a cryptographic accelerator, may be needed for greater
2754   throughput, but this may limit the algorithm options. Another potential issue is export restrictions
2755   involving the use of encryption algorithms in certain countries.[52] In addition, some IPsec
2756   components may not provide support for a particular algorithm or key size.

2757   For integrity checking of non-AEAD algorithms, most IPsec implementations offer HMAC-
2758   SHA-1 or the HMAC with the SHA-2 hashing algorithms[53] (referred to as the HMAC-SHA2s).
2759   Even though HMAC-SHA1 is still a NIST-approved option, the HMAC-SHA2s are
2760   recommended due to the fact that the HMAC-SHA2s have stronger security than HMAC-SHA1.
2761   HMAC-MD5 has never been a NIST-approved algorithm and shall not be used.

2762   In some implementations of IPsec, the cryptographic policy settings are not immediately
2763   apparent to administrators. The default settings for encryption and integrity protection, as well as
2764   the details of each setting, are often located down several levels of menus or are split among
2765   multiple locations. It is also challenging with some implementations to alter the settings once

---

[52]   More information on export restrictions is available from the Bureau of Industry and Security, U.S. Department of
       Commerce, at https://www.bis.doc.gov/index.php/policy-guidance/encryption.
[53]   HMAC-SHA256, HMAC-384 or HMAC-SHA-512.

2766   they have been located. For example, by having portions of the settings in multiple locations,
2767   administrators may need to go back and forth between different configuration screens to ensure
2768   that the settings are correct and consistent.

2769   ### 7.2.4   High Speed and Large Server Considerations

2770   While network devices such as routers and firewalls will already be optimized for network
2771   performance, generic operating systems will require tuning for optimized network performance.
2772   Enough RAM should be made available to the network stack. CPU power saving and throttling
2773   should be disabled and, on non-uniform memory access (NUMA) systems, further optimizations
2774   might be possible. Check with the hardware vendor for specific instructions.

2775   Network card settings can also have a large impact on throughput. Check that the network card's
2776   transmit queue (txqueuelen) is set large enough to accommodate the amount of traffic. Check the
2777   network card settings for TCP Segmentation Offload (TSO), Generic Segmentation Offload
2778   (GSO), checksum offloading, and virtual local area network (VLAN) settings. If using a network
2779   card with IPsec hardware acceleration support, follow the vendor's instructions on how to
2780   optimize the host.

2781   When using virtualization, ensure that the virtualization layer is using as much direct hardware
2782   access as possible. For performance, it will be better to configure a hardware network card inside
2783   a virtual machine than to configure the virtual machine with a virtual network card. On some
2784   hardware, this needs to be enabled in the Basic Input/Output System (BIOS). For example, on
2785   Intel systems, ensure that Intel Virtualization Technology for Directed I/O (Intel VT-d) is
2786   enabled. Ensure that the virtualization is not emulating a slightly different CPU than the real
2787   hardware because it will not be able to use the hardware virtualization instructions of the CPU
2788   and instead will have to perform full emulation in software.[54]

2789   Ideally, when not using IPsec, the system should be able to utilize line-speed unencrypted traffic.
2790   A popular network tool to perform network performance tests is *iperf*. Once the system is
2791   performing well without IPsec, IPsec can be enabled.

2792   IPsec hosts that are busy will spend the bulk of their computational resources on encrypting and
2793   decrypting ESP traffic. The performance of the algorithms for IKE is less important, as there are
2794   far fewer IKE packets than ESP packets in most deployments of IPsec VPNs.

2795   ### 7.2.4.1   ESP performance considerations

2796   If the host's CPU usage is the limiting factor, it is particularly important to use the right
2797   algorithms. Using an AEAD algorithm for encryption and integrity protection is much faster than
2798   using two non-AEAD algorithms. Likely the best algorithm choice will be AES-GCM because
2799   modern CPUs have hardware support for it. Both 256-bit and 128-bit AES keys currently

---

[54]   This usually happens when a virtual machine configuration with a specific CPU sub-type is migrated to different hardware
       without the configuration being updated.

2800   provide strong protection, so when CPU load becomes an issue, one could consider switching
2801   from 256-bit to 128-bit keys, provided that this is allowed by the deployment policy.

2802   If the host is running a few high-speed IPsec SAs, it could be that multiple CPUs on the host are
2803   not utilized properly to spread the cryptographic load of a single IPsec SA over multiple CPUs.
2804   When multiple CPUs are used for a single IPsec SA, there will be an increase in out-of-order
2805   packets being sent, and the replay-window will need to be increased to accommodate this at both
2806   endpoints. IPsec replay-protection can be disabled to test if that is the limiting factor for the
2807   server performance. This is less of a concern on busy servers that act as a remote access VPN,
2808   since these will be serving many users' IPsec SAs per CPU. For high-speed IPsec SAs, it is also
2809   important to use ESNs to avoid excessive rekeying.

2810   If the application is sending packets close to the MTU size, using ESP encryption (which adds a
2811   few bytes in size compared to the unencrypted packet size) might lead to fragmentation, which
2812   will reduce performance. If the IPsec SA is a connection within a data center or over a dedicated
2813   fiber cable, it might be possible to increase the MTU (e.g., to 9000 bytes) to prevent
2814   fragmentation. The MTU of the internal-facing network card can also be reduced to force the
2815   LAN to send packets that are smaller than 1500 bytes, so once the host encrypts the packet to
2816   send it out over the external interface, the ESP packet will not exceed an MTU of 1500 bytes.
2817   TCP MSS clamping can be used on both IPsec endpoints to ensure that TCP sessions will use a
2818   lower MTU that prevents fragmentation.

7.2.4.2 IKE performance considerations

2820   While IKE performance in most cases does not matter, it does matter for remote access VPN
2821   servers that have a continuous stream of clients connecting and disconnecting. If IKE uses too
2822   much of the CPU resources, this will impact ESP processing times as well. If a remote access
2823   VPN server is too busy and has degraded to the point where an IKE session takes more than a
2824   few seconds to establish, the server will completely collapse under the load. IKE clients usually
2825   timeout after five to ten seconds and will start a new IKE attempt. This will put even more load
2826   on the already loaded server. That is, the load based on the number of IKE clients connecting
2827   will slowly go up until it hits a breaking point. If the IKE REDIRECT [38] extension is
2828   supported, the server can be configured to start redirecting clients to another server before it
2829   becomes too busy. See Section 3.8 for more information.

2830   The most computationally expensive part of IKE is the DH calculation performed during a key
2831   exchange. DH implemented using ECP groups (elliptic curve group modulo a prime) take less
2832   resources than the use of finite field groups (modular exponential, or MODP groups) such as DH
2833   group 14. The DH 19, DH 20, and DH 21 ECP groups are also considered to be more secure
2834   [61]. DH groups 1, 2, 5, and 22 are not NIST-approved because these groups do not supply the
2835   minimum of 112 bits of security. See NIST SP 800-56A [62] for further information about
2836   approved DH groups.

2837   MOBIKE should be enabled on remote access VPN servers. Mobile devices will switch between
2838   WiFi and mobile data, and without MOBIKE ,this requires a new IKE session for each network
2839   switch. This will increase the number of DH calculations that need to be supported. IKE clients

2840   on unreliable WiFi can end up restarting IKE many times. When MOBIKE is used, an encrypted
2841   informational exchange message is sent to modify the existing IKE and ESP sessions to use the
2842   new IP address of the other interface and avoid starting new sessions with new expensive DH
2843   group calculations.

2844   Liveness[55] probes can be used by a server to detect remote clients that have vanished without
2845   sending a delete notification. The timer for these probes should not be set too short, or else the
2846   server will need to send frequent IKE packets with DPD probes for idle IKE clients. If the
2847   timeout value is set very short (in the order of a few seconds), there is the additional risk of IKE
2848   clients on unreliable networks not receiving the DPD probes. The server will disconnect the IKE
2849   client when a response to the probe is not returned. That client will experience packet loss and
2850   declare the IPsec connection dead. This will lead to the creation of another new IKE session and
2851   an increased load on the VPN server. In general, keeping a few IKE and IPsec states alive for
2852   vanished VPN clients is cheap. It takes very little memory and no CPU resources. A reasonable
2853   DPD timeout value is in the range of 10 to 60 minutes.

2854   The IKE SA and IPsec SA lifetimes are not negotiated. Each endpoint decides when it wants to
2855   rekey or expire an existing SA. Using longer IKE SA and IPsec SA lifetimes can reduce the
2856   amount of IKE rekeying required. IKE rekeying and IPsec rekeying with PFS require a new DH
2857   calculation as well, so extending the IKE and IPsec lifetimes can help reduce the server load.

2858   Another option on busy servers with many remote access users is to support IKE session
2859   resumption [63]. A mobile device that is going to sleep can send the server a sleep notification to
2860   prevent DPD-based disconnections. The server and client keep the cryptographic state of the IKE
2861   session. When the device wakes up, it can send an encrypted session resumption request. This
2862   avoids the need for a new IKE session with the expensive DH calculation to establish a new
2863   connection; the server is triggered via a DPD timeout to delete the IKE and IPsec SA if the sleep
2864   period exceeds the timeout period.

2865   If a provisioning system is used to generate and install configurations for the IKE clients,
2866   optimized settings could be pushed automatically to all IKE clients to ensure optimal
2867   performance. This would avoid manual configurations that, when performed by inexperienced
2868   users, could result in less optimized settings because the user did not enable or disable certain
2869   features.

2870   Enabling IKE debugging can cause a lot of logging data to be generated. That in itself can cause
2871   a significant performance impact on the system. Always check to see if debugging has
2872   accidentally been left enabled on systems experiencing a high work load.

2873   **7.2.4.3 IKE denial of service attack considerations**

2874   DDoS attacks are a separate issue of concern. Such attacks also put an additional load on the
2875   server, but the characteristics are different from a legitimate user load.

---

[55]   This was formerly called Dead Peer Detection (DPD).

2876 An attack from an authenticated user with valid credentials is assumed to be a readily solvable
2877 problem—simply revoke such users' access to the VPN infrastructure. One exception to this is
2878 when anonymous IPsec is in use, because in that case, the connection cannot be terminated or
2879 prevented based on the user credentials. Vendors of IPsec equipment supporting anonymous
2880 IPsec connections should take countermeasures, for example by limiting the number of IPsec SA
2881 requests that are accepted or by limiting the number of rekeys or anonymous connections
2882 allowed based on an IP address.

2883 IKEv2 has built-in protection against DDoS attacks, but IKEv1 does not. When the number of
2884 incomplete IKE sessions (sometimes called half-open IKE SAs) reaches a threshold, indicating a
2885 possible DDoS attack, IKEv2 can enable DDoS COOKIES. Each new IKE_SA_INIT request
2886 will be answered with a reply that only contains a COOKIE based on a local secret[56] and the
2887 client's IP address and port. The client will have to resend its original IKE_SA_INIT request
2888 with the COOKIE added to the request. The server can calculate the value of the COOKIE
2889 without needing to store any state in memory for the original IKE_SA_INIT request. The IKE
2890 server will only perform the expensive DH calculations after the client has retransmitted its
2891 IKE_SA_INIT packet with the COOKIE, proving to the server that the client was not simply a
2892 spoofed IP packet.

2893 Additionally, IKEv1 can be coerced into an amplification attack. With IKEv1, the responder and
2894 initiator are each responsible for retransmission when a packet is lost. A malicious user can send
2895 a single spoofed IKEv1 packet to an IKEv1 server and cause that IKEv1 server to send several
2896 retransmit packets to the spoofed IP address. Some IKEv1 implementations defend against this
2897 by never responding more than once to an initial IKEv1 request, but this can break legitimate
2898 IKEv1 clients using Aggressive Mode when there is actual packet loss happening.

2899 **7.2.5 Packet Filter**

2900 The purpose of the packet filter is to specify how each type of incoming and outgoing traffic
2901 should be handled—whether the traffic should be permitted or denied (usually based on IP
2902 addresses, protocols, and ports), and how permitted traffic should be protected (if at all). By
2903 default, IPsec implementations typically provide protection for all traffic. In some cases, this
2904 may not be advisable for performance reasons. Encrypting traffic that does not need protection or
2905 is already protected (e.g., encrypted by another application) can be a significant waste of
2906 resources. For such traffic, the packet filter could specify the use of the null encryption algorithm
2907 for ESP, which would provide integrity checks and anti-replay protection, or the packet filter
2908 could simply pass along the traffic without any additional protection. One caveat is that the more
2909 complex the packet filter becomes, the more likely it is that a configuration error may occur,
2910 which could permit traffic to traverse networks without sufficient protection.

---

[56] The secret is usually a random value refreshed every hour to prevent attackers from attempting to guess the secret by trying different possibilities until the correct value is found. The server needs to remember the current and previous secret and to perform two calculations so that clients caught at a secret refresh will not be locked out. [rephrase "caught"]

An issue related to packet filters is that certain types of traffic are incompatible with IPsec. For example, IPsec cannot negotiate security for multicast and broadcast traffic.[57] This means that some types of applications, such as multicast-based video conferencing, may not be compatible with IPsec. Attempting to use IPsec to secure such traffic often causes communication problems or impairs or breaks application functionality. Other traffic such as multicast DNS (mDNS) and DNS Service Discovery (DNS-SD) broadcast requests should not be forwarded to other networks because they have no meaning or relevance beyond the local network. For example, ICMP error messages are often generated by an intermediate host such as a router, not a tunnel endpoint; because the source IP address of the error message is the intermediate host's address, these ICMP packets do not have confidentiality or integrity protection, and the receiving host cannot make security policy decisions based on unprotected packets. Packet filters should be configured to not apply IPsec protection to types of traffic that are incompatible with IPsec—they should let the traffic pass through unprotected if that does not compromise security. If the IPsec gateway cannot block broadcasts and other traffic that should not be passed through it, it may also be effective to configure firewalls or routers near the IPsec gateway to block that particular type of traffic.

7.2.6 Other Design Considerations

A particularly important consideration in design decisions is the identification and implementation of other security controls. Organizations should have other security controls in place that support and complement the IPsec implementation. For example, organizations should configure packet filtering devices (e.g., firewalls, routers) to restrict direct access to IPsec gateways. Organizations should have policies in place regarding the acceptable usage of IPsec connections and software. Organizations may also set minimum security standards for IPsec endpoints, such as mandatory host hardening measures and patch levels, and specify security controls that must be employed by every endpoint.

For endpoints outside the organization's control, such as systems belonging to business partners, users' home computers, and public internet access networks, organizations should recognize that some of the endpoints might violate the organization's minimum security standards. For example, some of these external endpoints might be compromised by malware and other threats occasionally; malicious activity could then enter the organization's networks from the endpoints through their IPsec connections. To minimize risk, organizations should restrict the access provided to external endpoints as much as possible, and also ensure that policies, processes, and technologies are in place to detect and respond to suspicious activity. Organizations should be prepared to identify users or endpoint devices of interest and disable their IPsec access rapidly as needed.

IPsec packet filters can be helpful in limiting external IPsec endpoints' accesses to the organization. Using packet filters to limit acceptable traffic to the minimum necessary for untrusted hosts, along with other network security measures (e.g., firewall rulesets, router access control lists), should be effective in preventing certain types of malicious activity from reaching

---

[57] Section 10.1 contains information on current research efforts to create IPsec solutions for multicast traffic.

2950 　their targets. Administrators may also need to suspend access temporarily for infected hosts until
2951 　appropriate host security measures (e.g., antivirus software update, patch deployment) have
2952 　resolved the infection-related issues. Another option in some environments is automatically
2953 　quarantining each remote host that establishes an IPsec connection, checking its host security
2954 　control settings, and then deciding if it should be permitted to use the organization's networks
2955 　and resources. It is advisable to perform these checks not only for hosts connecting to the
2956 　organization's VPN from external locations, but also for mobile systems connecting to the
2957 　organization's internal network that are also sometimes connected to external networks.

2958 　In addition to endpoint security, there are many other possible design considerations. The
2959 　following items describe specific IPsec settings not addressed earlier in this section:

2960 　　　• **SA Lifetimes.** The IPsec endpoints should be configured with lifetimes that balance
2961 　　　　security and overhead.[58] In general, shorter SA lifetimes tend to support better security,
2962 　　　　but every SA creation involves additional overhead. In IKEv1, the appropriate lifetime is
2963 　　　　somewhat dependent on the authentication method—for example, a short lifetime may be
2964 　　　　disruptive to users in a remote access architecture that requires users to authenticate
2965 　　　　manually, but not disruptive in a gateway-to-gateway architecture with automatic
2966 　　　　authentication. IKEv2 also decouples rekeying from reauthentication, so rekeying can be
2967 　　　　performed more frequently without affecting the user. During testing, administrators
2968 　　　　should set short lifetimes (perhaps 5 to 10 minutes) so the rekeying process can be tested
2969 　　　　more quickly. In operational implementations, IPsec SA lifetimes should generally be set
2970 　　　　to a few hours, with IKE SA lifetimes set somewhat higher. A common default setting for
2971 　　　　IKE SAs is a lifetime of 24 hours (86400 seconds), and for IPsec SAs a lifetime of 8
2972 　　　　hours (28800 seconds). It is important to ensure that the peers are configured with
2973 　　　　compatible lifetimes; some configurations will terminate an IKE negotiation if the peer
2974 　　　　uses a longer lifetime than its configured value. Some IKEv2 implementations, especially
2975 　　　　minimum IKEv2 implementations used with embedded devices, might not support the
2976 　　　　CREATE_CHILD_SA exchange, and therefore do not support rekeying without
2977 　　　　reauthentication.

2978 　　　• **IKE Version.** IKEv2 should be used instead of IKEv1 where possible. If using IKEv1,
2979 　　　　the aggressive mode (see RFC 2409 [94] for detail) should be avoided because it provides
2980 　　　　much weaker security compared to main mode.

2981 　　　• **Diffie-Hellman Group Number.** DH group numbers 14, 15, 16, 17, and 18 [64], 19, 20,
2982 　　　　and 21 [61] are NIST-approved groups. The DH group 22 is not a NIST-approved option
2983 　　　　because it provides less than 112 bits of security; see [47]. The ECP DH groups 19, 20,
2984 　　　　and 21 are preferred for security and performance reasons. The DH group used to
2985 　　　　establish the secret keying material for IKE and IPsec should be consistent with current
2986 　　　　security requirements for the strength of the encryption keys generated by the IKE KDF.

---

[58]　In most cases, lifetimes should be specified by both time and bytes of traffic so that all SAs, regardless of the volume of
　　　traffic, have a limited lifetime. Organizations should not specify a lifetime by bytes of traffic only, because an SA that is not
　　　used or used lightly might exist indefinitely.

2987   • **Extra Padding.** As described in Section 4.1.5, ESP packets can contain optional padding
2988   that alters the size of the packet to conceal how many bytes of actual data the packet
2989   contains, which is helpful in deterring traffic analysis. Having larger packets increases
2990   bandwidth usage and the endpoints' processing load for encrypting and decrypting
2991   packets, so organizations should only use extra padding if traffic analysis is a significant
2992   threat (in most cases, it is not) and costs are not an important factor.

2993   • **Perfect Forward Secrecy (PFS).** Because the PFS option provides stronger security, it
2994   should be used unless the additional computational requirements of the additional DH
2995   key exchanged would pose a problem. For IPsec servers with permanent IPsec tunnels,
2996   this is usually not a problem, but a remote access VPN with thousands of users might
2997   experience additional work load if PFS is enabled on all VPN clients.

2998   Design decisions should incorporate several other considerations, as described below:

2999   • **Current and Future Network Characteristics.** This document has already described
3000   issues involving the use of NAT. Organizations should also be mindful of other network
3001   characteristics, such as the use of IPv6 and wireless networking, when designing an IPsec
3002   implementation. For example, if the organization is planning on deploying IPv6
3003   technologies in the near future, it may be desirable to deploy an IPsec solution that
3004   supports IPv4 in IPv6 and IPv6 in IPv4 configurations as well as an IPv6-only mode.

3005   • **Incident Response.** Organizations should consider how IPsec components may be
3006   affected by incidents and create a design that supports effective and efficient incident
3007   response activities. For example, if an IPsec user's system is compromised, this should
3008   necessitate canceling existing credentials used for IPsec authentication, such as revoking
3009   a digital certificate or deleting a PSK.

3010   • **Log Management.** IPsec should be configured so it logs sufficient details regarding
3011   successful and failed IPsec connection attempts to support troubleshooting and incident
3012   response activities. IPsec logging should adhere to the organization's policies on log
3013   management, such as requiring copies of all log entries to be sent through a secure
3014   mechanism to centralized log servers and preserving IPsec gateway log entries for a
3015   certain number of days.

3016   • **Redundancy.** Organizations should carefully consider the need for a robust IPsec
3017   solution that can survive the failure of one or more components. If IPsec is supporting
3018   critical functions within the organization, the IPsec implementation should probably have
3019   some duplicate or redundant components. For example, an organization could have two
3020   IPsec gateways configured so that when one gateway fails, users automatically switch
3021   over to the other gateway (assuming that the gateways support such a failover capability).
3022   Redundancy and failover capabilities should be considered not only for the core IPsec
3023   components, but also for supporting systems such as authentication servers and directory
3024   servers.

3025   **7.2.7   Summary of Design Decisions**

3026   Table 2 provides a checklist that summarizes the major design decisions made during the first
3027   two phases of the IPsec planning and implementation process.

3028   **Table 2: Design Decisions Checklist**

Completed	Design Decision
Identify Needs (Section 7.1)	
	Determine which communications need to be protected
	Determine what protective measures are needed for each type of communication
	Select an IPsec architecture
	Identify other current and future requirements
	Consider the possible technical solutions and select the one that best meets the identified needs
Design the Solution—Architecture (Section 7.2.1)	
	Determine where IPsec hosts and gateways should be located within the network architecture
	Select appropriate IPsec client software for hosts
	Determine whether split tunneling should be permitted
	Determine whether IPsec hosts should be issued virtual IP addresses
Design the Solution—IKE Authentication (Section 7.2.2)	
	Decide which authentication methods should be supported
Design the Solution—Cryptography (Section 7.2.3)	
	Set the cryptographic policy
Design the Solution—High Speed and Large Server Considerations (Section 7.2.4)	
	Tune the operating system for optimized network performance
Design the Solution—Packet Filter (Section 7.2.5)	
	Determine which types of traffic should be permitted and denied
	Determine what protection and compression measures (if any) should be applied to traffic
Design the Solution—Other Design Considerations (Section 7.2.6)	
	Select maximum lifetimes for IKE and IPsec SAs
	Choose IKEv2 or IKEv1. If using IKEv1, choose between main or aggressive mode
	Select an appropriate DH group number for each chosen encryption algorithm and key size
	Determine whether extra padding should be used to thwart traffic analysis
	Enable PFS if it would not negatively impact performance too much

3029   **7.3   Implement and Test Prototype**

3030   After the solution has been designed, the next step is to implement and test a prototype of the
3031   design. This could be done in one or more environments, including lab, test, and production
3032   networks.[59] Aspects of the solution to evaluate include the following:

---

[59]   Ideally, implementation and testing should first be performed with a lab network, then a test network. Only implementations

3033
3034
3035
3036
3037
3038
3039
3040
3041
- **Connectivity.** Users can establish and maintain connections that use IPsec for all types of traffic that are intended to be protected by IPsec and cannot establish connections for traffic that IPsec is intended to block. It is important to verify that all of the protocols that need to flow through the connection can do so. This should be tested after initial SA negotiation as well as after the original SAs have expired and new IKE and IPsec SAs have been negotiated. (During testing, it may be helpful to temporarily shorten the SA lifetimes so that renegotiation occurs more quickly.) Connectivity testing should also evaluate possible fragmentation-related issues for IKE (e.g., certificates) and ESP (e.g., TCP flow issues).

3042
3043
3044
3045
- **Protection.** Each traffic flow should be protected in accordance with the information gathered during the Identify Needs phase. This should be verified by monitoring network traffic and checking IPsec endpoint logs to confirm that the packet filter rules are ensuring that the proper protection is provided for each type of traffic.

3046
3047
3048
3049
- **Authentication.** Performing robust testing of IKE authentication is important because if authentication services are lost, IPsec services may be lost as well. Authentication solutions such as using digital signatures may be complex and could fail in various ways. See Section 7.2.2 for more information on IKE authentication.

3050
3051
3052
3053
- **Application Compatibility.** The solution should not break or interfere with the use of existing software applications. This includes network communications between application components, as well as IPsec client software issues (e.g., a conflict with host-based firewall or intrusion detection software).

3054
3055
3056
3057
3058
3059
3060
3061
- **Management.** Administrators should be able to configure and manage the solution effectively and securely. This includes all components, including gateways, management servers, and client software. For remote access architectures, it is particularly important to evaluate the ease of deployment and configuration. For example, most implementations do not have fully automated client configuration; in many cases, administrators manually configure each client. Another concern is the ability of users to alter IPsec settings, causing connections to fail and requiring administrators to manually reconfigure the client, or causing a security breach.

3062
3063
- **Logging.** The logging and data management functions should function properly in accordance with the organization's policies and strategies.

3064
3065
3066
3067
3068
3069
- **Performance.** The solution should be able to provide adequate performance during normal and peak usage. Performance issues are among the most common IPsec-related problems. It is important to consider not only the performance of the primary IPsec components, but also that of intermediate devices, such as routers and firewalls. Encrypted traffic often consumes more processing power than unencrypted traffic, so it may cause bottlenecks.[60] Also, because IPsec headers and tunneling increase the packet

---

in final testing should be placed onto a production network. The nature of IPsec allows a phased introduction on the production network as well.

[60] The additional resources necessitated by IPsec vary widely based on several factors, including the IPsec mode (tunnel or

3070　length, intermediate network devices might need to fragment them, possibly slowing
3071　network activity.[61] In many cases, the best way to test the performance under load of a
3072　prototype implementation is to use simulated traffic generators on a live test network to
3073　mimic the actual characteristics of expected traffic as closely as possible. Testing should
3074　incorporate a variety of applications that will be used with IPsec, especially those that are
3075　most likely to be affected by network throughput or latency issues, such as Voice Over
3076　IP.[62] Addressing performance problems generally involves upgrading or replacing
3077　hardware, offloading cryptographic calculations from software-based cryptographic
3078　modules to hardware-based cryptographic modules, or reducing processing needs (e.g.,
3079　using a more efficient encryption algorithm or only encrypting sensitive traffic).

3080　● **Security of the Implementation.** The IPsec implementation itself may contain
3081　vulnerabilities and weaknesses that attackers could exploit. Organizations with high
3082　security needs may want to perform extensive vulnerability assessments against the IPsec
3083　components. At a minimum, the testers should update all components with the latest
3084　patches and configure the components following sound security practices. Section 7.3.2
3085　presents some common IPsec security concerns.

3086　● **Component Interoperability.** The components of the IPsec solution must function
3087　together properly. This is of the greatest concern when a variety of components from
3088　different vendors may be used. Section 7.3.1 contains more information on
3089　interoperability concerns.

3090　● **Default Settings.** Besides the IPsec settings described in Section 7.2, IPsec
3091　implementations may have other configuration settings. IPsec implementers should
3092　carefully review the default values for each setting and alter the settings as necessary to
3093　support their design goals. They should also ensure that the implementation does not
3094　unexpectedly "drop back" to default settings for interoperability or other reasons.

3095　**7.3.1　Component Interoperability**

3096　Another facet of testing to consider is the compatibility and interoperability of the IPsec
3097　components. Although there have been improvements in the industry, especially with IKEv2-
3098　based IPsec implementations, some vendors make it difficult to interoperate with, or manage,
3099　other IPsec devices. Because many vendors offer IPsec clients and gateways, implementation
3100　differences among products and the inclusion of proprietary solutions can lead to interoperability
3101　problems. Although IPsec vendors use the term "IPsec compliant" to state that they meet the
3102　current IETF IPsec standards, they may implement the standards differently, which can cause
3103　subtle and hard-to-diagnose problems. Also, some products provide support for components
3104　(e.g., encryption algorithms) that are not part of the IPsec standards; this is done for various

---

transport), the encryption algorithm, and the use of IPComp, UDP encapsulation, or optional padding.
[61]　Similar problems can occur when tunnels are within other tunnels, so that packets are encapsulated multiple times. Typically, the solution for these types of problems is to reduce the size of the MTU value on the host originating the network traffic. The MTU is the maximum allowable packet size. The MTU can be lowered so the IPsec-encapsulated packets are not large enough to require fragmentation.
[62]　For more information on Voice Over IP, see [66].

reasons, including enhancing ease-of-use, providing additional functionality, and addressing weak or missing parts of the standards. Examples of compatibility issues are as follows:

- The endpoints support different encryption algorithms, compression algorithms, or authentication methods.

- One endpoint requires the usage of a proprietary feature for proper operation.

- The endpoints may encode or interpret certain digital certificate fields or data differently.

- The endpoints default to different parameters, such as DH group 14 versus DH group 19.

- The endpoints implement different interpretations of ambiguous or vaguely worded standards, such as performing SA rekeying in different ways.

- Most gateway implementations interoperate with other vendors' implementations, but many client implementations only interoperate with their own vendor's gateway implementation.

The following are some IKE-related interoperability issues:

- **Certificate Contents.** Different implementations may encode or interpret certificate data fields (e.g., peer identity) differently, or handle certificate extensions such as EKU extensions in conflicting ways. Some vendors have also implemented sending intermediary certificates in a non-standard way.

- **Rekeying Behavior.** When implementations re-negotiate IKE or IPsec SAs, different rekeying behavior can result in lost traffic. One potential area of difficulty is timing-related: when to start using the new SA and when to delete the old SA. In addition, when an IKEv1 SA expires, some implementations delete all IPsec SAs that were negotiated using that IKEv1 SA. Other implementations allow the IPsec SAs to continue until they, in turn, expire. This can also cause interoperability problems. In IKEv1, an expired IKE SA leaving an IPsec SA can also no longer send or respond to DPD packets. IKEv2 resolved these issues by specifying that the deletion of an IKE SA causes the deletion of all its IPsec SAs.

- **Initial Contact Messages.** Some implementations send an Initial Contact notification message when they begin an IKE negotiation with a peer for whom they have no current SAs. This can also be an indication that the sending implementation has rebooted and lost previously negotiated SAs. There can be incompatibility issues if one implementation sends and expects to receive this message, and the other one has not implemented this feature.

- **Dead Peer Detection (DPD).** DPD enables an endpoint to ensure that its peer is still able to communicate. This can help the endpoint to avoid a situation in which it expends processing resources to send IPsec-protected traffic to a peer that is no longer available. If no traffic is sent through an SA, some implementations will delete the SA, even if the negotiated lifetime has not elapsed. DPD messages can be sent to ensure that an otherwise unused SA is kept alive. This can avoid NAT mapping timeouts and the deletion of inactive SAs.

3144   • **Vendor ID.** One endpoint may depend upon a proprietary custom Vendor ID IKE
3145   payload to enable a feature that is either absent or inconsistently implemented. This has
3146   led some vendors to include Vendor IDs of other vendors in their product to gain
3147   compatibility with the other vendor. This can lead to unexpected side effects when one
3148   vendor adds a different customization that is activated when the same Vendor ID value is
3149   seen.

3150   • **Lifetimes.** Peers may be configured with different values for IKE or IPsec SA lifetimes.
3151   IKEv2 allows the sending of the maximum accepted authentication lifetime, so a client
3152   connecting to a server will be told within which period of time it is supposed to re-
3153   authenticate.

3154   In IKEv1, a misconfiguration of the mode (transport or tunnel) or compression would lead to a
3155   failure in establishing the IPsec SA. With IKEv2, transport mode and compression can only be
3156   requested. If not confirmed, the IPsec SA must be established in tunnel mode or without
3157   compression.

3158   The best way to determine interoperability between vendors is to actually test them in a lab
3159   environment. Another approach is to research issues with the products by using Web sites that
3160   provide interoperability testing configuration and results, as well as the ability to perform real-
3161   time testing.

3162   ### 7.3.2   Security of the Implementation

3163   Another topic to keep in mind during testing is the security of the IPsec implementation itself.
3164   IPsec was built with careful thought and consideration for security; however, no protocol or
3165   software is completely bulletproof. Security concerns regarding IPsec include the following:

3166   • Some IPsec implementations store PSKs in plain text on the system. This can be accessed
3167   by legitimate users and anyone else who gains access to the system. The use of such
3168   implementations should be avoided if unauthorized physical access to the system is a
3169   concern. However, if it is necessary to use such a product, be sure to apply the
3170   appropriate system hardening measures and deploy host-based firewalls and intrusion
3171   detection software.

3172   • IPsec allows some traffic to pass unprotected, such as broadcast, multicast, IKE, and
3173   Kerberos. Attackers could potentially use this knowledge to their advantage to send
3174   unauthorized malicious traffic through the IPsec filters. Be sure to carefully monitor the
3175   traffic that is passing through the IPsec tunnel, as well as that which is bypassing it. For
3176   example, network-based intrusion detection system or intrusion prevention system
3177   devices can typically be configured to alert when non-tunneled traffic appears.

3178   • Periodically, vulnerabilities are discovered in IPsec implementations. Organizations such
3179   as the United States Computer Emergency Readiness Team (US-CERT) notify vendors
3180   of new vulnerabilities and, at the appropriate time, also notify the public of the issues and
3181   the recommended resolutions, such as installing vendor-supplied patches. Information on
3182   known vulnerabilities is provided by various online databases, including the National

3183   Vulnerability Database (NVD)[63] and the Common Vulnerabilities and Exposures (CVE)
3184   database.[64]

3185   **7.4   Deploy the Solution**

3186   Once testing is complete and any issues have been resolved, the next phase of the IPsec planning
3187   and implementation model involves deploying the solution. A prudent strategy is to gradually
3188   migrate existing network infrastructure, applications, and users to the new IPsec solution. The
3189   phased deployment provides administrators an opportunity to evaluate the impact of the IPsec
3190   solution and resolve issues prior to enterprise wide deployment. Most of the issues that can occur
3191   during IPsec deployment are the same types of issues that occur during any large IT deployment.
3192   Typical issues that are IPsec-specific are as follows:

3193   •   Encrypted traffic can negatively affect services such as firewalls, intrusion detection,
3194   QoS, remote monitoring (RMON) probes, and congestion control protocols.

3195   •   Unexpected performance issues may arise, either with the IPsec components themselves
3196   (e.g., gateways) or with intermediate devices, such as routers.

3197   •   IPsec may not work properly on some production networks because of firewalls, routers,
3198   and other intermediate packet filtering devices that block IPsec traffic. For example, the
3199   devices might have been misconfigured for IPsec traffic or not configured at all—for
3200   example, if the IPsec implementers were not aware of the existence of a device.
3201   Misconfigured devices are more likely to be an issue with organizations that use a wider
3202   variety of network devices or have decentralized network device administration and
3203   management. In such environments, the changes needed to permit IPsec could vary
3204   widely among devices.

3205   •   The environment may change during the deployment. For example, IPsec client software
3206   may be broken by a new operating system update. This issue can be handled rather easily
3207   in a managed environment, but it can pose a major problem if users have full control over
3208   their systems and can select their own client software.

3209   **7.5   Manage the Solution**

3210   The last phase of the IPsec planning and implementation model is the longest lasting. Managing
3211   the solution involves maintaining the IPsec architecture, policies, software, and other
3212   components of the deployed solution. Examples of typical maintenance actions are testing and
3213   applying patches to IPsec software, deploying IPsec to additional remote sites, configuring
3214   additional user laptops as IPsec clients, performing key management duties (e.g., issuing new
3215   credentials, revoking credentials for compromised systems or departing users) and adapting the
3216   policies as requirements change. It is also important to monitor the performance of the IPsec
3217   components so that potential resource issues can be identified and addressed before the
3218   components become overwhelmed. Another important task is to perform testing periodically to

---

[63]   https://nvd.nist.gov/
[64]   https://cve.mitre.org/

3219   verify that the IPsec controls are functioning as expected. Any new hardware, software, or
3220   significant configuration changes starts the process again at the Identify Needs phase. This
3221   ensures that the IPsec solution lifecycle operates effectively and efficiently.

3222   Another aspect of managing the IPsec solution is handling operational issues. For example, a
3223   common problem is poor performance caused by undesired fragmentation or by not utilizing
3224   enough resources (e.g., other available CPUs or sufficient memory) to perform networking tasks.
3225   When troubleshooting IPsec connections, a network sniffer such as tcpdump or Wireshark can be
3226   very helpful. A sniffer allows the administrator to analyze the communications as they take place
3227   and correct problems. IPsec gateway logs and client logs may also be valuable resources during
3228   troubleshooting; firewall and router logs may validate whether the IPsec traffic is reaching them,
3229   passing through them, or being blocked.

3230   **7.6   Summary**

3231   This section has described a phased approach to IPsec planning and implementation and
3232   highlighted various issues that may be of significance to implementers. The following
3233   summarizes the key points from the section:

3234   - The use of a phased approach for IPsec planning and implementation can help to achieve
3235   successful IPsec deployments. The five phases of the approach are as follows:

3236   1. **Identify Needs**—Identify the need to protect network communications and determine
3237   how that need can best be met.

3238   2. **Design the Solution**—Make design decisions in four areas: architectural
3239   considerations, authentication methods, cryptographic policy, and packet filters.

3240   3. **Implement and Test a Prototype**—Test a prototype of the designed solution in a lab
3241   or test environment to identify any potential issues.

3242   4. **Deploy the Solution**—Gradually deploy IPsec throughout the enterprise.

3243   5. **Manage the Solution**—Maintain the IPsec components and resolve operational
3244   issues; repeat the planning and implementation process when significant changes
3245   need to be incorporated into the solution.

3246   - The placement of an IPsec gateway has potential security, functionality, and performance
3247   implications. Specific factors to consider include device performance, traffic
3248   examination, gateway outages, and NAT.

3249   - Although IPsec clients built into operating systems may be more convenient than
3250   deploying third-party client software, third-party clients may offer features that built-in
3251   clients do not.

3252   - When IPsec hosts are located outside the organization's networks, it may be desirable to
3253   assign them virtual internal IP addresses to provide compatibility with existing IP
3254   address-based security controls.

3255   - Authentication options include PSKs, digital signatures, and (in some implementations)
3256   external authentication services such as EAP and Generic Security Services Application

3257
3258

Program Interface (GSSAPI)/Kerberos. An authentication solution should be selected based primarily on ease of maintenance, scalability, and security.

3259
3260
3261
3262
3263

- Cryptographic algorithms and key lengths that are considered secure for current practice should be used for encryption and integrity protection. AES-GCM with a 128-bit key or 256-bit key is recommended for encryption and integrity. DH ECP groups and the MODP group 14 (2048) are recommended. More than one algorithm can be specified to ease the transition to new updated algorithms.

3264
3265

- Packet filters should apply appropriate protections to traffic and not protect other types of traffic for performance or functionality reasons.

3266
3267
3268
3269
3270
3271

- Specific design decisions include IKE and IPsec SA lifetimes, DH group numbers, extra packet padding, and the use of PFS. When IPsec is going to be used with third parties, design decisions should take the capabilities of those third parties into account, as long as their capabilities are using NIST-approved algorithms and methods. Additional design considerations include current and future network characteristics, incident response, log management, redundancy, and other security controls already in place.

3272
3273
3274
3275

- Testing of the prototype implementation should evaluate several factors, including connectivity, protection, IKE authentication, application compatibility, management, logging, performance, the security of the implementation, component interoperability, and default settings.

3276
3277
3278

- Existing network infrastructure, applications, and users should gradually be migrated to the new IPsec solution. This provides administrators an opportunity to evaluate the impact of the IPsec solution and resolve issues prior to enterprise wide deployment.

3279
3280
3281

- After implementation, the IPsec solution needs to be maintained, such as applying patches and deploying IPsec to additional networks and hosts. Operational issues also need to be addressed and resolved.

3282
3283
3284
3285

- Organizations should implement technical, operational, and management controls that support and complement IPsec implementations. Examples include having control over all entry and exit points for the protected networks, ensuring the security of all IPsec endpoints, and incorporating IPsec considerations into organizational policies.

3286

3287 | **8   Alternatives to IPsec**

3288 This section lists several VPN protocols that are used as alternatives to IPsec and groups them by
3289 the layer of the IP model (as shown in Figure 16)[65] at which they function, although the
3290 distinction between layers is not always clear. For each VPN protocol, a brief description is
3291 provided, along with a description of the circumstances under which it may be more
3292 advantageous than IPsec. Some alternatives have specifications and implementations, but some
3293 of the alternatives are implementations with some documentation that does not provide a full
3294 specification.

Application Layer. This layer sends and receives data for particular applications, such as Domain Name System (DNS), web traffic via Hypertext Transfer Protocol (HTTP) and HTTP Secure (HTTPS), and email via Simple Mail Transfer Protocol (SMTP) and the Internet Message Access Protocol (IMAP).
Transport Layer. This layer provides connection-oriented or connectionless services for transporting application layer services between networks. The transport layer can optionally assure the reliability of communications. Transmission Control Protocol (TCP) and User Datagram Protocol (UDP) are commonly used transport layer protocols.
Network Layer. This layer routes packets across networks. Internet Protocol (IP) is the fundamental network layer protocol for TCP/IP. Other commonly used protocols at the network layer are Internet Control Message Protocol (ICMP) and Internet Group Management Protocol (IGMP).
Data Link Layer. This layer handles communications on the physical network components. The best-known data link layer protocols are Ethernet and the various WiFi standards such as the Institute of Electrical and Electronics Engineers (IEEE) 802.11.

3295   **Figure 16: IP Model**

3296 If only one or two applications need protection, a network layer control may be excessive.
3297 Transport layer protocols such as TLS are most commonly used to provide security for
3298 communications with individual HTTP-based applications, although they are also used to
3299 provide protection for communication sessions of other types of applications such as SMTP, Post
3300 Office Protocol (POP), IMAP, and FTP. Because all major web browsers include support for
3301 TLS, users who wish to use web-based applications that are protected by TLS normally do not
3302 need to install any client software or reconfigure their systems. Web-based systems have gained
3303 considerable integration support that reaches outside the browser. One common example is the
3304 virtual network drive, where the browser takes on the role of a file manager application to
3305 securely transmit files.

3306 **8.1   Data Link Layer VPN Protocols**

3307 Data link layer VPN protocols function below the network layer in the TCP/IP model. These
3308 types of VPNs are also known as layer 2 VPNs (L2VPN). This means non-IP network protocols
3309 can also be used with a data link layer VPN. Most VPN protocols (including IPsec) only support
3310 IP, so data link layer VPN protocols may provide a viable option for protecting networks running

---

[65] Figure 16 repeats Figure 1 for additional clarity.

84

3311   non-IP protocols. (As the name implies, IPsec is designed to provide security for IP traffic only.).
3312   Protection at the link layer means that the security added is limited to the devices that share this
3313   link layer, such as an Ethernet-based LAN or WiFi network. However, various virtual link layers
3314   now exist to facilitate network virtualization, allowing a link layer VPN protocol to secure nodes
3315   in different physical (and virtual) locations. Since confidentiality and integrity happen at the link
3316   layer, deploying a link layer VPN protocol requires no specific support in the application.
3317   However, this also means that the application is generally not aware of the link layer protection
3318   and cannot make decisions based on whether the communication is secure or not.

8.1.1   WiFi Data Link Protection

3320   All devices that support WiFi technology support a number of link layer protocols that provide
3321   confidentiality and integrity protection. Wireless connections broadcast their data, so from the
3322   start there has been a push to send data using confidentiality and integrity protection. The initial
3323   security protocol was Wired Equivalent Privacy (WEP), deprecated in 2004 for Wi-Fi Protected
3324   Access (WPA). WEP uses 40-bit or 128-bit RC4 PSKs and is easily broken, whereas WPA2[66]
3325   uses AES-CCM. The Enterprise versions of WPA use IEEE 802.1X for authentication instead of
3326   a PSK. WPA supports a number of EAP extensions, such as EAP-TLS, EAP-MSCHAPv2, and
3327   EAP-Subscriber Identity Module (EAP-SIM). In WPA3, the PSK is replaced by Password
3328   Authenticated Key Exchange (PAKE) which offers more protection against the use of weak
3329   passwords. WPA3 also offers PFS.[67]

3330   The strength of the link layer protection for WiFi depends strongly on the configuration and the
3331   implementation of the various 802.11 standards. WiFi encryption only protects the data from the
3332   wireless device to the wireless access point. It is good practice to consider WiFi encryption to be
3333   insufficient and to not trust the access point. Devices on a WiFi network should use a remote
3334   access VPN like IPsec to communicate with resources on the wired network. This is especially
3335   true for WiFi access points belonging to third parties, such as restaurants and hotels.

8.1.2   Media Access Control Security (MACsec)

3337   MACsec is an industry standard defined in IEEE 802.1AE. It creates point-to-point security
3338   associations within an Ethernet network. MACsec is the Ethernet version of WiFi WPA security.
3339   It uses AES-GCM with 128-bit keys for confidentiality and integrity. It protects regular IP
3340   traffic, as well as ARP, IPv6 Neighbor Discovery (ND), and DHCP. For key exchange and
3341   mutual authentication, MACsec uses the IEEE 802.1X extension MACsec Key Agreement
3342   (MKA) protocol. New devices have to authenticate themselves to the authentication server
3343   before being able to join the network, and communication with other hosts on the network are
3344   encrypted between each pair of hosts. This allows MACsec to be used with virtual network

---

[66]   WPA version 1 was designed as a compromise between security and being able to run on old hardware that implemented
       WEP. It uses the Temporal Key Integrity Protocol (TKIP) which was a stopgap replacement for the broken WEP protocol,
       but TKIP is also no longer considered secure. WPA2 mandated the support for the Counter Mode with Cipher Block
       Chaining Message Authentication Code Protocol (CCMP), which uses AES-CCM.
[67]   See also NIST SP 800-153, *Guidelines for Securing Wireless Local Area Networks (WLANs)* [67].

3345   technologies such as Virtual eXtensible LAN (VXLAN) and GEneric NEtwork Virtualization
3346   Encapsulation (GENEVE).

3347   MACsec can protect two machines via a switch even if the switch itself does not support
3348   MACsec. However, if the switch supports MACsec, each individual Ethernet port of the switch
3349   can become a node in the MACsec network for devices connected to those ports that do not
3350   support MACsec natively. In that case, all traffic between this device and the LAN is encrypted,
3351   except from the Ethernet port to the actual device.

3352   The Ethernet packet change to support MACsec is similar to the change of an IP packet to
3353   support IPsec. The Ethernet header is extended with the SecTAG header, which contains the
3354   equivalent to the ESP SPI number and Sequence Number. This is followed by the (now
3355   encrypted) original payload, followed by the ICV.[68] To a switch that does not support MACsec,
3356   the SecTAG and ICV look like just part of the regular Ethernet frame payload.

3357   Similar to IPsec, MACsec can be configured to use manual keying. It suffers from all the same
3358   problems as IPsec manual keying: no PFS, and no protection from reusing the same counters as
3359   nonces for AES-GCM.

8.2   Transport Layer VPN Protocols (SSL VPNs)

3361   Transport layer VPNs are what people usually think of when describing a VPN. The host obtains
3362   a new virtual interface configured with one or more IP addresses. Packets to and from this virtual
3363   interface use a transport protocol to encapsulate the packets securely to the remote endpoint of
3364   the VPN. The packets are then further routed, just like packets that arrived on a physical network
3365   interface. The most common IPsec alternative is the Secure Sockets Layer (SSL) VPN. Although
3366   these are still called SSL VPNs, most actually use the TLS protocol and not the older SSL
3367   protocol. This can be TLS [16] based on TCP or DTLS [68] based on UDP. The advantage is
3368   that SSL VPNs' traffic is much harder to be blocked, as it can run on any (preconfigured) port
3369   number. Usually, it is run over port 443 (HTTPS) since most networks pass on this traffic
3370   without attempting any kind of deep packet inspection. When using TCP, it can suffer from
3371   severe performance degrading due to dueling TCP layers when there is congestion or packet loss;
3372   DTLS does not have this problem. SSL VPNs are usually implemented as an application,
3373   resulting in significantly lower performance compared to kernel-based VPNs such as IPsec or
3374   WireGuard.

3375   NIST provides specific guidance for SSL VPN deployments in NIST SP 800-113, *Guide to SSL*
3376   *VPNs* [69].

8.2.1   Secure Socket Tunneling Protocol (SSTP)

3378   Secure Socket Tunneling Protocol (SSTP) is the Microsoft version of an SSL VPN. It uses
3379   SSL/TLS over port 443 and can use TCP or UDP as the underlying protocol. It uses the SSTP

---

[68]   In ESP, the ICV is only used for non-AEAD protocols. For AEAD protocols such as AES-GCM, the ICV is implicit and
         generated from the IKE session and not transmitted over the wire.

3380   protocol to run a Point-to-Point Protocol (PPP) session that handles the IP assignment and IP
3381   encapsulation. Microsoft calls this a Point-to-Site VPN, which is another name for remote access
3382   VPN. It supports the standard encryption and integrity algorithms that SSL/TLS support.

8.2.2   OpenConnect

3384   OpenConnect originated as an open source replacement implementation for the Cisco
3385   AnyConnect SSL VPN client using the Cisco proprietary AnyConnect protocol. OpenConnect is
3386   now a protocol specification and a client and server implementation. While it remains backwards
3387   compatible with Cisco AnyConnect, it has added its own features and has been submitted to the
3388   IETF as a draft to become an Informational RFC [70]. It uses DTLS but can fall back to TLS
3389   over TCP when needed. The server is authenticated via a machine certificate. Clients can
3390   authenticate using a user/password, certificate, or Kerberos (GSSAPI). The OpenConnect client
3391   also supports other proprietary SSL VPN protocols that are similar to Cisco AnyConnect, such as
3392   Palo Alto GlobalProtect and Juniper SSL-VPN. OpenConnect is a relatively new SSL VPN and
3393   has not been deployed as much as other SSL VPNs.

8.2.3   OpenVPN

3395   OpenVPN is a popular SSL VPN protocol/implementation that was originally written in 2001. It
3396   uses SSL or TLS over any preconfigured port and can use TCP or UDP as the transport protocol.
3397   The supported algorithms are the common SSL/TLS algorithms. For authentication, it supports
3398   certificates, PSKs, and user/password. It can act as a link layer VPN or as a transport layer VPN.
3399   The server can send the client commands to be executed, which can be dangerous. OpenVPN has
3400   a larger attack surface because the entire protocol runs as a user process and has had
3401   vulnerabilities in the past. It is one of the more widely used SSL VPNs.

8.3   WireGuard

3403   WireGuard[69] is a fairly new VPN implementation originally written for the Linux kernel. It is a
3404   minimalistic VPN implementation that is less complex than IPsec, but as a result is also not as
3405   flexible as IPsec. There is no formal protocol specification or publication in static form, which
3406   makes it harder to find compatibility issues between different versions, although it does provide
3407   extensive documentation of the current implementation. The code base is small compared to
3408   other VPN implementations. It combines the control and data plane over a single preconfigured
3409   UDP port.

3410   WireGuard uses the Noise Protocol Framework[70] for its key exchange and the HMAC-Based
3411   Key Derivation Function (HKDF) [71] to generate symmetric encryption keys. It uses
3412   Curve25519 [72] as its DH group and supports authentication only via public keys. It uses
3413   CHACHA20POLY1305 [73] as its encryption and integrity algorithm. None of these algorithms

---

[69]   https://www.wireguard.com
[70]   https://www.noiseprotocol.org/

3414   are NIST-approved at the moment. However, NIST plans to allow Edwards Curve DSA
3415   (EdDSA) digital signatures [74].

3416   There are many similarities with IPsec and IKE. WireGuard uses IKEv2-style DDoS COOKIES
3417   and DPD/Keepalives. The data packet looks very similar to ESP in tunnel mode. Transport mode
3418   is not supported. Its replay attack protection is the same as IPsec, using a replay window of 2000
3419   (continuous packet ids). It supports PPK and has the same seamless reconnection properties as
3420   MOBIKE where a device can switch network interfaces without losing the VPN connection.
3421   WireGuard takes advantage of multiple CPUs when present, unlike typical SSL VPNs that are
3422   bound to one CPU.

3423   The protocol does not allow for DHCP-style IP address allocation, and IP addresses are hard-
3424   coded in its configuration file on the client and server. DNS configuration has to be conveyed via
3425   a provisioning protocol. WireGuard lacks authentication support using certificates or PSKs. It
3426   does not support a transport mode configuration, making it less suitable for mesh encryption. It
3427   does not support AES-GCM.

3428   WireGuard is mostly intended as a remote access VPN. As such, it does a much better job
3429   compared to SSL VPNs and SSH. While it can be used in a gateway-to-gateway or host-to-host
3430   architecture, it misses the optimizations and flexibility of IPsec in these architectures.

3431   **8.4   Secure Shell (SSH)**

3432   SSH is a commonly used application layer protocol suite. While it is commonly used as a secure
3433   remote login application and a secure file transfer application, it can also be used to tunnel
3434   specific ports via an SSH connection to allow either a local connection to access a remote
3435   resource, or a remote connection to access a local resource. SSH is often used on intermediary
3436   hosts (also called bastion hosts) to jump to other hosts, but that jump does not need to be to the
3437   remote login (SSH) host itself. For instance, port 25 on localhost (127.0.0.1) could be made
3438   available to locally running mail clients, with SSH tunneling this traffic over the SSH VPN to the
3439   bastion host, where the SSH client running will forward the traffic to a remote mail server's port
3440   25. Because a single SSH tunnel can provide protection for several applications at once, it is
3441   technically a transport layer VPN protocol, not an application layer protocol.

3442   While SSH could be used to start a PPP daemon to create a more traditional VPN with an
3443   interface, recent versions of OpenSSH have added native functionality for binding the SSH
3444   protocol to tun interfaces on the hosts. An SSH tunnel creates a tun interface on the local and
3445   remote host, and these tun interfaces can be configured with other IP addresses, providing a true
3446   remote access VPN.

3447   As with SSL VPNs, SSH VPNs perform badly if there is packet loss, due to multiple TCP layers
3448   independently retransmitting packets.

3449   SSH tunnel-based VPNs are resource-intensive and complex to set up. They require the
3450   installation and configuration of SSH client software on each user's machine, as well as the
3451   reconfiguration of client applications to use the tunnel. Each user must also have login privileges

3452 on a server within the organization; because this server typically needs to be directly accessible
3453 from the Internet, it is susceptible to attack. Generally, users need to have solid technical skills so
3454 that they can configure systems and applications themselves, as well as troubleshoot problems
3455 that occur. The most common users of SSH tunnel-based VPNs are small groups of IT
3456 administrators.

3457 ## 8.5 Obsoleted and Deprecated VPN Protocols

3458 A number of commonly used VPN protocols are no longer suitable for use. Some of these were
3459 designed for dial-up internet connections. Some used encryption techniques that were broken or
3460 have become too weak to withstand current computational attacks. Early VPN protocols were
3461 implemented on top of PPP [75]. These solutions were built as extensions to secure modem-
3462 based connections and are no longer appropriate to deploy, both from an architectural point of
3463 view and from a cryptographic point of view. The protocols listed in this section must not be
3464 used.

3465 ### 8.5.1 Point-to-Point Tunneling Protocol (PPTP)

3466 The Point-to-Point Tunneling Protocol (PPTP) [76] uses Generic Routing Encapsulation (GRE,
3467 IP protocol 47) as its transport protocol. The GRE tunnel is used to send PPP packets. Similar to
3468 the ESP protocol, NAT routers often do not forward this protocol. PPTP uses TCP port 1723 as
3469 its control plane. It uses the Microsoft Point-to-Point Encryption (MPPE) mechanism at the PPP
3470 layer for encryption. MPPE uses the deprecated RSA RC4 algorithm with 40-bit or 128-bit keys
3471 [77]. For authentication it can use the Password Authentication Protocol (PAP) [78] or Challenge
3472 Handshake Authentication Protocol (CHAP) [79]. Microsoft created MS-CHAPv1 and MS-
3473 CHAPv2 to provide stronger forms of authentication, but researchers have found serious
3474 weaknesses in MS-CHAP.[71] The original version of PPTP contained serious security flaws.
3475 PPTP version 2 addressed many of these issues, but researchers have identified weaknesses with
3476 this version as well (in addition to the MS-CHAP issues).[72] PPTP should not be used, and if it is
3477 used regardless, it should be considered as a plaintext protocol with no functional confidentiality
3478 or integrity protection.

3479 ### 8.5.2 Layer 2 Tunneling Protocol (L2TP)

3480 The Layer 2 Tunneling Protocol (L2TP) [80] is the successor to PPTP. Instead of using the GRE
3481 protocol, it encapsulates PPP packets inside UDP on port 1701. For confidentiality and integrity
3482 of the data plane, it depends on IPsec. Some implementations support encryption at the PPP
3483 layer, meaning that to enable IPsec support, one has to (confusingly) disable "L2TP encryption".
3484 L2TP without IPsec is used by some ISPs as the replacement of PPTP connections, but this
3485 usage is not a VPN. L2TP VPNs all use IPsec in transport mode, commonly referred to as
3486 L2TP/IPsec. In addition to the PPP-provided authentication methods, L2TP can also use other

---

[71] One paper discussing MS-CHAP weaknesses is "Exploiting Known Security Holes in Microsoft's PPTP Authentication Extensions (MS-CHAPv2)" by Jochen Eisinger (http://www2.informatik.uni-freiburg.de/~eisinger/paper/pptp_mschapv2.pdf).

[72] For more information on PPTP security issues, see Bruce Schneier's "Analysis of Microsoft PPTP Version 2" page, located at https://www.schneier.com/academic/pptp/.

3487   methods, such as RADIUS [81], although it commonly uses the PPP-based MS-CHAPv2 for
3488   authentication of the PPP layer. IPsec is established using IKEv1, often using a weak group PSK,
3489   but it can be deployed using X.509 certificates as well. Even when deployed securely,
3490   L2TP/IPsec offers no advantage over IKEv2-based IPsec VPNs. It adds a number of unnecessary
3491   encapsulation layers that reduce the effective MTU and increase network issues related to packet
3492   fragmentation. Additionally, because it uses IPsec in transport mode, it works poorly behind
3493   NAT. Some vendors switch to tunnel mode when behind NAT, but not all L2TP/IPsec servers
3494   are configured to support tunnel mode.

3495   One advantage of L2TP/IPsec used to be that it was shipped as part of popular operating
3496   systems, which meant no separate VPN software needed to be purchased and installed. Up-to-
3497   date versions of those operating systems now support IKEv2-based IPsec VPNs. Additionally,
3498   L2TP/IPsec VPNs usually do not support AEAD algorithms such as AES-GCM, which increases
3499   the CPU usage compared to IKEv2-based IPsec VPNs. On mobile devices this means using more
3500   battery power. L2TP/IPsec deployments should be migrated to IKEv2-based IPsec VPNs.

3501   ## 8.6   Summary

3502   Section 8 describes the main alternatives to IPsec. SSL VPNs are popular because they are not as
3503   easily blocked as IPsec VPNs, although this advantage will be negated once IKEv2-based IPsec
3504   implementations add support for TCP and TLS encapsulation as specified in [49]. Traditionally,
3505   SSL VPNs were easier to set up and use than IPsec VPNs, but IKEv2 configurations and
3506   provisioning systems have improved considerably making IPsec VPNs as easy to set up and use
3507   as SSL VPNs. WireGuard is an interesting upcoming remote access VPN protocol, but at the
3508   moment has no support for NIST-approved algorithms.

3509   **9   Planning and Implementation Case Studies**

3510   This section presents a few typical IPsec solution planning and implementation case studies.
3511   Each case study begins by describing a real-world security requirement scenario, such as
3512   protecting network communications between two offices. The case study then discusses possible
3513   solutions for the security requirement and explains why IPsec was selected over the alternatives.
3514   The next section of each case study discusses the design of the solution and includes a simple
3515   network diagram that shows the primary components of the solution (e.g., IPsec gateways and
3516   hosts, routers, switches). Each case study also provides some details of the implementation of the
3517   solution prototype, which include examples of configuring the solution using commonly
3518   available equipment and software, based on an implementation performed in a lab or production
3519   environment. Each case study ends with a brief discussion that points out noteworthy aspects of
3520   the implementation, indicates when another case study model may be more effective, and
3521   discusses variants on the case study scenario that might be of interest to readers.

3522   The case studies are not meant to endorse the use of particular products, nor are any products
3523   being recommended over other products. Several common products were chosen so the case
3524   studies would demonstrate a variety of solutions. **Organizations and individuals should not**
3525   **replicate and deploy the sample configuration files or entries.** They are intended to illustrate
3526   the decisions and actions involved in configuring the solutions, not to be deployed as-is onto
3527   systems.

3528   The case studies presented in this section are as follows:

3529   • Protecting communications between two local area networks (remote office, main office)

3530   • Protecting wireless communications in a small office/home office environment

3531   • Protecting communications between remote users (e.g., telecommuters, road warriors)
3532   and the main office's network

3533   • Protecting a datacenter or cloud network using mesh encryption

3534   **9.1   Connecting a Remote Office to the Main Office**

3535   An organization with a single office location is planning the creation of a small remote office,
3536   which includes identifying any needs to protect network communications. To perform various
3537   job functions, most users at the remote office will need to access several information technology
3538   (IT) resources located at the main office, including the organization's email, intranet web server,
3539   databases, and file servers, as well as several business applications. Currently, email is the only
3540   one of these resources that can be accessed from outside the main office (it is available through
3541   the Internet using a web-based email client). Communications with most of the IT resources will
3542   involve transferring sensitive data (such as financial information) between systems. To support
3543   its mission, the organization needs to maintain the confidentiality and integrity of the data in a
3544   cost-effective manner. (At this time, the need is to protect communications initiated by remote
3545   office hosts to the main office network only; in the future, the solution might be extended to
3546   protect communications initiated by main office hosts to the remote office network.) The

3547 following sections describe how the organization evaluates its options, identifies a viable
3548 solution, creates a design, and implements a prototype.

9.1.1   Identifying Needs and Evaluating Options

3550 As described below, the organization considers a few options for providing access from the
3551 remote office to IT resources at the main office and protecting the data:

3552 • **Data Link Layer Solution: Leased Line.** The organization could establish a dedicated
3553   leased line between the remote office and the main office. This would provide a private
3554   communications mechanism for all the network traffic between the offices. (If the
3555   organization were concerned about security breaches of the leased line, additional
3556   protection measures such as a data link layer VPN protocol could be used to provide
3557   another layer of security.) Unfortunately, because the remote office is geographically
3558   distant from the main office, a leased line would be prohibitively expensive.

3559 • **Network Layer Solution: Network Layer VPN.** The organization could establish a
3560   network layer VPN between the remote office and main office. Connecting the remote
3561   office to the Internet and establishing a VPN tunnel over the Internet between the offices
3562   could provide access to the resources and protect the communications. The VPN could
3563   have a remote access architecture, which would reduce hardware costs (only one gateway
3564   needed) but increase labor costs (deploying and configuring clients on each remote office
3565   system). A gateway-to-gateway architecture would increase hardware costs and decrease
3566   labor costs; in effect, the VPN would be invisible to users. The two models also differ in
3567   terms of authentication. In a gateway-to-gateway VPN, the gateways would authenticate
3568   with each other; in a remote access VPN, each user would need to authenticate before
3569   using the VPN. A gateway-to-gateway VPN could also be configured to permit
3570   authorized users from the main office to access resources on the remote office's network.
3571   Although this is not a current need, it could be in the future.

3572 • **Transport Layer Solution: Web-Based Applications.** The organization could provide
3573   web-based access to all required IT resources. This could be done either by creating or
3574   acquiring web-based clients for each resource, or by deploying a terminal server that
3575   provides access to the resource and providing a web-based terminal server client to
3576   employees. All web-based applications would use the TLS protocol over HTTP (transport
3577   layer security controls) to protect the confidentiality and integrity of data and
3578   authentication credentials. By connecting the remote office to the Internet and making the
3579   web-based applications available from the Internet, users at the remote office could use
3580   the required IT resources, and the communications would be protected. The main office's
3581   network perimeter could be configured to permit external access to the resources only
3582   from the remote office's IP address range, which would reduce the risk of external parties
3583   gaining unauthorized access to the resources. Users would need to be authenticated by the
3584   terminal server, the individual applications, or both the server and the applications.

3585 • **Application Layer Solution: Application Modification.** The organization could
3586   purchase add-on software and modify existing applications to provide protection for data
3587   within each application. However, a brief review of the required IT resources shows that

3588   several of them are off-the-shelf applications that cannot be modified and cannot be
3589   protected by third-party application add-ons. Even if the applications could be deployed
3590   to protect their own communications, the applications would have to be directly
3591   accessible by remote users, which would significantly increase their exposure to threats.
3592   The organization is also concerned about the effectiveness of application layer controls in
3593   protecting data. Application layer controls may also conceal information from network
3594   layer security controls such as network-based intrusion detection systems, necessitating
3595   the use of additional host-based security controls that can monitor application layer
3596   activity. Having separate controls for each application also complicates or precludes
3597   centralized enforcement of security policies across multiple applications, as well as
3598   centralized authentication (unless each application supports the use of a third-party
3599   authentication server.)

3600   The organization considers the network layer and transport layer options to be the most feasible
3601   for meeting its remote access needs. The data link layer and application layer solutions are too
3602   expensive, compared to the network and transport layer solutions. Further investigation of the
3603   transport layer solution determines that it is not possible or practical to provide web-based
3604   interfaces for several of the desired IT resources. For example, some of the desired applications
3605   are off-the-shelf products that offer no web-based client. A terminal server solution could
3606   provide access, but this would require users to connect to the terminal server and authenticate
3607   before accessing any applications. Also, each host would need the terminal server client to be
3608   installed and configured.

3609   After comparing the three remaining solutions (remote access network layer VPN, gateway-to-
3610   gateway network layer VPN, and terminal server transport layer VPN) and considering how each
3611   solution would be deployed in the organization's environment, the organization chooses the
3612   gateway-to-gateway network layer VPN. Its primary advantages are that it should be relatively
3613   easy for the organization to deploy and maintain, and it will be transparent to users. The
3614   organization expects to be able to configure the Internet routers at the main office and remote
3615   office to act as VPN gateways, so no additional hardware will be needed. Also, each office
3616   already routes internally generated network traffic designated for another office's network to its
3617   Internet router, so routing changes should need to be made only on the Internet routers
3618   themselves. Another advantage of the gateway-to-gateway VPN is that in the future, users at the
3619   main office could use it to access resources at the remote office. There is no current need for this,
3620   but it is likely that as the remote office matures, this may become a necessity.

3621   **9.1.2   Designing the Solution**

3622   The organization hopes to use its Internet routers as endpoints for the VPN solution, see Figure
3623   17 below. Both routers support IPsec, and IPsec should be able to protect confidentiality and
3624   integrity adequately for the organization's needs, so the plan is to configure the routers to
3625   provide an IPsec tunnel. Based on the organization's performance requirements, the routers

3626   should be able to handle any additional load because they are currently lightly utilized.[73] Figure
3627   17 illustrates the planned design for the VPN architecture. The main office and remote office
3628   networks are on separate private networks, each with an IPv4 network. Each private network is
3629   connected to the Internet through a router that provides NAT services. The plan is to establish an
3630   IPsec tunnel between the external interfaces of the two routers. Desktop computers on the remote
3631   office network will send unencrypted information to the office's Internet router. The router acts
3632   as a VPN gateway, encrypting the traffic and forwarding it to the destination router at the main
3633   office, which also acts as a VPN gateway. The main office router decrypts the traffic and
3634   forwards it to its final destination, such as a file server or email server. Responses from the
3635   servers to the desktops are returned through the tunnel between the gateways.

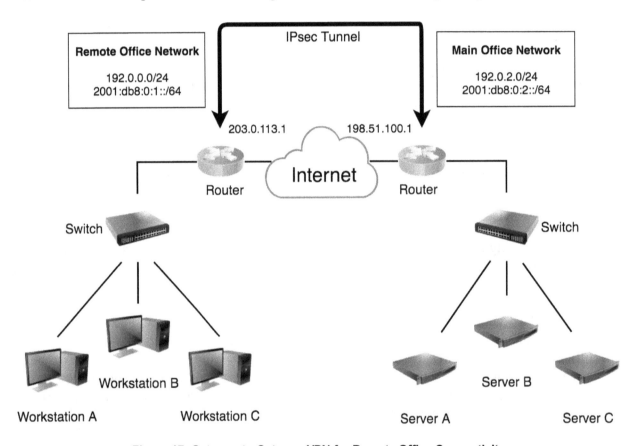

3636
3637   **Figure 17: Gateway-to-Gateway VPN for Remote Office Connectivity**

3638   In this scenario, NAT is an important architectural consideration. If possible, the design should
3639   keep NAT services out of the IPsec tunnel path to avoid potential NAT-related incompatibilities
3640   and to simplify the design. This means that outgoing packets to the remote network needing to
3641   pass through the IPsec tunnel should be excluded from NAT.

---

[73]   If the load on the routers increases significantly in the future, cryptographic accelerator cards possibly could be added to the
       routers. (Not all routers support the use of such cards.)

3642   After designing the architecture, the network administrators next consider other elements of the
3643   design, including the following:

3644   • **Authentication.** Because the VPN is being established between only two routers, a
3645   strong PSK with entropy of at least 112 bits should provide adequate authentication with
3646   minimal effort (as compared to alternatives such as digital certificates). The routers will
3647   encrypt the PSK in storage to protect it.

3648   • **IKE and ESP Algorithms.** Since 128-bit AES provides sufficiently strong encryption, it
3649   is chosen initially for ESP to prevent potentially overloading the gateways. The AES-
3650   GCM algorithm is a good choice for IKE and ESP, because it is an AEAD algorithm
3651   providing encryption and integrity together in an efficient and more secure manner. It is
3652   preferred over the older combined algorithms with separate encryption and integrity
3653   algorithms, such as AES-CBC with HMAC-SHA-2. The PRF used is SHA-256-HMAC.
3654   If the DH group chosen is DH 19, a modern and strong ECP group that provides 128 bits
3655   of security strength. PFS is enabled to ensure that a compromise of one of the routers will
3656   not cause all previously captured encrypted traffic to be vulnerable to decryption. A
3657   fallback proposal using AES-CBC with HMAC-SHA-2 is added to ensure maximum
3658   interoperability with other devices, as not all devices support AES-GCM for IKE and
3659   ESP. The initiator must use a DH group that is also supported by the responder.

3660   • **Packet Filters.** The network administrators work with the security staff to design packet
3661   filters that will permit only the necessary network traffic between the two networks and
3662   will require adequate protection for traffic. To make initial testing of the solution easier,
3663   the administrators decide that the packet filters should allow all IP-based communications
3664   from the remote office's hosts to the main office's hosts. Once initial testing has been
3665   completed, more restrictive packet filters will be added and tested. The packet filters
3666   should permit only the necessary communications and specify the appropriate protection
3667   for each type of communication.

3668   • **MTU and Fragmentation.** Since the IPsec tunnel is using an ISP, and the network might
3669   not support packets larger than 1500 bytes, both routers are set to use TCP MSS clamping
3670   at 1440 bytes, as path MTU discovery might not work properly across the network.

3671   **9.1.3   Implementing a Prototype**

3672   Because the organization has limited network equipment and does not have a test lab, the IT staff
3673   decides the best option for validating the solution is to test it after hours using the production
3674   routers once the remote office network infrastructure is in place and Internet connectivity has
3675   been established. If the testing causes a connectivity outage, the impact should be minimal. The
3676   network administrators perform the following steps to configure and test a prototype of the IPsec
3677   solution:

3678   1. **Back up the routers.** Backing up the router operating system and configuration files is a
3679   necessity since the prototype is being implemented on production equipment. Even in a
3680   test environment, performing a backup before making any changes is often very helpful
3681   because the routers can be restored quickly to a "clean" state.

3682 2. **Update the firmware of the routers.** To ensure that no known bugs are left unfixed, the
3683   routers are updated to the latest firmware and assessed for regular operation without any
3684   other changes in configuration. One endpoint is updated and rebooted. Once the network
3685   is confirmed to be operating properly, the other endpoint's firmware is updated, and the
3686   router is rebooted. Once both routers are confirmed to be working properly on the latest
3687   firmware, the process of configuring the routers for IPsec can be started.

3688 3. **Verify the security of the routers.** The network administrators should perform a
3689   vulnerability assessment to identify any existing security issues with the routers, such as
3690   unneeded user accounts or inadequate physical security controls. The administrators
3691   should then address all identified issues before proceeding, or the IPsec implementation
3692   may be compromised quickly.

3693 4. **Update the endpoints to support IPsec.** This could involve patching the operating
3694   system, installing or enabling IPsec services, or making other changes to the endpoints so
3695   that they can support IPsec services. In this case, both endpoints happen to be Cisco
3696   routers, so the administrators double-check each router to confirm that it can support
3697   IPsec and the desired encryption algorithm.

3698 5. **Specify the IKE cryptographic algorithms.** For our preferred proposal, use AES-GCM,
3699   since it is an AEAD algorithm; specify a PRF. For the fallback proposal, use AES-CBC
3700   with HMAC-SHA-256. It will use SHA-256 (in HMAC) for integrity protection as well.
3701   The following ECP DH group (19) is specified.

```
3702  crypto ikev2 proposal 1
3703    encryption aes-gcm 256
3704    prf sha256
3705    group 19

3706  crypto ikev2 proposal 2
3707    encryption aes-cbc-256
3708    integrity sha256[74]
3709    group 19[75]

3710  crypto ikev2 policy default
3711    proposal 1
3712    proposal 2
3713    match fvfr any
```

3714 6. **Specify the IKE authentication method.** In this case, each router needs to be configured
3715   to use a PSK, as illustrated by the following configuration entries[76]. Instead of IP

---

[74] For AEAD algorithms, a PRF needs to be specified. For non-AEAD algorithms, the PRF defaults to the integrity algorithm.
[75] Change this value to 14 and/or 15 if DH 19 is not supported by the other device.
[76] Secure transport for the PSK is provided by one of the network administrators, who physically carries a copy of the key
      from the main office to the remote office.

3716   addresses as identifiers, Fully Qualified Domain Names (FQDNs) will be used. An easy
3717   way to create a strong random PSK is to use the openssl command: `openssl rand -`
3718   `base64 64`

3719   ```
       crypto ikev2 profile default
3720   identity local fqdn west.example.gov
3721   match identity remote fqdn east.example.gov
3722   authentication local pre-share key XXXXXXXX
3723   authentication remote pre-share key XXXXXXXX
       ```

3724   7. **Specify the IPsec mode and cryptographic algorithms.** The following configuration
3725      entry on each router specifies ESP tunnel mode, preferring AES-GSM instead of AES-
3726      CBC-128 encryption with HMAC-SHA-256 integrity protection:

3727   ```
       crypto ipsec transform-set 1 esp-gcm-128[77]
3728     mode tunnel
3729   crypto ipsec transform-set 2 esp-cbc-128
3730     mode tunnel
       ```

3731   8. **Define the packet filters.** The following configuration entry tells the routers which
3732   packets should be permitted to use IPsec:

3733   ```
       ip access-list extended 100
3734   permit ip 192.0.0.0 0.0.0.255 192.0.2.0 0.0.0.255
3735   permit ipv6 2001:db8:0:1::/64 2001:db8:0:2::/64
       ```

3736   9. **Tie the IPsec settings together in a crypto map.** On Cisco routers, the settings created
3737      in steps 5, 6, and 7 need to be connected. This can be done through the following
3738      configuration settings, which create a crypto map called *west-east*:

3739   ```
       crypto map west-east 1 ipsec-isakmp
3740     set peer 203.0.113.1
3741     set transform-set 1 2
3742     set pfs group19[78]
3743     set ikev2-profile default
3744   match address 100
       ```

3745   10. **Apply the IPsec settings to the external interface.** Because the external interface of the
3746   router will provide IPsec services, the crypto map created in the previous step must be
3747   applied to the external interface. This is done through the following commands:

3748   ```
       interface g1/1
       ```

---

[77]   The term *transform set* refers to the VPN algorithms and security protocols.
[78]   For devices not supporting DH 19, use DH 14 and/or DH 15.
       ```

3749   `crypto map west-east`

3750   11. **Review the configuration.** After configuring both routers, the administrators review the
3751   routers' configurations to ensure that all the necessary settings are in place.[79] The
3752   following commands can be used to display the policies:

3753   `show crypto ikev2 policy`
3754   `show crypto map`

3755   12. **Test the solution.** Administrators can test the solution by attempting to gain access to
3756   main office resources from a desktop at the remote office. The test should also include
3757   using packet sniffers to monitor the network traffic at both offices and confirm it is
3758   properly protected. If successful, the configuration could be updated to use 256-bit keys
3759   for ESP encryption. If the test is unsuccessful, the administrators should troubleshoot the
3760   problem, make any necessary corrections or changes, then test the solution again.[80]
3761   Additional test actions should include implementing the restrictive packet filters and
3762   verifying them, and verifying that the correct algorithms are used. For example, some
3763   IPsec implementations have a fallback policy that causes weaker algorithms to be used if
3764   the user-selected settings cannot be negotiated successfully; this could provide inadequate
3765   protection for communications.

3766   **9.1.4 Analysis**

3767   Setting up an IPsec tunnel between Internet routers can be effective in connecting remote offices
3768   with multiple users to another network. It can reduce costs because remote offices need only
3769   Internet connectivity instead of a leased line. In addition, all traffic from the remote office could
3770   be routed though the main corporate firewall, which could decrease the costs and risks associated
3771   with the administration of multiple firewalls. To set up this type of implementation, both routers
3772   need to have a static IP address because the addresses would have to be entered into the IPsec
3773   configurations. In most cases, this is not an issue for the router at the main office, but it may be a
3774   problem for locations such as home offices that often use DSL or cable modem services, which
3775   may offer only dynamic IP addresses. Remote access solutions may be more practical for such
3776   situations.

3777   In this case study, a gateway-to-gateway VPN was established between a remote office and the
3778   main office. An interesting variant on this scenario is a gateway-to-gateway VPN between the
3779   main office and the network of a business partner. In such a case, more stringent security
3780   measures may be needed to satisfy each organization's requirements for communication. Also,
3781   the organizations should establish a formal interconnection agreement that specifies the technical
3782   and security requirements for establishing, operating, and maintaining the interconnection, as

---

[79]   Appendix C.1 contains a sample configuration file from one of the routers.
[80]   The **debug crypto ikev2**, **debug crypto ipsec**, and **debug crypto engine** commands cause the router to display any errors
       related to the crypto implementation in the terminal window. This can be useful in determining why a connection is failing.
       Also, the **clear crypto sa** command can be used to clear part or all of the SA database, which may clear some errors.

3783   well as documenting the terms and conditions for sharing data and information resources in a
3784   secure manner. Appendix B contains more information on interconnection agreements.

3785   In a gateway-to-gateway VPN between the organization and a business partner, each
3786   organization typically has control over its own VPN gateway. Accordingly, the organizations
3787   need to identify an acceptable out-of-band method for provisioning each other's gateways with
3788   the necessary authentication information, such as PSKs or digital certificates. Another possible
3789   difference from the original scenario is that in the business partner scenario, both organizations
3790   should configure their packet filters to be as restrictive as possible from the beginning of the
3791   implementation. The organizations also need to coordinate their testing efforts and determine
3792   how a prototype for the solution can best be tested.

3793   **9.1.4.1 Direct remote branch access versus hub-spoke**

3794   The solution for one remote location can be extended with additional remote office locations. If
3795   one remote office needs to be able to communicate to other remote offices, another design
3796   decision needs to be made. Either each remote office can build an IPsec tunnel to each other
3797   remote office and bypass the main office, or each remote office can contact other remote offices
3798   via the main office. This latter setup is called a *hub-spoke setup*.

3799   The advantage of the hub-spoke architecture is that the main office is the central hub that can
3800   dictate policies and inspect all traffic. If a remote office wants to communicate with another
3801   remote office, it involves two separate IPsec tunnels. The hub server decrypts the traffic from the
3802   first remote office, performs network inspection and packet filter restrictions on the network
3803   traffic, and then re-encrypts the traffic to send it via the second IPsec tunnel to the second remote
3804   office. Adding a branch does not require any other branches to be reconfigured for the new
3805   branch.

3806   The disadvantage of the hub-spoke architecture is the main office requires a lot more bandwidth
3807   to facilitate all the remote branches' traffic to each other. It might require an IPsec service with
3808   additional hardware acceleration network cards to be able to handle all the IPsec traffic. It also
3809   becomes a single point of failure. When the branches communicate via their own IPsec
3810   connections, the branches are more independent of the main office. It does require more
3811   management, since whenever a branch office is added or modified, all other branches need to
3812   have their IPsec configurations updated. Any network inspection configurations and packet
3813   filters can still be centrally managed but need to be pushed out to the branch locations.

3814   **9.2 Protecting Communications for Remote Users**

3815   A system administrator of a federal agency has been giving out SSH access to individual
3816   developers who sometimes work from home. While usable for remote logins via SSH, reaching
3817   various reporting servers required complicated port forwarding configurations for SSH that were
3818   prone to misconfiguration. It was decided that a proper remote access VPN should be deployed.
3819   It would allow the remote users to directly access the agency's servers from their browser once
3820   connected to the VPN, without needing SSH.

3821 The system administrator had also learned that the WiFi at the office was using WPA2 security,
3822 which had seen a number of attacks and was no longer considered secure enough. However, the
3823 WiFi hardware vendor had no plans to support WPA3 for the hardware they used. The system
3824 administrator wanted to treat the office WiFi as insecure and require the remote access VPN to
3825 connect to the office network, even from the office WiFi network.

3826 9.2.1 Identifying Needs and Evaluating Options

3827 As described below, a federal agency may consider a few options for protecting the connections
3828 to their secure internal network for remote users as well as local WiFi users.

3829 • **Network Layer Solution: Network Layer VPN.** The organization could establish
3830   network layer VPNs between the developers and the agency's main office. The VPN
3831   tunnels would provide access to the agency internal resources without the need for
3832   hopping through a number of servers via SSH. The organization considers each possible
3833   network layer VPN architecture, as follows:

3834   o A gateway-to-gateway VPN solution is not suitable because the developers work
3835   from a number of remote locations, such as co-sharing spaces, hotels, and coffee
3836   shops. The developers need access from their laptops and phones, not desktops at
3837   home.

3838   o The agency already has a flexible FreeBSD-based internet gateway. A remote
3839   access VPN solution for FreeBSD would allow the agency to use its existing
3840   gateway, eliminating additional hardware costs. Each remote device would need
3841   VPN client software installed, but their laptops and phones already support IKEv2
3842   remote access VPNs, so additional labor would be limited to supporting the
3843   developers in performing the configuration and troubleshooting issues. The
3844   agency would not even need to pay for additional VPN client licenses.

3845 • **Transport Layer Solution: Web-Based Access Solution.** The agency could provide
3846   web-based access to resources. This could be accomplished by deploying secured web-
3847   based services. This solution would meet the requirement to protect the data in transit, but
3848   it would require the agency to deploy, secure, and maintain a public web server
3849   connected to the internet. Additionally, all HTTPS services would need to be
3850   reconfigured to require a new kind of authentication system, as currently it is assumed
3851   that anyone who can reach the internal services is authorized to use the services.

3852 • **Application Layer Solution: File Encryption.** Instead of encrypting communications,
3853   an application layer solution could encrypt the data itself, which could then be transferred
3854   through non-encrypted communications. Using a public key from the agency, the external
3855   developers could encrypt their data and then transfer the data to the server over public
3856   networks. The data on the server could be decrypted by the developers as needed.
3857   Although file encryption is a reasonable solution for transferring files to the agency's
3858   server, it is not well-suited for protecting reports and other files that may be downloaded
3859   from the server by the external organizations. Such files would need to be encrypted so
3860   the external organizations could decrypt them. As developers join or leave the agency, or
3861   other changes occur to the set of valid keys, all files would need to be encrypted using the

3862   new set of keys. The agency could establish a shared key for all external developers, but
3863   this would increase the risk of unauthorized access, reduce accountability, and still
3864   require considerable maintenance effort, such as distributing new keys in an out-of-band
3865   manner.

3866   After further investigations into security, ease of deployment, and cost, the agency selects the
3867   network layer VPN solution and chooses to use its existing remote access architecture. It is
3868   important to note that this solution protects traffic only between the external developers' laptops
3869   (at home or on the corporate WiFi) and the main office's VPN gateway; the traffic between the
3870   VPN gateway and the local servers is not encrypted, unless the developers use the SSH protocol
3871   to provide encryption.

3872   **9.2.2 Designing the Solution**

3873   The solution is based on the agency's existing FreeBSD Internet router and will only require
3874   installing the additional strong Swan IPsec software to become an IPsec VPN gateway. The
3875   router is lightly utilized, so an additional VPN device is not needed for the external developers'
3876   usage. The strongSwan IPsec implementation supports EAP-TLS for authentication, which can
3877   use the same AAA backend as the WiFi WPA2 solution. Certificates can be easily added and
3878   revoked when developers join or leave the agency. The VPN requirement for the internal WiFi
3879   network can be rolled out as optional first and made mandatory later by deploying a packet filter
3880   on the firewall that connects the WiFi access point to only allow IKE and ESP packets from the
3881   WiFi clients.

3882   Figure 18 illustrates the planned design for the VPN architecture. The internal WiFi and the
3883   remote access clients are considered external (and insecure) networks and are on a different
3884   segment from the internal networks of the main office. The strategy is to establish an IPsec
3885   tunnel from the external devices to connect to the main office VPN router. Data sent between the
3886   developers' laptops and the VPN router will be encrypted, while data between the VPN router
3887   and the internal servers (A, B, and C) will not. The tunnel will stay intact until the external
3888   system or the VPN router manually terminates the tunnel, or the connection is inactive for a
3889   certain period of time. The VPN router and VPN client software on the developers' laptops
3890   support UDP encapsulation and MOBIKE, so remote clients that are on NAT networks or have
3891   multiple interfaces (WiFi and mobile data) can negotiate UDP encapsulation and MOBIKE to
3892   use the IPsec solution.

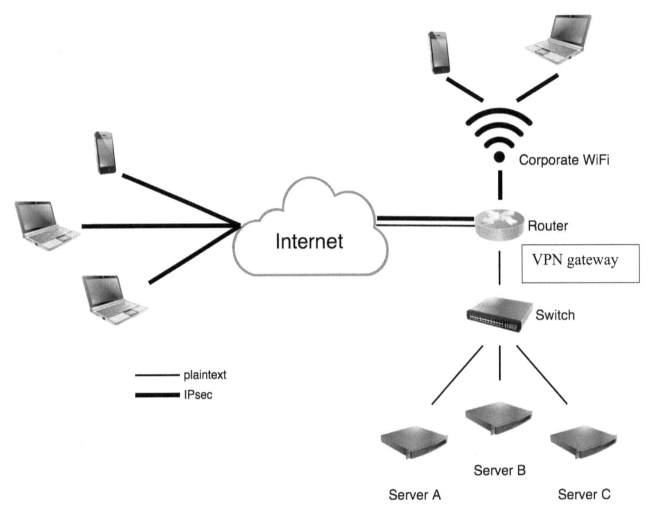

3893

Figure 18: Remote Access VPN for Protecting Communications

3895   After designing the architecture, the company next considers other elements of the design and
3896   makes several decisions, including the following:

3897   •   **Authentication.** In the actual deployment of the solution, the clients will be authenticated
3898   through digital certificates issued by the company's CA. The VPN router will be
3899   provisioned with a machine certificate. The certificates will be installed on the
3900   developers' laptops when these devices are locally present at the office. The IPsec client
3901   software will be configured to use the digital certificate as a user-based certificate, as this
3902   would not require any administrator privileges. When a tunnel needs to be established,
3903   the client will send its user certificate using EAP-TLS to the VPN gateway for
3904   authentication as part of the IKE exchange. The strongSwan IPsec software in the VPN
3905   gateway will act as a AAA server initially. When the company extends the solution to
3906   multiple VPN gateways for remote access to a number of remote access locations, a
3907   separate AAA backend will be set up to handle the EAP-TLS authentication. The VPN
3908   gateway will send its certificate via IKE to the remote clients as a machine certificate, so
3909   the clients do not need to contact the AAA server to authenticate the VPN's server

3910   certificate. Instead, the client uses the CA certificate to validate the VPN gateway
3911   certificate and that this certificate matches the IKE ID of the VPN gateway.

3912   • **Encryption and Integrity Protection Algorithms.** The VPN gateway supports multiple
3913   encryption algorithms for IKE and ESP, including AES-CBC and AES-GCM. Since not
3914   all IKEv2 clients support AES-GCM for IKE, the gateway will also allow AES-CBC
3915   with HMAC-SHA-2 for IKE. However, since most IKEv2 clients support AES-GCM for
3916   ESP, the server normally does not permit AES-CBC with HMAC-SHA-2 as a default for
3917   ESP because that would put an additional load on the server.

3918   • **Packet Filters.** To restrict the external developers' usage as much as possible, the IPsec
3919   packet filters should be configured to permit only access to the development network
3920   over the VPN tunnel. This would ensure that the agency's internal network is minimally
3921   impacted by the remote VPN clients.

3922   • **Split Tunneling.** The IPsec client configuration could offer split tunnel configurations.
3923   Since the developers' laptops are issued for agency use only, their configurations do not
3924   allow split tunneling. The split tunnel configuration would also not make sense on the
3925   corporate WiFi, since all traffic will always first reach the corporate gateway regardless,
3926   so it makes sense to encrypt everything for the additional security it provides in case the
3927   native WiFi link layer security is compromised. For mobile phones, the IPsec
3928   configuration could allow split-tunnel configurations, as the network traffic generated by
3929   different applications on a phone are usually isolated from each other, and the VPN could
3930   be provisioned in such a way that only the corporate application is allowed to send traffic
3931   over the corporate VPN tunnel.

3932   ### 9.2.3 Implementing a Prototype

3933   The VPN gateway administrator performs the following steps to configure and test a prototype of
3934   the IPsec solution between an external test system and the FreeBSD VPN gateway. Section
3935   9.2.3.1 describes the configuration of the VPN gateway device, while Section 9.2.3.2 describes
3936   the external system's configuration. The testing of the whole solution is detailed in Section
3937   9.2.3.3.

3938   ### 9.2.3.1 Configuring the Server

3939   The administrator performs the following steps to configure the FreeBSD VPN gateway for use
3940   with strongSwan. It is assumed that there is an existing CA system that can issue certificates.

3941   1. **Create a separate certificate for each device.** Device certificates use a subjectAltName
3942   (SAN) for the FQDN based on the user, a user-device@example.com like syntax, or a
3943   random globally unique identifier (GUID). For maximum compatibility, it will also set
3944   the EKU attribute for serverAuth.

3945   2. **Create a VPN gateway machine certificate.** This certificate must have the full DNS
3946   hostname as SAN included with the certificate. Because the gateway has a static IP, a
3947   SAN for the IP address is added as well. For maximum compatibility, the EKU attribute
3948   for serverAuth is set as well.

3949
3950
3951

3. **Configure global VPN server parameters.** The global parameters in the configuration files in the `/usr/local/etc/strongswan.d/` directory are reviewed. The system administrator decides to set logging to use a file instead of the default syslog.

3952
3953
3954
3955
3956
3957

4. **Configure the VPN server's IPsec connection and EAP-TLS RADIUS backend.** A new configuration file `remote-access.conf` is created in the `/usr/local/etc/swanctl/ipsec.d/` directory. It contains the server's IKEv2 parameters, such as the IKE ID, public IP address, local subnet (0.0.0.0/0 and/or ::0), configuration for DNS servers, lease IP addresses for clients, and tunnel. The radius server is located at IP address 10.10.10.10.

```
# /usr/local/etc/swanctl/ipsec.d/remote-access.conf
connections {
    remote-clients-eap {
        local_addrs = 192.0.2.1
        local {
            auth = pubkey
            certs = vpn.example.gov.pem
            id = vpn.example.gov
        }
        remote {
            auth = eap-tls
        }
        children {
            net {
                local_ts = 0.0.0.0/0
                updown = /usr/local/libexec/ipsec/_updown iptables
                esp_proposals = aes256gcm256-ecp256, aes256gcm256-
modp2048
            }
        }
        version = 2
        send_certreq = no
        proposals = aes256gcm256-prfsha2-ecp256, aes256-sha256-
modp2048
    }
}

pools {
    connections_pool {
        addrs = 10.11.0.0/16
    }
}
```

The EAP-TLS configuration is configured in strongswan.conf by editing the libtls{} and plugins{} section:

```
# /usr/local/etc/strongswan.conf
```

```
3994            plugins {
3995                eap-radius {
3996                    secret = XXXXXXXXX
3997                    server = 10.10.10.10
3998                }
3999            }
4000
4001        libtls {
4002            suites = TLS_DHE_RSA_WITH_AES_128_GCM_SHA256,
4003                            TLS_DHE_RSA_WITH_AES_256_GCM_SHA384
4004        }
```

4005   5. **Ensure that the VPN service is started**. To ensure the strongSwan IKE daemon is
4006   started when booting the system, the file `/etc/rc.conf` is updated and the server is
4007   rebooted as a test.

4008   6. **Create provisioning profiles for those IKEv2 clients that support it**. Using
4009   provisioning profiles can save a lot of time for the administrator and make it easier on the
4010   users to configure their system for IPsec. Unfortunately, not all common IKEv2 clients
4011   support this. The administrator uses the vendor enterprise tools from Apple, Microsoft,
4012   and others to generate profiles for easy installation.

4013   7. **Update the firewall settings**. The firewall settings need to be updated to allow the IKE
4014   and IPsec traffic and to allow the decrypted traffic to be inspected and then forwarded to
4015   the right interfaces. The `/etc/rc.conf` file is updated to set
4016   `firewall_enable="YES"`, and the file `/etc/rc.firewall` is updated to allow
4017   protocol 50, UDP port 500, and UDP and TCP port 4500.

4018   ### 9.2.3.2 Configuring the Clients

4019   After completing the VPN gateway configuration, the administrator configures an externally
4020   located test system to be an IPsec client. The steps performed to achieve this are as follows:

4021   1. **If required, install IKEv2 software on the device.** On most phones and laptops, an
4022   IKEv2-based IPsec client comes pre-installed. Because some people inside the company
4023   use Android-based phones, and they do not have native support for IKEv2, the
4024   strongSwan IKEv2 client is installed on them.

4025   2. **Configure the IPsec clients.** Each vendor's IPsec client has its own type of
4026   configuration. Clients that support provisioning can usually install a profile configuration
4027   file from universal serial bus (USB) media or an email attachment. Such profiles are
4028   usually encrypted by a password to ensure that the file can be sent over an insecure
4029   network. If provisioning is not supported, the configuration menu on the client will have
4030   an option to add a "VPN configuration". This configuration will then ask for the remote
4031   VPN server's DNS name, the type of configuration required, and some optional
4032   information. Some IPsec clients have an option to import a certificate bundle, while other
4033   IPsec clients require the user to import certificates separately from the VPN connection.

4034 Certificates usually are transported using the PKCS#12 format, which consists of an
4035 encrypted bundle consisting of a certificate, private key, and CA certificate that are
4036 protected by symmetric key wrapping using a key derived from a strong password.

4037 **3. Test the tunnel settings.** Once the parameters have been entered, the administrator starts
4038 the VPN connection.

9.2.3.3 Testing the Solution

4039

4040 After completing the configuration of the VPN router and the external test clients, the VPN
4041 gateway administrator tests the solution to ensure that the external system can successfully
4042 establish a secure tunnel to the VPN router and transfer encrypted traffic through the tunnel.
4043 While ping commands are a good initial test to see if things appear to be working, it is not
4044 enough, as these packets are unusually small and will give no indication whether a large TCP
4045 stream will work as well. Using a web browser to generate traffic is a better test. If the remote
4046 access server provides both IPv4 and IPv6 lease IP addresses to the VPN clients, both types
4047 should be verified to work properly. Traffic to both the corporate servers and the Internet should
4048 be tested to ensure proper functioning of the (lack or presence of) split tunnel configuration.

4049 Tests should also ascertain that the VPN gateway will only negotiate IPsec tunnels for the
4050 approved algorithm and will block traffic that is not encrypted. The administrator should monitor
4051 the VPN gateway's logs for errors that indicate problems with the connection. The gateway's log
4052 report generation tool can be useful when troubleshooting issues because it can indicate where
4053 connections are failing or where traffic is being dropped. The administrator also deploys a packet
4054 sniffer on the gateway or an external test device to confirm that the traffic is being protected.

4055 MOBIKE is tested by using a phone that has mobile data and WiFi connectivity. The phone
4056 establishes a VPN connection to the VPN server using the WiFi interface. The WiFi interface is
4057 then disabled. The VPN connection should still be working. Logs on the VPN server can be
4058 checked to see if the VPN client's public IP address changed through a MOBIKE message. Re-
4059 enabling WiFi should cause the VPN client to switch back to WiFi, since that is usually the
4060 preferred connection, as it will be faster and cheaper.

9.2.4 Analysis

4061

4062 IPsec tunnels established from external systems to a trusted gateway can be effective for
4063 protecting sensitive information from eavesdroppers. Providing secure remote access for laptops,
4064 phones, or industrial equipment can be done using standard IKEv2 and IPsec software. Using the
4065 existing IPsec client software and IPsec gateway eliminates the need to purchase additional
4066 hardware or software and greatly reduces design and implementation time.

4067 Reusing the remote access VPN architecture to provide additional protection to the local WiFi
4068 network requires less reliance on the WiFi hardware manufacturers and WiFi security protocols.
4069 The WEP and WPA2 link layer security protocols have been cryptographically broken on a few
4070 occasions, requiring protocol updates that are not always possible on older hardware models.
4071 Using an IPsec solution provides confidence that the WiFi network cannot be abused or broken

4072 into to gain access to the corporate network, as the WiFi network is as untrusted as any other
4073 host on the internet. Visitors to the office can be given guest internet access to the WiFi network
4074 using the link layer credentials without endangering the corporate network, as access to the
4075 corporate network is not possible from the office WiFi network without using the IPsec remote
4076 access VPN.

4077, **9.3   Remote Access to a Cloud Server Instance**

4078 An agency has outsourced some of its public facing web pages to a cloud provider. A number of
4079 virtual machines are used to provide the service from the cloud. This private cloud uses private
4080 IP addresses. The agency has one public IP address that terminates at the cloud provider. The
4081 cloud provider allows the agency to forward specific protocols and ports to one of its virtual
4082 machines. The agency forwards TCP port 80 and TCP port 443 to one of the virtual machines
4083 running the haproxy software configured as a service that load balances these connections to a
4084 number of virtual machine web servers. These web servers connect to another set of virtual
4085 machines running a database server. During peak seasons for this agency, the number of database
4086 and web servers can be increased to match demand. To update the database content on these
4087 virtual machines from the agency internal network, a VPN connection is desired. This would
4088 allow the database servers to be replicated from the agency's network to the private cloud.

4089 The virtual cloud is using the IPv4 private space IP network 10.0.2.0/24. The cloud provider runs
4090 a virtual router on the IP address 10.0.2.254. Traffic for the cloud uses one of the cloud
4091 provider's public IP addresses, 192.1.2.78. This is the IP address for the agency's cloud
4092 webserver at cloud.example.gov. Web traffic using ports 80 and 443 to the IP address 192.1.2.78
4093 uses NAT and is sent to the internal IP 10.0.2.2 running the haproxy service. The agency itself
4094 uses the private space IP network 192.168.0.0/16, but only wants select parts of their network to
4095 have direct access to the private cloud—192.168.103.0/24 and 2001:db8:0:2::/64. While the
4096 agency could get public IPv6 addresses for its virtual private cloud, it decides it would be safer to
4097 use private space IPv6 addresses as well, similar to how it rolled out private space IPv6 at the
4098 agency network for its database servers and workstation machines. The IPv6 private cloud will
4099 use 2001:db8:0:1::/64.

4100 **9.3.1   Identifying Needs and Evaluating Options**

4101 As there is no dedicated link between the agency and the cloud provider, link-based VPNs
4102 cannot be used. The agency also wants to keep the ability to move to another cloud provider, so
4103 it does not want to use the cloud provider's VPN solution. An additional advantage of using a
4104 virtual VPN server inside the private cloud is that all traffic inside the cloud provider's network,
4105 but outside the private cloud itself, would be encrypted. Only the virtual machines of the agency
4106 would be able to see the unencrypted traffic.

4107 Using a network layer VPN would allow the agency to extend the solution by adding IPsec VPN
4108 tunnels to other cloud providers or new physical locations. It could extend the solution to
4109 building more VPN tunnels to other physical locations or other cloud providers. A VPN tunnel
4110 could even be used to move a single server to another cloud provider without reconfiguration of
4111 any other virtual servers in the private cloud.

4112   **9.3.2   Designing the Solution**

4113   Since the agency is using Linux-based virtual machines at the cloud provider, it will also use a
4114   Linux-based virtual machine as its VPN server in the private cloud. It decides to use the
4115   libreswan IPsec software that comes with the Linux distribution it is using for its cloud instances.
4116   The agency already has an enterprise Linux-based server as its internet access and firewall
4117   server, so it is decided to extend that server to build an IPsec VPN to the private cloud network.
4118   This enterprise Linux server is also using libreswan. See Figure 19 for illustration of the network
4119   setting.

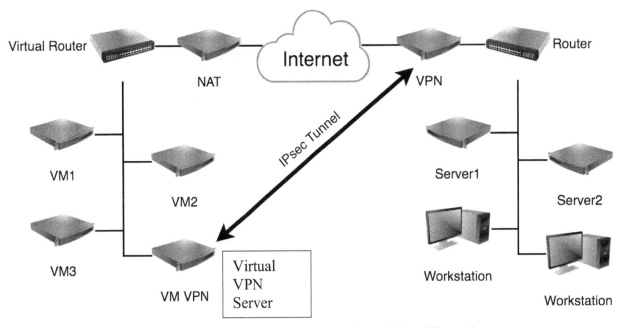

4120

4121   **Figure 19: Remote Access to a Cloud-Based Virtual Network**

4122   After designing the architecture, the company next considers other elements of the design and
4123   makes several decisions, including the following:

4124   •   **Authentication.** Libreswan supports and defaults to using IKEv2. Since both VPN
4125   endpoints are controlled by the agency, it decides to use public keys for authentication
4126   without using certificates. This will prevent the situation where certificates would expire.
4127   Using public keys without a CA is also much simpler.

4128   •   **Encryption and Integrity Protection Algorithms.** Since both ends use the same
4129   enterprise Linux solution that supports libreswan running a cryptographic module
4130   operating in FIPS mode, it is decided to leave the IKE and ESP options with their default
4131   values. That means that the VPN will start out using AES-GCM with 256-bit keys for
4132   IKE and ESP, SHA-256 as the IKE PRF, and DH 14 with PFS. When NIST-approved
4133   algorithms change in the future, the Linux enterprise solution will update the libreswan
4134   software, and the configuration on the VPN servers will be automatically updated to use
4135   the new stronger algorithm requirements.

- **Packet Filters.** To restrict the VPN access to the cloud from the agency's internal network, it is decided that only workstations and servers at some specific IP addresses are allowed to have access to the private cloud, such as only two IPv4 networks and one IPv6 network for the developer workstations using 192.168.100.0/24 and the database servers using the IPv4 range 192.168.103.0/24 and the IPv6 range 2001:db8:0:2::/64.

- **MTU and TCP settings.** It is not known exactly how many layers of encapsulations are happening at the cloud provider and at the agency's Internet service provider (ISP) itself. It is known that a digital subscriber line (DSL) service adds at least one encapsulation using PPP at the data link layer. To prevent unnecessary fragmentation and possible flow issues on the database and remote SSH login connections that will use TCP, it is decided to use TCP MSS clamping and slightly reduce the MTU for packets across the VPN connection.

9.3.3 Implementing a Prototype

A new virtual machine instance is requested from the cloud provider. The cloud security policy is updated to temporarily allow SSH connections from port 2222 of the public IP to reach the SSH port 22 on the new VPN virtual machine. An administrative SSH public key is configured to be allowed to log in to the server, and password-based SSH logins are disabled.

Using SSH to remotely log in, the virtual machine is configured as a VPN gateway. The configuration options of libreswan uses the terms *left* and *right*. The left side of our diagram is the virtual machine VPN and the administrator uses left* options to refer to it. Similarly, the agency's office VPN is on the right side of the diagram and denoted by *right*.

9.3.3.1 Configuring the VPN gateways

The cloud instance and the office gateway are prepared to run libreswan by:

- Updating the operating system: `yum update`

- Installing Libreswan: `yum install libreswan`

- Initializing Libreswan's NSS database: `ipsec initnss`

- Generating a new host key: `ipsec newhostkey --output /etc/ipsec.d/hostkey.secrets`

- Using the host key's ckaid from the previous step to obtain the public key:
  - On the cloud instance: `ipsec showhostkey --left --ckaid <ckaid>`
  - On the office gateway: `ipsec showhostkey --right --ckaid <ckaid>`

- Creating the configuration file `cloud-office.conf` with a *conn* definition for the connection named cloud-office-ipv4 and cloud-office-ipv6, then uploading it to both VPN servers and placing it in the directory */etc/ipsec.d/*

4172   • Customizing the left= entry on both servers, as indicated in the configuration file below

4173   • Updating firewall rules to allow traffic from the subnets and exempt these IP destination
4174   ranges from being NAT'ed. Adding a firewall rule for TCP MSS clamping.[81]

4175   • Enabling IP forwarding on the cloud instance. The built-in rp_filter is disabled to avoid
4176   false positives, otherwise the kernel will drop or try to redirect traffic due to the
4177   encrypted and decrypted traffic using the same (single) virtual ethernet card.

```
4178    # /etc/ipsec.d/cloud-office.conf
4179
4180    conn cloud-office-base
4181        # On the cloud gateway, use left=%defaultroute to pick up its
4182        # internal IP address
4183        # left=%defaultroute
4184        # on the office gateway, use left=<IP of the cloud's public IP>
4185        left=192.1.2.78
4186        leftid=@cloud-vpn
4187        leftrsasigkey=<value from above ipsec showhostkey  --left command>
4188        right=office-gw.example.gov
4189        righted=@office-gw
4190        leftrsasigkey=<value from above ipsec showhostkey  --left command>
4191        ikev2=insist
4192        mtu=1440
4193
4194    conn cloud-office-ipv4
4195        also=cloud-office-base
4196        leftsubnets=10.0.2.0/24
4197        rightsubnets=192.168.100.0/24,192.168.103.0/24
4198        auto=add
4199
4200    conn cloud-office-ipv6
4201        also=cloud-office-base
4202        leftsubnet=2001:db8:0:1::/64
4203        rightsubnet=2001:db8:0:2::/64
4204        auto=add
```

4205

4206   ### 9.3.4 Testing the Solution

4207   The administrator is at the office, so they use SSH to log in to a third-party host that is neither
4208   behind the office VPN nor within the private cloud. From that machine, they use SSH to log in to
4209   the cloud instance VPN server. Now if the IPsec tunnels fail to come up due to a
4210   misconfiguration and drop all packets between the two locations, they are not locked out from
4211   fixing the configuration.

---

[81]   Different Linux systems use different firewall management tools. These could be based on iptables, firewalld, or shorewall.
        Consult the vendor's documentation.

- On both ends, start libreswan: `systemctl start ipsec`

- On one end, start the IPv4 connection manually: `ipsec auto --up cloud-office-ipv4`

- If the connection fails, it should show what happened. Consult the libreswan documentation and Frequently Asked Questions (FAQ) if the error is unclear.

- Once the connection establishes, a ping from one of the workstations in the office can be used to test: ping 10.0.2.78.

- Once confirmed to work, a database replication is started to test performance.

- Byte counters on the tunnel are confirmed using the command `ipsec trafficstatus`

- Next, the IPv6 connection can be brought up and tested: `ipsec auto --up cloud-office-ipv6`

With the tunnels have been confirmed to be working correctly, the configuration is updated to automatically start the tunnels when the libreswan IPsec service starts by changing `auto=add` to `auto=start`. The ipsec service is enabled to start at bootup on both gateways using the command `systemctl enable ipsec`.

The port forwarding for SSH into the private cloud is disabled using the cloud management tools to prevent the virtual machines from being scanned by attackers from the internet. SSH access is still possible, as long as the connections are made from the office through the VPN connection.

9.3.5   Analysis

A private cloud can be safely accessed remotely by adding a virtual machine acting as a VPN gateway. The private cloud can be used and protected just like physical servers at a data center. Additionally, by requiring the use of the VPN, remote access control can be further limited to legitimate sources and prevent the cloud instances from being susceptible to port scanning attacks via port forwarding on the public IP through which the private cloud is reachable.

In the future, the VPN configuration can be extended to connect to other private clouds or other data centers. It can also be extended to act as a remote access VPN for developers so they can safely connect to the private cloud from their laptops even if not at the office.

Both IPv4 and IPv6 can be used, even if the cloud provider does not provide IPv6 themselves. This allows the agency to be proactive and compliant to regulations that mandate IPv6 readiness on all their equipment.

9.4   Cloud Encryption

A large enterprise has a number of data centers and is renting virtual machines from various cloud providers. While it has connected the different networks using a gateway-to-gateway architecture, it is concerned that traffic within these networks is not encrypted. Furthermore, its

4247 global size makes it hard to monitor and ensure that all fiber cables and satellite links it deploys
4248 use proper data link security. For example, the agency might be renting an inter-city fiber cable
4249 to create a VLAN network that uses MPLS to connect a number of physically separate locations.
4250 It might be using MPLS without any link security. As nodes would not be aware when traffic
4251 would be local or would be traversing a fiber cable, such a network is vulnerable to unauthorized
4252 wiretaps. The desire is to encrypt as much traffic as possible between all nodes worldwide
4253 without creating chokepoints or single point of failures for encryption.

4254 ### 9.4.1   Identifying Needs and Evaluating Options

4255 The goal of the project is for all network traffic to be protected by network layer-based security
4256 to ensure that a compromised segment of its global data link security would not result in
4257 plaintext data being obtained by an attacker. As the goal is to encrypt all traffic, it is infeasible to
4258 perform this at the application layer. While part of the traffic can be protected by the
4259 application's use of the TLS protocol, this would not fulfill the requirement of ensuring that all
4260 traffic is encrypted at the network layer.

4261 As a first step for encrypting traffic between any two nodes, each node needs to have an identity.
4262 With various cloud deployments using virtualization and container technologies, it means that
4263 nodes are created and destroyed continuously. A provisioning system will need to be able to
4264 create and revoke identities for authorization. Ideally, the existing provisioning system that
4265 creates virtual machines and containers will be extended to give these services their
4266 cryptographic identity.

4267 To comply with legal requirements and corporate compliance policies, specific traffic between
4268 certain nodes must be monitored and stored. This traffic must be exempted from the network-
4269 wide encryption policy.

4270 Due to the sheer size of the project, it is inevitable that individual exceptions to policies need to
4271 be accommodated. A phased approach will be required where individual network managers can
4272 prepare their data center or cloud deployments for participation in the network-wide mesh
4273 encryption solution.

4274 **9.4.2   Designing the Solution**

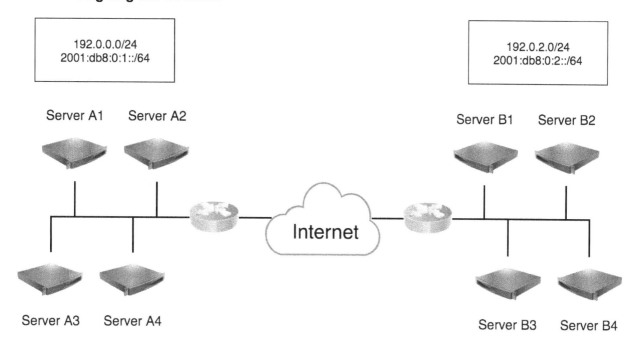

4275

4276   **Figure 20: Mesh Encryption Using Opportunistic IPsec**

4277 **Connection Establishment**. A packet triggered IPsec based solution is chosen. Since IPsec can
4278 be easily added to physical servers, virtual servers, and container-based instances, the solution
4279 should work across most of the global infrastructure.

4280 **Authentication.** As certificates are already used to identify many services, the IPsec nodes will
4281 be authenticated using machine certificates. At a later date, DNSSEC-based authentication using
4282 public keys will be evaluated, which will reduce the overhead of running a CA and remove the
4283 need for certificate renewal.

4284 **Confidentiality and Integrity**. As it is expected that some nodes will have hundreds of IPsec
4285 connections, it is important to pick the most optimum cryptography. AES-GCM with 128-bit
4286 keys is used for IKE and IPsec. For DH, the DH group 19 is used to provide 128 bits of security
4287 strength for the key exchange.

4288 **Lifetime and Idletime**. Standard IKE SA and IPsec SA lifetimes are used, although since these
4289 are not negotiated, individual managers can tune these later to optimum values depending on
4290 their traffic patterns. Similarly, idletimes are set to 15 minutes to prevent the accumulation of too
4291 many idle IKE and IPsec sessions per host, and idletimes can be tuned at a later stage as well.

4292 **IPsec Mode.** As all networks are already connected via IPsec gateways, no NAT is deployed and
4293 the IPsec connections can use the transport mode, resulting in a larger effective MTU than if an
4294 IPsec tunnel mode was used. Transport mode also prevents a node from creating a custom policy
4295 covering more than itself.

4296 **9.4.3   Implementing a Prototype**

4297 To make a realistic deployment prototype, the company decides to use two networks normally
4298 reserved as staging servers that test new code before it is deployed into production. Two staging
4299 networks at different data centers are used. These two networks are already connected in a
4300 gateway-to-gateway architecture. In a first step, servers in network A and servers in network B
4301 will each be configured for mesh encryption to their local nodes only. Once the mesh IPsec
4302 encryption is functional in one network, and the mesh IPsec encryption is functional in the other
4303 network, the mesh will be extended to incorporate both networks in a single mesh configuration.
4304 This allows for further testing of IPsec-in-IPsec packets when a server from network A starts an
4305 IPsec connection to a server in network B.

4306   • The opensource *ansible* software provisioning system is extended to create a PKCS#12
4307   certificate for each new virtual machine that is created for network A and network B.

4308   • An opportunistic IPsec configuration file is created and added to the ansible script to be
4309   installed on new virtual machines deployed in networks A and B.

```
4310    # /etc/ipsec.d/mesh.conf
4311    conn private-or-clear
4312          left=%defaultroute
4313          leftcert=provisioned-cert
4314          leftid=%fromcert
4315          rightid=%fromcert
4316          rightrsasigkey=%cert
4317          right=%opportunisticgroup
4318          type=transport
4319          failureshunt=passthrough
4320          auto=ondemand
4321
```

4322   • As part of the new virtual machine provisioning, libreswan is installed, and the generated
4323   file containing the PKCS#12 bundle with *friendly_name* "provisioned-cert" is imported
4324   into libreswan using the `ipsec import` command.

4325   • Opportunistic IPsec is enabled using the "private-or-clear" connection by adding the IP
4326   network ranges of the participating networks to the file:

```
4327
4328    /etc/ipsec.d/policies/private-or-clear:
4329
4330    # /etc/ipsec.d/policies/private-or-clear
4331    192.0.0.0/24
4332    192.0.2.0/24
4333    2001:db8:0:1::/64
4334    2001:db8:0:2::/64
4335
```

4336   **9.4.4   Testing the Solution**

4337   Traffic is generated and nodes are inspected using the `ipsec trafficstatus` command.
4338   Once the basic mesh encryption is working, more advanced scenarios are tested.

4339   • A single IP address is added to the exception policy
4340   `/etc/ipsec.d/policies/clear` to confirm communication only happens in
4341   cleartext.

4342   • Both network A and network B add each other's IP ranges to the policy file for
4343   opportunistic IPsec in `/etc/ipsec.d/policies/private-or-clear` to test
4344   mesh encryption across the two networks.

4345   • Some servers are tested with a policy in `/etc/ipsec.d/policies/private`,
4346   which mandates IPsec encryption.

4347   • TCP streams are tested between network A and B to confirm that there are no issues with
4348   double encryption (a VPN over another VPN) and packet sizes.

4349   • An IPsec mesh IP connection is triggered, and no more traffic is sent between the nodes.
4350   The connection is monitored to be expired due to idleness within the configured
4351   timeframe.

4352   • To harden against attacks where one compromised server takes over the IKE identity of
4353   another server while using its non-matching certificate, the `dns-match-id` option is
4354   enabled. After testing that the mesh connections still work, one host is configured with
4355   another host's certificate, and a mesh connection is attempted again. The connection is
4356   tested for proper rejection.

4357   **9.4.5   Analysis**

4358   The additional provisioning to add IPsec to the virtual machines and containers are minimal and
4359   working. However, it was found that packet filters on the networks were no longer able to filter
4360   traffic because most of it was encrypted. This necessitated an extension of the provisioning
4361   system to push firewall rules to each virtual machine and container.

4362   While the initial deployment of using certificates works, using raw keys in DNSSEC would work
4363   better for a large-scale deployment, but it would require a way to update DNS dynamically after
4364   generating host keys for newly generated virtual machines and containers. A follow-up project is
4365   planned for a DNSSEC-based deployment.

4366   **10   Work In Progress**

4367   This section briefly discusses some of the future directions of IPsec. At this time, the IETF is
4368   working on various IKE and IPsec extensions. This section provides a brief discussion of the
4369   new standards and pointers to additional information.

4370   **10.1 Support for Multicast and Group Authentication**

4371   *Multicast traffic* refers to sending a packet to an IP address that is designated as a multicast
4372   address; one or more hosts that are specifically interested in the communication then receive
4373   copies of that single packet. This differs from *broadcast traffic*, which causes packets to be
4374   distributed to all hosts on a subnet, because multicast traffic will only be sent to hosts that are
4375   interested in it. Multicasting is most often used to stream audio and video. For the sender, there
4376   are two primary advantages of using multicast. First, the sender only needs to create and send
4377   one packet, instead of creating and sending a different packet to each recipient. Second, the
4378   sender does not need to keep track of who the actual recipients are. Multicasting can also be
4379   advantageous from a network perspective, because it reduces network bandwidth usage.

4380   RFC 4301 [40] describes IPsec processing for multicast traffic. RFC 5374 [82] extends the
4381   IKEv1 protocol to apply to groups and multicast traffic. It defines a new class of SAs (Group
4382   Security Associations, GSAs) and additional databases used to apply IPsec protection to
4383   multicast traffic [83]. The secret key to these GSAs is distributed to the group members. Once a
4384   member leaves the group, any secret key shared with other members has to be replaced with a
4385   new group key unknown to the group member that just left. For large groups that always have
4386   members joining and leaving, this can be complicated.

4387   At the time of writing, IKEv2 does not support this, but a draft document is under development
4388   to add this support [84]. It defines a new G-IKEv2 extension that conforms with the Multicast
4389   Group (MEC) Security Architecture [83] and the Multicast Security (MSEC) Group Key
4390   Management Architecture [85]. G-IKEv2 replaces Group Domain of Interpretation (GDOI) [86],
4391   which defines a similar group key management protocol for IKEv1.

4392   **10.2 Labeled IPsec**

4393   Labeled IPsec is a mechanism to convey a security label or context that is associated with an
4394   IPsec stream. Both endpoints can apply further restrictions on the type of traffic allowed to be
4395   transmitted via the IPsec connection. Some vendors had a proprietary extension to IKEv1 to
4396   support labeled IPsec. The IETF is currently working on a draft to add this extension to IKEv2.
4397   The extension takes the form of an additional Traffic Selector with the security context that
4398   needs to be matched. This work is discussed in [87].

4399   **10.3 ESP Implicit IV**

4400   For IoT devices, as well as other battery-powered network devices, there is a desire to reduce the
4401   number of bytes sent over a network to save battery power. When IPsec is deployed using an
4402   AEAD such as AES-GCM, each packet contains an IV, also called a nonce. This value must be

4403   unique but may be predictable. The recommended implementation is to use a simple counter.
4404   However, the ESP protocol itself already has a counter, which is used to defend against replay
4405   attacks. A proposal is being developed by the IETF to define AES-GCM and AES-CCM variants
4406   that omit sending the AEAD IV and use the ESP replay counter instead. These variants are only
4407   defined for ESP algorithms, not the IKE algorithms. This work is discussed in [88].

4408   **10.4 The INTERMEDIATE Exchange**

4409   Classic DH key exchanges could become vulnerable to quantum computing attacks. There is a
4410   need to replace the DH key exchange with a quantum-safe key exchange. Current proposals for
4411   such algorithms all require the use of large public keys that need to be exchanged in IKE during
4412   the IKE_SA_INIT phase. During this phase of the exchange, IKEv2 fragmentation cannot yet be
4413   used, because a confidential channel that can identify fragments as legitimate has not yet been
4414   established. A new INTERMEDIATE exchange is placed between the IKE_SA_INIT and
4415   IKE_AUTH exchanges, which can support fragmentation. This work is discussed in [89].

4416   **10.5 IPv4 and IPv6 Support in Remote Access VPNs**

4417   The telecom networks (LTE/5G) can provide notifications about whether a network connection
4418   should be attempted with IPv4, IPv6, or both. However, IKEv2 does not offer a similar
4419   notification structure or rich enough error notification for clients to determine if they should
4420   attempt IPv4 or IPv6 only, or address both families (IPv4 and IPv6) for use with IPsec. A new
4421   draft is proposing to clarify this, for better integration of 3GPP standards with IKEv2. This work
4422   is discussed in [90].

4423   **10.6 Post Quantum Key Exchange**

4424   Once there are quantum-safe key exchange algorithms that can replace the classic DH key
4425   exchanges, the IKEv2 protocol will need to be extended to support this. One suggestion is to
4426   keep the existing (EC)DH exchange and add on one or more quantum-safe key exchanges to the
4427   protocol in such a way that the resulting hybrid key exchange is at least as strong as the strongest
4428   component. This guarantees that even if a quantum-safe algorithm candidate is used and later
4429   turns out to be unsafe, the security of the connection is still at least as strong as the known
4430   classical DH key exchange. This design also ensures that a NIST-approved IPsec implementation
4431   that adds a quantum-safe algorithm for protection still complies to all current NIST requirements.
4432   This work is discussed in [91].

4433   **Appendix A—Required Configuration Parameters for IKE and IPsec**

4434   The table below can be used as a checklist of information required to set up a gateway-to-
4435   gateway VPN tunnel. Example values are NIST approved and ranked from most preferred to
4436   least preferred. IKE and IPsec lifetimes and maximum bytes are local values only and not
4437   negotiated.

Information	Value(s)		
Local network name:			
Remote network name:			
IKE parameters:			
IKE version: (e.g., IKEv2, IKEv1)			
IKEv1 mode: (if applicable) (e.g., Main, Aggressive)			
Local ID: (type can be: IPv4, IPv6, FQDN, email or DN[82]. Default is often IPv4/IPv6)	type:	value:	
Local Peer IP address or DNS name:			
Remote Peer ID: (type can be: IPv4, IPv6, FQDN, email or DN[83]. Default is often IPv4/IPv6)	type:	value:	
Remote Peer IP address or DNS name:			
Encryption algorithm(s): (e.g., AES-GCM, AES-XCBC, 3DES (deprecated))			
Encryption key size(s): (e.g., 128, 192, 256)			
Integrity algorithm(s): (None when using an AEAD such as AES-GCM) (e.g., HMAC-SHA-2-512, HMAC-SHA-2-384, HMAC-SHA-2-256)			
Diffie-Hellman Group: (e.g., DH 19 (ecp256), DH 20 (ecp384), DH 21 (ecp512), DH 14 (modp2048), DH 15 (modp3072), DH 16 (modp4096), DH 17 (modp6144), DH 18 (8192), DH 23, DH 24, DH 25 (ecp192), DH 26 (ecp224)	group(s):	PFS (yes/no):	
Authentication type: (e.g., ECDSA >=256, RSA-Probabilistic Signature Scheme (RSA-PSS) (>= 2048), RSA-v1.5 (legacy) (>=2048), PSK)			
If PSK: (minimum 32 random characters)			
IPsec parameters:			
DH Group for PFS: must be equal strength (or stronger) as IKE above			
Local network(s):			
Remote network(s):			
Encryption algorithm(s): (e.g., AES-GCM, AES-XCBC, 3DES (deprecated)			
Encryption key size(s): (e.g., 128, 192, 256)			
Integrity algorithm(s): (None when using an AEAD such as AES-GCM) (e.g., HMAC-SHA-2-512, HMAC-SHA-2-384, HMAC-SHA-2-256)			

4438

---

[82]   When using a certificate, instead of specifying its DN, it is often easier and more robust to use its SubjectAltName.
[83]   When using a certificate, instead of specifying its DN, it is often easier and more robust to use its SubjectAltName.

118

4439   **Appendix B—Policy Considerations**

4440   As mentioned in Section 6, organizations should develop IPsec-related policies and use them as
4441   the foundation for their IPsec planning and implementation activities. This appendix presents
4442   examples of common IPsec-related policy considerations that address the confidentiality,
4443   integrity, and availability of the IPsec implementation, as well as the conditions constituting its
4444   acceptable use. The appendix focuses on policy considerations for three sample scenarios: a
4445   gateway-to-gateway VPN between two offices of a single organization, a gateway-to-gateway
4446   VPN between two business partners, and a remote access VPN for telecommuting employees of
4447   an organization.

4448   The examples provided in this appendix are intended only to provide a starting point for
4449   developing IPsec-related policy. Each organization needs to develop its own policy based on its
4450   environment, requirements, and needs. Also, many of the policy considerations in this section
4451   might already be addressed through an organization's existing policies. The examples in this
4452   appendix are not comprehensive; organizations should identify additional IPsec-related
4453   considerations that apply to their environments.

4454   **B.1   Communications with a Remote Office Network**

4455   In this scenario, an organization wants to establish an IPsec VPN to protect communications
4456   between its main office's network and a remote office's network. This VPN would be created by
4457   having the organization deploy and manage an IPsec gateway on each network and configuring
4458   the gateways so that they protect communications between the networks through an IPsec tunnel
4459   as needed. This scenario assumes that the same policies apply to the main office and remote
4460   office networks. The policy consideration examples listed in this section are divided into two
4461   groups: items specific to the IPsec gateway devices and management servers, and items specific
4462   to the hosts and people using the IPsec tunnel.

4463   **B.1.1 IPsec Gateway Devices and Management Servers**

4464   Items that are typically part of VPN policy for gateway devices and management servers include
4465   the following:

4466   •   Roles and responsibilities related to IPsec gateway operations.

4467   •   Definition for where VPN tunnels should terminate (e.g., between the border router and
4468   firewall, on the firewall).

4469   •   Security controls that are required to monitor the unencrypted network traffic, such as
4470   network-based intrusion detection systems or antivirus software, and their acceptable
4471   placement in the network architecture relative to the IPsec gateways.

4472   •   Authentication requirements for IPsec gateway administrators (e.g., two-factor
4473   authentication). This could also include requirements to change all default manufacturer
4474   passwords on the gateways and management servers, to have a separate account for each
4475   administrator, to change administrator passwords on a regular basis, and to disable or
4476   delete an administrator account as soon as it is no longer needed.

4477
4478
- Authentication requirements for IPsec tunnel users, if any. This should include a requirement for how often user accounts are audited.

4479
- Authentication requirements for the IPsec gateway devices.

4480
4481
4482
4483
4484
4485
- Security requirements for the IPsec gateway devices and IPsec management servers. For example, an organization might require a firewall to be deployed between an IPsec gateway device and its users and be configured to block all traffic not explicitly approved for use with the IPsec implementation. An organization might also require certain security controls on the IPsec gateway devices and management servers, such as host-based firewalls and antivirus software.

4486
4487
- What information should be kept in audit logs, how long it should be maintained, and how often it should be reviewed.

4488
4489
- Requirements for remediating vulnerabilities in the IPsec gateway devices and management servers.

4490
4491
- Which types of traffic should be protected by IPsec tunnels, and what types of protection should be applied to each type of traffic.

4492
4493
- What types of protection should be applied to communications between an IPsec gateway and an IPsec management server.

4494 **B.1.2 Hosts and People Using the IPsec Tunnel**

4495
4496
4497
4498
4499
4500
4501
Because the hosts and people using the IPsec tunnel are assumed to be using the organization's equipment and networks, existing policies regarding acceptable use of the organization's systems should already address most policy needs regarding IPsec tunnel use. Examples include host access requirements (e.g., authentication) and vulnerability mitigation requirements (e.g., patching OS and application vulnerabilities). Existing policy also typically specifies technical controls that must be used on each host, as well as the minimum acceptable configuration for the technical controls.

4502 **B.2   Communications with a Business Partner Network**

4503
4504
4505
4506
4507
4508
4509
4510
In this scenario, an organization wants to establish an IPsec VPN to protect certain communications between a system on its network and a system on a business partner's network. This VPN would be created by having each organization deploy and manage an IPsec gateway on its own network and configuring the gateways so that they protect communications between the organizations through an IPsec tunnel. This section focuses on the formal agreements made between the two organizations, and also summarizes policy considerations related to the organization's IPsec gateway and management server, and the people and hosts within the organization using the IPsec tunnel.

B.2.1 Interconnection Agreement

Federal policy requires Federal agencies to establish interconnection agreements for connections with business partners.[84] Specifically, OMB Circular A-130, Appendix III, requires agencies to obtain written management authorization before connecting their IT systems to other systems, after determining that there is an acceptable level of risk of doing so. The written authorization should define the rules of behavior and controls that must be maintained for the system interconnection and should be included in the organization's system security plan. It is critical that the organization and the business partner establish an agreement between themselves regarding the management, operation, and use of the interconnection, and that they formally document this agreement. The agreement should be reviewed and approved by appropriate senior staff from each organization.

An interconnection agreement is typically composed of two documents: an Interconnection Security Agreement (ISA) and a Memorandum of Understanding or Agreement (MOU/A).[85] The ISA is a security document that specifies the technical and security requirements for establishing, operating, and maintaining the interconnection. It also supports the MOU/A between the organizations. Specifically, the ISA documents the requirements for connecting the systems, describes the security controls that will be used to protect the systems and data, contains a topological drawing of the interconnection, and provides a signature line. The MOU/A documents the terms and conditions for sharing data and information resources in a secure manner. Specifically, the MOU/A defines the purpose of the interconnection; identifies relevant authorities; specifies the responsibilities of both organizations; and defines the terms of agreement, including the apportionment of costs and the timeline for terminating or reauthorizing the interconnection. The MOU/A should not include technical details on how the interconnection is established or maintained; that is the function of the ISA.

Items that are typically part of the ISA include the following:

- The information and data that will be made available, exchanged, or passed in only one direction between the systems through the IPsec gateways, and the sensitivity of that information

- The services offered over the VPN by each organization, if any

- The user community that will be served by the VPN

- A description of all system security technical services pertinent to the secure exchange of data between the systems; examples include the use of NIST-approved encryption

---

[84] NIST SP 800-47, *Security Guide for Interconnecting Information Technology Systems*, contains information on interconnection agreements, as well as extensive guidance on planning, establishing, maintaining, and disconnecting system interconnections, and developing an interconnection agreement [92].

[85] Appendices A and B of NIST SP 800-47 [92] contain detailed guidance on developing an ISA and an MOU/A as well as a sample of each. Rather than develop an ISA and MOU/A, organizations may choose to incorporate this information into a formal contract, especially if the interconnection is to be established between a Federal agency and a commercial organization. Also, in some cases, organizations may decide to use established organizational procedures for documenting the agreement, in lieu of an ISA and MOU/A.

4543   mechanisms to protect communications, and the use of physical security controls to
4544   restrict access to the IPsec gateway devices and the systems

4545   • A summary of the behavior expected from users who will have access to the
4546   interconnection; for example, each system is expected to protect information belonging to
4547   the other through the implementation of security controls that protect against intrusion,
4548   tampering, and viruses, among others

4549   • The titles of formal security policies that govern each system

4550   • A description of the agreements made regarding the reporting of and response to
4551   information security incidents for both organizations

4552   • An explanation of how the audit trail responsibility will be shared by the organizations
4553   and what events each organization will log; this should include the length of time that
4554   audit logs will be retained.

4555   Items that are typically part of the MOU/A include the following:

4556   • A description of the systems communicating through the VPN

4557   • A discussion of the types of formal communications that should occur among the owners
4558   and the technical leads for the systems

4559   • A statement regarding the security of the systems, including an assertion that each system
4560   is designed, managed, and operated in compliance with all relevant federal laws,
4561   regulations, and policies.

4562   As a foundation for the interconnection agreement, the organization should have general policy
4563   statements regarding the appropriate and necessary use of IPsec, so that it is clear when and how
4564   IPsec should be used to protect an interconnection.

B.2.2 IPsec Gateway Devices and Management Servers

4566   Each organization should have policy statements that apply to the security and acceptable use of
4567   its IPsec gateway devices and management servers, as described in Appendix B.1.1.

B.2.3 Hosts and People Using the IPsec Tunnel

4569   As described in Appendix B.1.2, existing policies regarding the acceptable use and security of
4570   the organization's systems should already address most or all policy needs regarding IPsec
4571   tunnel use by hosts and people within the organization.

B.3   Communications for Individual Remote Hosts

4573   In this scenario, an organization wants to establish an IPsec VPN to protect communications
4574   between individual remote hosts used by telecommuting employees and its main network. This
4575   VPN would be created by having the organization deploy and manage an IPsec gateway on its
4576   main network. Employees' computers would be configured with IPsec clients that would
4577   establish tunnels with the IPsec gateway as needed to protect communications between the

4578 laptops and the organization's main network. This section presents policy consideration
4579 examples for remote hosts and the organization's IPsec gateway and management server.[86]

4580 **B.3.1 Remote Access Policy**

4581 The organization should have a remote access policy that includes IPsec usage by employees
4582 from both organization-controlled and other systems. The organization might also choose to have
4583 each employee that will use the IPsec implementation sign a remote access agreement or a copy
4584 of the remote access policy before being permitted to use the systems.[87]

4585 IPsec-related items that are typically in a remote access policy include the following:

4586 • A description of appropriate and inappropriate usage of the IPsec connection (e.g.,
4587   forbidding personal use and forbidding use by other individuals)

4588 • Pointers to other organization policies that apply to remote access, such as an acceptable
4589   use policy or a VPN policy

4590 • Remote access authentication requirements, such as two-factor authentication or strong
4591   passwords

4592 • Requirements for the networking profile of remote hosts; for example, the policy might
4593   forbid a host from being connected to the organization's network and another network at
4594   the same time, as well as forbidding split tunneling

4595 • Minimum hardware and software requirements for remote hosts, including acceptable
4596   operating systems and patch levels

4597 • Required security controls for remote hosts; this could also include required
4598   configuration settings for the controls, such as scanning all files before placing them onto
4599   the host

4600 Organizations might also wish to require remote hosts to be checked automatically for
4601 vulnerabilities, malware, or other security problems immediately after establishing an IPsec
4602 connection. This should be stated in the remote access policy.

4603 **B.3.2 IPsec Gateway Devices and Management Servers**

4604 The organization should have policy statements that apply to the security and acceptable use of
4605 its IPsec gateway devices and management servers, as described in Appendix B.1.1. In addition,
4606 the organization might add policy statements specific to IPsec usage by remote hosts, such as the
4607 following:

4608 • An automatic termination and disconnection of idle connections after X minutes

---

[86] Additional guidance on policy and security considerations for remote access users is available from NIST SP 800-46 [93].
[87] The policy and agreement could also be utilized for the use of the IPsec implementation by non-employees. Depending on
      the details of the policy and agreement, some changes might be needed to make them suitable for addressing non-employee
      use.

4609   • A requirement for creating and maintaining a list of authorized users, disabling access for
4610   individual users as soon as it is no longer needed, and auditing the list of authorized users
4611   periodically.

4612

4613   **Appendix C—Case Study Configuration Files**

4614   This section contains configuration files that are referenced in the Section 9 case studies.

4615   **C.1   Section 9.1 Case Study Cisco Configuration**

4616   The following lists the contents of one of the Cisco router configuration files used in the Section
4617   9.1 gateway-to-gateway case study.

```
4618    !
4619    version 12.0
4620    service timestamps debug uptime
4621    service timestamps log uptime
4622    no service password-encryption
4623    !
4624    hostname west.example.gov
4625    !
4626    enable secret 5 $1$rMk2$5fPj5s3CvYE35OSW0qkLD.
4627    !
4628    ip subnet-zero
4629    no ip finger
4630    !
4631    crypto ikev2 proposal 1
4632     encryption aes-gcm 256
4633     prf sha256
4634     group 19
4635    !
4636    crypto ikev2 proposal 2
4637     encryption aes-cbc-256
4638     integrity sha256
4639     group 19
4640    !
4641    crypto ikev2 policy default
4642    proposal 1
4643    proposal 2
4644    match fvfr any
4645    !
4646    crypto ikev2 profile default
4647    identity local fqdn west.example.gov
4648    match identity remote fqdn east.example.gov
4649    authentication local pre-share key XXXXXXXXX
4650    authentication remote pre-share key XXXXXXXXX
4651    !
4652    crypto ipsec transform-set 1 esp-gcm-128
4653    mode tunnel
4654    crypto ipsec transform-set 2 esp-cbc-128
4655    mode tunnel
4656    !
4657    crypto map west-east 1 ipsec-isakmp
4658    set peer 203.0.113.1
```

125

```
4659   set transform-set 1 2
4660   set pfs group19
4661   set ikev2-profile default
4662   match address 100
4663   !
4664   interface g1/1
4665    ip address 198.51.100.1  255.255.255.0
4666    no ip directed-broadcast
4667   !
4668   ip classless
4669   ip route 0.0.0.0 0.0.0.0 20.20.20.20
4670   no ip http server
4671   !
4672   ip access-list extended 100
4673    permit ip 192.0.0.0 0.0.0.255 192.0.2.0 0.0.0.255
4674    permit ipv6 2001:db8:0:1::/64 2001:db8:0:2::/64
4675   !
4676   line con 0
4677   login
4678    transport input none
4679   line aux 0
4680   line vty 0 4
4681   login
4682   !
4683   end
```

4684

4685 C.2   Section 9.1 Case Study Alternative Using strongSwan on FreeBSD

4686 The following lists the contents of the same configuration as provided in Appendix C.1, but
4687 using strongSwan on FreeBSD:

```
4688   # /usr/local/etc/swanctl/swanctl.conf
4689   connections {
4690       west-east {
4691           local_addrs = 198.51.100.1
4692           remote_addrs = 203.0.113.1
4693           local {
4694               auth = psk
4695               id = west.example.gov
4696           }
4697           remote {
4698               auth = psk
4699               id = east.example.gov
4700           }
4701           children {
4702               net4-net4 {
4703                   local_ts = 192.0.0.0/24
4704                   remote_ts = 192.0.2.0/24
4705                   esp_proposals = aes128gcm128-ecp256
4706               }
```

```
4707                    net6-net6 {
4708                        local_ts = 2001:db8:0:1::/64
4709                        remote_ts = 2001:db8:0:2::/64
4710                        esp_proposals = aes128gcm128-ecp256
4711                    }
4712                }
4713            version =2
4714            mobike = no
4715            proposals = aes128gcm128-prfsha256-ecp256
4716        }
4717    }
4718    secrets {
4719        ike-1 {
4720            id-1 = west.example.gov
4721            secret = XXXXXXXXXXXXXX
4722        }
4723        ike-2 {
4724            id-2 = east.example.gov
4725            secret = XXXXXXXXXXXXXX
4726        }
4727    }
4728
```

4729 **C.3 Section 9.1 Case Study Alternative Using libreswan on Linux**

4730 The following lists the contents of the same configuration as provided in Appendix C.1, but
4731 using libreswan on Linux:

```
4732    # /etc/ipsec.d/west-east.conf
4733    # left and right are arbitrary choices and auto-detected.
4734    # The identical configuration can be used on both gateways
4735    conn west-east
4736        left=198.51.100.1
4737        leftid=@west.example.gov
4738        right=203.0.113.1
4739        rightid=@east.example.gov
4740        ikev2=insist
4741        authby=secret
4742        auto=add
4743    conn westnet-eastnet-ipv4
4744        also=west-east
4745        leftsubnet=192.0.0.0/24
4746        rightsubnet=192.0.2.0/24
4747        auto=start
4748    conn westnet-eastnet-ipv6
4749        also-west-east
4750        leftsubnet=2001:db8:0:1::/64
4751        rightsubnet=2001:db8:0:2::/64
4752        auto=start
4753    # /etc/ipsec.d/west-east.secrets
4754    @west.example.gov @east.example.gov : PSK "XXXXXXXXXXX"
```

4755
4756   **C.4   Section 9.1 Case Study Alternative Using iked on OpenBSD**

4757   The following lists the contents of the same configuration as was provided for Appendix C.1 but
4758   using OpenIKED on OpenBSD. Note that this IKE daemon does not support AES-GCM for IKE,
4759   only for ESP. The order of the keywords matter.

```
4760    # /etc/iked.conf
4761    ikev2 westnet-eastnet esp \
4762    from 192.0.0.0/24 to 192.0.0.0/24 \
4763    from 2001:db8:0:1::/64 to 2001:db8:0:2::/64 \
4764    local 198.51.100.1 peer 203.0.113.1 \
4765    ikesa enc aes-256 auth hmac-sha2-256 group ecp256 group modp2048 \
4766    childsa enc aes-128-gcm \
4767    childsa enc aes-128 auth hmac-sha2_512
4768    srcid west.example.gov dstid east.example.gov \
4769    psk XXXXXXXX \
4770    tag west-east
```

4771

4772

4773   **Appendix D—Glossary**

4774   Selected terms used in the publication are defined below.
4775

Asymmetric Cryptography	Cryptography that uses two separate keys to exchange data, one to encrypt or digitally sign the data and one for decrypting the data or verifying the digital signature. Also known as *public key cryptography*.
Authentication Header (AH)	A deprecated IPsec security protocol that provides integrity protection (but not confidentiality) for packet headers and data.
Encapsulating Security Payload (ESP)	The core IPsec security protocol; can provide encryption and/or integrity protection for packet headers and data.
Extensible Authentication Protocol (EAP)	A framework for adding arbitrary authentication methods in a standardized way to any protocol.
Internet Key Exchange (IKE)	A protocol used to negotiate, create, and manage its own (IKE) and IPsec security associations.
IP Payload Compression Protocol (IPComp)	A protocol used to perform lossless compression for packet payloads.
Keyed Hash Algorithm	An algorithm that creates a message authentication code based on both a message and a secret key shared by two endpoints. Also known as a *hash message authentication code algorithm*.
Mobile Internet Key Exchange (MOBIKE)	A form of IKE supporting the use of devices with multiple network interfaces that switch from one network to another while IPsec is in use.
Network Layer Security	Protecting network communications at the layer of the IP model that is responsible for routing packets across networks.
Perfect Forward Secrecy (PFS)	An option that causes a new secret key to be created and shared through a new Diffie-Hellman key exchange for each IPsec SA. This provides protection against the use of compromised old keys that could be used to attack the newer derived keys still in use for integrity and confidentiality protection.
Preshared Key (PSK)	A single secret key used by IPsec endpoints to authenticate endpoints to each other.
Security Association (SA)	A set of values that define the features and protections applied to a connection.

Security Association Database (SAD)	A list or table of all IPsec SAs, including those that are still being negotiated.
Security Parameters Index (SPI)	An arbitrarily chosen value that acts as a unique identifier for an IPsec connection.
Security Policy Database (SPD)	A prioritized list of all IPsec policies.
Symmetric Cryptography	A cryptographic algorithm that uses the same secret key for its operation and, if applicable, for reversing the effects of the operation (e.g., an AES key for encryption and decryption).
Traffic Flow Confidentiality (TFC) Padding	Dummy data added to real data in order to obfuscate the length and frequency of information sent over IPsec.
Transport Mode	An IPsec mode that does not create an additional IP header for each protected packet.
Tunnel Mode	An IPsec mode that creates an additional outer IP header for each protected packet.
Virtual Private Network (VPN)	A virtual network built on top of existing physical networks that can provide a secure communications mechanism for data and IP information transmitted between networks or between different nodes on the same network.

4776

4777   **Appendix E—Acronyms and Abbreviations**

4778   Acronyms and abbreviations used in this publication are defined below.

3DES	Triple Data Encryption Standard
3GPP	3rd Generation Partnership Project
5G	5th Generation
6LowPAN	Low-Power Wireless Personal Area Network
AAA	Authentication, Authorization, and Accounting
AEAD	Authenticated Encryption with Associated Data
AES	Advanced Encryption Standard
AES-CBC	Advanced Encryption Standard-Cipher Block Chaining
AES-CCM	Advanced Encryption Standard-Counter with CBC-MAC
AES-CMAC	Advanced Encryption Standard-Cipher-Based Message Authentication Code
AES-GCM	Advanced Encryption Standard-Galois Counter Mode
AES-GMAC	Advanced Encryption Standard-Galois Message Authentication Code
AES-SHA-2	Advanced Encryption Standard-Secure Hash Algorithm-2
AES-XCBC	Advanced Encryption Standard-eXtended Cipher Block Chaining
AH	Authentication Header
ALG	Application Layer Gateway
API	Application Programming Interface
ARP	Address Resolution Protocol
BGP	Border Gateway Protocol
BIOS	Basic Input/Output System
BMP	BGP Monitoring Protocol
CA	Certificate Authority
CAVP	Cryptographic Algorithm Validation Program
CBC	Cipher Block Chaining
CCMP	Counter Mode with Cipher Block Chaining Message Authentication Code Protocol
CGN	Carrier Grade NAT
CHAP	Challenge Handshake Authentication Protocol
CIDR	Classless Inter-Domain Routing
CMVP	Cryptographic Module Validation Program
CoAP	Constrained Application Protocol
COTS	Commercial-Off-the-Shelf
CP	Configuration Payload
CPU	Central Processing Unit
CRL	Certificate Revocation List
CSE	Communications Security Establishment
CVE	Common Vulnerabilities and Exposures
DDoS	Distributed Denial of Service
DES	Data Encryption Standard
DH	Diffie-Hellman

DHCP	Dynamic Host Configuration Protocol
DNS	Domain Name System
DNS-SD	Domain Name System Service Discovery
DNSSEC	Domain Name System Security Extensions
DPD	Dead Peer Detection
DSA	Digital Signature Algorithm
DSL	Digital Subscriber Line
DTLS	Datagram Transport Layer Security
EAP	Extensible Authentication Protocol
EAP-MSCHAPv2	Extensible Authentication Protocol-Microsoft Challenge Handshake Authentication Protocol version 2
EAP-SIM	Extensible Authentication Protocol-Subscriber Identity Module
EAP-TLS	Extensible Authentication Protocol-Transport Layer Security
ECDH	Elliptic Curve Diffie-Hellman
ECDSA	Elliptic Curve Digital Signature Algorithm
ECP	Elliptic Curve Groups Modulo a Prime
EdDSA	Edwards Curve Digital Signature Algorithm
EKU	Extended Key Usage
ESN	Extended Sequence Number
ESP	Encapsulating Security Payload
ESPinUDP	ESP encapsulated in UDP
ESP-NULL	Encapsulating Security Payload without encryption
EVPN	Ethernet Virtual Private Network
FAQ	Frequently Asked Questions
FIDO	Fast Identity Online
FIPS	Federal Information Processing Standards
FISMA	Federal Information Security Modernization Act
FOIA	Freedom of Information Act
FQDN	Fully Qualified Domain Name
FTP	File Transfer Protocol
GDOI	Group Domain of Interpretation
GENEVE	Generic Network Virtualization Encapsulation
GMAC	Galois Message Authentication Code
GRE	Generic Routing Encapsulation
GSA	Group Security Association
GSO	Generic Segmentation Offload
GSSAPI	Generic Security Services Application Program Interface
GUID	Globally Unique Identifier
HKDF	HMAC Key Derivation Function
HMAC	Keyed-Hash Message Authentication Code
HMAC-MD5	Keyed-Hash Message Authentication Code-Message Digest
HMAC-SHA-1	Keyed-Hash Message Authentication Code-Secure Hash Algorithm
HMAC-SHA-2	Keyed-Hash Message Authentication Code-Secure Hash Algorithm
HTTP	HyperText Transfer Protocol
HTTPS	HyperText Transfer Protocol Secure

ICMP	Internet Control Message Protocol
ICV	Integrity Check Value
IEEE	Institute of Electrical and Electronics Engineers
IGMP	Internet Group Management Protocol
IETF	Internet Engineering Task Force
IKE	Internet Key Exchange
IMAP	Internet Message Access Protocol
Intel VT-d	Intel Virtualization Technology for Directed I/O
IoT	Internet of Things
IP	Internet Protocol
IPComp	IP Payload Compression Protocol
IPsec	Internet Protocol Security
IPv4	Internet Protocol version 4
IPv6	Internet Protocol version 6
ISA	Interconnection Security Agreement
ISAKMP	Internet Security Association and Key Management Protocol
ISP	Internet Service Provider
IT	Information Technology
ITL	Information Technology Laboratory
IV	Initialization Vector
KDF	Key Derivation Function
KE	Key Exchange
L2TP	Layer 2 Tunneling Protocol
L2VPN	Layer 2 VPN
LAN	Local Area Network
LDAP	Lightweight Directory Access Protocol
LTE	Long-Term Evolution
LZS	Lempel-Ziv-Stac
MAC	Message Authentication Code
MACsec	Media Access Control Security
MD	Message Digest
mDNS	Multicast Domain Name System
MEC	Multicast Group
MKA	MACsec Key Agreement
MOBIKE	Mobile Internet Key Exchange
MODP	Modular Exponential
MOU/A	Memorandum of Understanding or Agreement
MPLS	Multi-Protocol Label Switching
MPPE	Microsoft Point-to-Point Encryption
MS-CHAP	Microsoft Challenge-Handshake Authentication Protocol
MS-CHAPv1	Microsoft Challenge-Handshake Authentication Protocol version 1
MS-CHAPv2	Microsoft Challenge-Handshake Authentication Protocol version 2
MSEC	Multicast Security
MSS	Maximum Segment Size
MTU	Maximum Transmission Unit

NAPT	Network Address Port Translation
NAT	Network Address Translation
ND	Neighbor Discovery
NETCONF	Network Configuration Protocol
NIC	Network Interface Card
NIST	National Institute of Standards and Technology
NSA	National Security Agency
NUMA	Non-Uniform Memory Access
NVD	National Vulnerability Database
NVO3	Network Virtualization Overlay
OAuth	Open Authorization
OCSP	Online Certificate Status Protocol
OMB	Office of Management and Budget
OSPF	Open Shortest Path First
OTP	One-Time Password
P.L.	Public Law
PAKE	Password Authenticated Key Exchange
PAM	Pluggable Authentication Module
PAP	Password Authentication Protocol
PFS	Perfect Forward Secrecy
PKCS	Public Key Cryptography Standards
PKI	Public Key Infrastructure
POP	Post Office Protocol
PPK	Postquantum Preshared Key
PPP	Point-to-Point Protocol
PPTP	Point-to-Point Tunneling Protocol
PRF	Pseudo Random Function
PSK	Preshared Key
PSS	Probabilistic Signature Scheme
QoS	Quality of Service
RADIUS	Remote Authentication Dial In User Service
RAM	Random Access Memory
RFC	Request for Comment
RMON	Remote Monitoring
S/MIME	Secure/Multipurpose Internet Mail Extensions
SA	Security Association
SAD	Security Association Database
SAN	subjectAltName
SDN	Software-Defined Networking
SDWAN	Software-Defined Wide Area Network
SHA	Secure Hash Algorithm
SIP	Session Initiation Protocol
SMTP	Simple Mail Transfer Protocol
SNMP	Simple Network Management Protocol
SP	Special Publication

SPD	Security Policy Database
SPI	Security Parameters Index
SPKI	SubjectPublicKeyInfo
SSH	Secure Shell
SSL	Secure Sockets Layer
SSTP	Secure Socket Tunneling Protocol
TCP	Transmission Control Protocol
TCP/IP	Transmission Control Protocol/Internet Protocol
TCP-TLS	Transmission Control Protocol-Transport Layer Security
TFC	Traffic Flow Confidentiality
TKIP	Temporal Key Integrity Protocol
TLS	Transport Layer Security
TSi	Traffic Selector for Initiator
TSO	TCP Segmentation Offload
TSr	Traffic Selector for Responder
TTL	Time to Live
UDP	User Datagram Protocol
URI	Uniform Resource Indicator
USB	Universal Serial Bus
US-CERT	United States Computer Emergency Readiness Team
VLAN	Virtual Local Area Network
VM	Virtual Machine
VoIP	Voice over IP
VPN	Virtual Private Network
VXLAN	Virtual eXtensible Local Area Network
WEP	Wired Equivalent Privacy
WiFi	Wireless Fidelity
WPA	Wi-Fi Protected Access
WPA2	Wi-Fi Protected Access version 2
WPA3	Wi-Fi Protected Access version 3
XCBC	eXtended Cipher Block Chaining

4779

4780   **Appendix F—References**

4781   This appendix contains the references for the document.

[1]   Eggert L, Fairhurst G, Shepherd G (2017) *UDP Usage Guidelines*. (Internet
        Engineering Task Force (IETF)). Request for Comments (RFC) 8085 and Best
        Current Practice 145. https://doi.org/10.17487/RFC8085

[2]   van Elburg J, Drage K, Ohsugi M, Schubert S, Arai K (2014) *The Session Initiation
        Protocol (SIP) P-Private-Network-Indication Private Header (P-Header)*. (Internet
        Engineering Task Force (IETF)). Request for Comments (RFC) 7316.
        https://doi.org/10.17487/RFC7316

[3]   Saito M, Wing D, Toyama M (2011) *Media Description for the Internet Key
        Exchange Protocol (IKE) in the Session Description Protocol (SDP)*. (Internet
        Engineering Task Force (IETF)). Request for Comments (RFC) 6193.
        https://doi.org/10.17487/RFC6193

[4]   Mahalingam M, Dutt D, Duda K, Agarwal P, Kreeger L, Sridhar T, Bursell M,
        Wright C (2014) *Virtual eXtensible Local Area Network (VXLAN): A Framework
        for Overlaying Virtualized Layer 2 Networks over Layer 3 Networks*. (Internet
        Engineering Task Force (IETF)). Request for Comments (RFC) 7348.
        https://doi.org/10.17487/RFC7348

[5]   Filsfils C, Previdi S, Ginsberg L, Decraene B, Litkowski S, Shakir R (2018)
        Segment Routing Architecture. (Internet Engineering Task Force (IETF)). Request
        for Comments (RFC) 8402. https://doi.org/10.17487/RFC8402

[6]   Yong L, Dunbar L, Toy M, Isaac A, Manral V (2017) *Use Cases for Data Center
        Network Virtualization Overlay Networks*. (Internet Engineering Task Force
        (IETF)). Request for Comments (RFC) 8151. https://doi.org/10.17487/RFC8151

[7]   Gross J, Ganga I, Sridhar T (2019) *Geneve: Generic Network Virtualization
        Encapsulation*. (Internet Engineering Task Force (IETF) Network Working Group).
        Internet-Draft draft-ietf-nvo3-geneve-13. https://datatracker.ietf.org/doc/draft-ietf-
        nvo3-geneve/

[8]   Baker F, Meyer D (2011) *Internet Protocols for the Smart Grid*. (Internet
        Engineering Task Force (IETF)). Request for Comments (RFC) 6272.
        https://doi.org/10.17487/RFC6272

[9]   Pauly T, Touati S, Mantha R (2017) *TCP Encapsulation of IKE and IPsec Packets*.
        (Internet Engineering Task Force (IETF)). Request for Comments (RFC) 8229.
        https://doi.org/10.17487/RFC8229

[10]   Bhatia M, Manral V (2011) *Summary of Cryptographic Authentication Algorithm Implementation Requirements for Routing Protocols.* (Internet Engineering Task Force (IETF)). Request for Comments (RFC) 6094. https://doi.org/10.17487/RFC6094

[11]   Scudder J, Fernando R, Stuart S (2016) *BGP Monitoring Protocol (BMP).* (Internet Engineering Task Force (IETF)). Request for Comments (RFC) 7854. https://doi.org/10.17487/RFC7854

[12]   Gupta M, Melam N (2006) *Authentication/Confidentiality for OSPFv3.* (Internet Engineering Task Force (IETF) Network Working Group). Request for Comments (RFC) 4552. https://doi.org/10.17487/RFC4552

[13]   National Institute of Standards and Technology (2019) *Security Requirements for Cryptographic Modules.* Federal Information Processing Standard (FIPS) 140-3. https://nvlpubs.nist.gov/nistpubs/FIPS/NIST.FIPS.140-3.pdf

[14]   Ramsdell B, Turner S (2010) *Secure/Multipurpose Internet Mail Extensions (S/MIME) Version 3.2 Message Specification.* (Internet Engineering Task Force (IETF)). Request for Comments (RFC) 5751. https://doi.org/10.17487/RFC5751

[15]   Ylonen T, Lonvick C (2006) *The Secure Shell (SSH) Transport Layer Protocol.* (Internet Engineering Task Force (IETF) Network Working Group). Request for Comments (RFC) 4253. https://doi.org/10.17487/RFC4253

[16]   Rescorla E (2018) *The Transport Layer Security (TLS) Protocol Version 1.3.* (Internet Engineering Task Force (IETF)). Request for Comments (RFC) 8446. https://doi.org/10.17487/RFC8446

[17]   Rescorla E, Tschofenig H, Modadugu N (2019) *The Datagram Transport Layer Security (DTLS) Protocol Version 1.3.* (Internet Engineering Task Force (IETF)). Internet-Draft draft-ietf-tls-dtls13-31. https://datatracker.ietf.org/doc/draft-ietf-tls-dtls13/

[18]   Kaufman C, Hoffman P, Nir Y, Eronen P, Kivinen T (2014) *Internet Key Exchange Protocol Version 2 (IKEv2).* (Internet Engineering Task Force (IETF)). Request for Comments (RFC) 7296 and Internet Standard 79. https://doi.org/10.17487/RFC7296

[19]   Kent S (2005) *IP Encapsulating Security Payload (ESP).* (Internet Engineering Task Force (IETF)). Request for Comments (RFC) 4303. https://doi.org/10.17487/RFC4303

[20]   Nir Y, Kivinen T, Wouters P, Migault D (2017) *Algorithm Implementation Requirements and Usage Guidance for the Internet Key Exchange Protocol Version 2 (IKEv2).* (Internet Engineering Task Force (IETF)). Request for Comments (RFC) 8247. https://doi.org/10.17487/RFC8247

[21]   Wouters P, Migault D, Mattsson J, Nir Y, Kivinen T (2017) *Cryptographic Algorithm Implementation Requirements and Usage Guidance for Encapsulating Security Payload (ESP) and Authentication Header (AH)*. (Internet Engineering Task Force (IETF)). Request for Comments (RFC) 8221. https://doi.org/10.17487/RFC8221

[22]   Frankel S, Krishnan S (2011) *IP Security (IPsec) and Internet Key Exchange (IKE) Document Roadmap*. (Internet Engineering Task Force (IETF)). Request for Comments (RFC) 6071. https://doi.org/10.17487/RFC6071

[23]   Rosen E, Viswanathan A, Callon R (2001) *Multiprotocol Label Switching Architecture*. (Internet Engineering Task Force (IETF) Network Working Group). Request for Comments (RFC) 3031. https://doi.org/10.17487/RFC3031

[24]   National Institute of Standards and Technology (2008) *The Keyed-Hash Message Authentication Code (HMAC)*. (U.S. Department of Commerce, Washington, DC), Federal Information Processing Standards Publication (FIPS) 198-1. https://doi.org/10.6028/NIST.FIPS.198-1

[25]   National Institute of Standards and Technology (2015) *Secure Hash Standard (SHS)*. (U.S. Department of Commerce, Washington, DC), Federal Information Processing Standards Publication (FIPS) 180-4. https://doi.org/10.6028/NIST.FIPS.180-4

[26]   National Institute of Standards and Technology (2001) *Advanced Encryption Standard*. (U.S. Department of Commerce, Washington, DC), Federal Information Processing Standards Publication (FIPS) 197. https://doi.org/10.6028/NIST.FIPS.197

[27]   Dworkin M (2005) *Recommendation for Block Cipher Modes of Operation: The CMAC Mode for Authentication*. (National Institute of Standards and Technology, Gaithersburg, MD), NIST Special Publication (SP) 800-38B, Includes updates as of October 6, 2016. https://doi.org/10.6028/NIST.SP.800-38B

[28]   Dworkin M (2007) *Recommendation for Block Cipher Modes of Operation: Galois/Counter Mode (GCM) and GMAC*. (National Institute of Standards and Technology, Gaithersburg, MD), NIST Special Publication (SP) 800-38D. https://doi.org/10.6028/NIST.SP.800-38D

[29]   National Institute of Standards and Technology (2013) *Digital Signature Standard (DSS)*. (U.S. Department of Commerce, Washington, DC), Federal Information Processing Standards Publication (FIPS) 186-4. https://doi.org/10.6028/NIST.FIPS.186-4

[30] Enns R, Bjorklund M, Schoenwaelder J, Bierman A (2011) *Network Configuration Protocol (NETCONF)*. (Internet Engineering Task Force (IETF)). Request for Comments (RFC) 6241. https://doi.org/10.17487/RFC6241

[31] Carrel D, Weis B (2019) *IPsec Key Exchange using a Controller.* (Internet Engineering Task Force (IETF) Network Working Group). Internet-Draft draft-carrel-ipsecme-controller-ike-01. https://datatracker.ietf.org/doc/draft-carrel-ipsecme-controller-ike

[32] Eronen P (2006) *IKEv2 Mobility and Multihoming Protocol (MOBIKE)*. (Internet Engineering Task Force (IETF) Network Working Group). Request for Comments (RFC) 4555. https://doi.org/10.17487/RFC4555

[33] Aboba B, Calhoun P (2003) *RADIUS (Remote Authentication Dial In User Service) Support For Extensible Authentication Protocol (EAP)*. (Internet Engineering Task Force (IETF) Network Working Group). Request for Comments (RFC) 3579. https://doi.org/10.17487/RFC3579

[34] Eronen P, Hiller T, Zorn G (2005) *Diameter Extensible Authentication Protocol (EAP) Application*. (Internet Engineering Task Force (IETF) Network Working Group). Request for Comments (RFC) 4072. https://doi.org/10.17487/RFC4072

[35] Rekhter Y, Moskowitz B, Karrenberg D, de Groot G J, Lear E (1996) *Address Allocation for Private Internets*. (Internet Engineering Task Force (IETF) Network Working Group). Request for Comments (RFC) 1918 and Best Current Practice (BCP) 5. https://doi.org/10.17487/RFC1918

[36] Smyslov V (2014) *Internet Key Exchange Protocol Version 2 (IKEv2) Message Fragmentation*. (Internet Engineering Task Force (IETF)). Request for Comments (RFC) 7383. https://doi.org/10.17487/RFC7383

[37] Fluhrer S, McGrew D, Kampanakis P, Smyslov V (2019) *Postquantum Preshared Keys for IKEv2*. (Internet Engineering Task Force (IETF)). Internet-Draft draft-ietf-ipsecme-qr-ikev2-08. https://datatracker.ietf.org/doc/draft-ietf-ipsecme-qr-ikev2/

[38] Devarapalli V, Weniger K (2009) *Redirect Mechanism for the Internet Key Exchange Protocol Version 2 (IKEv2)*. (Internet Engineering Task Force (IETF) Network Working Group). Request for Comments (RFC) 5685. https://doi.org/10.17487/RFC5685

[39] Kent S, Atkinson R (1998) *IP Encapsulating Security Payload (ESP)*. (Internet Engineering Task Force (IETF) Network Working Group). Request for Comments (RFC) 2406. https://doi.org/10.17487/RFC2406

[40]   Kent S, Seo K (2005) *Security Architecture for the Internet Protocol*. (Internet Engineering Task Force (IETF)). Request for Comments (RFC) 4301. https://doi.org/10.17487/RFC4301

[41]   Krawczyk H, Bellare M, Canetti R (1997) *HMAC: Keyed-Hashing for Message Authentication*. (Internet Engineering Task Force (IETF) Network Working Group). Request for Comments (RFC) 2104. https://doi.org/10.17487/RFC2104

[42]   Frankel S, Herbert H (2003) *The AES-XCBC-MAC-96 Algorithm and Its Use With IPsec*. (Internet Engineering Task Force (IETF) Network Working Group). Request for Comments (RFC) 3566. https://doi.org/10.17487/RFC3566

[43]   Black D, McGrew D (2008) *Using Authenticated Encryption Algorithms with the Encrypted Payload of the Internet Key Exchange version 2 (IKEv2) Protocol*. (Internet Engineering Task Force (IETF) Network Working Group). Request for Comments (RFC) 5282. https://doi.org/10.17487/RFC5282

[44]   Viega J, McGrew D (2005) *The Use of Galois/Counter Mode (GCM) in IPsec Encapsulating Security Payload (ESP)*. (Internet Engineering Task Force (IETF) Network Working Group). Request for Comments (RFC) 4106. https://doi.org/10.17487/RFC4106

[45]   Frankel S, Glenn R, Kelly S (2003) *The AES-CBC Cipher Algorithm and Its Use with IPsec*. (Internet Engineering Task Force (IETF) Network Working Group). Request for Comments (RFC) 3602. https://doi.org/10.17487/RFC3602

[46]   Kelly S, Frankel S (2007) *Using HMAC-SHA-256, HMAC-SHA-384, and HMAC-SHA-512 with IPsec*. (Internet Engineering Task Force (IETF) Network Working Group). Request for Comments (RFC) 4868. https://doi.org/10.17487/RFC4868

[47]   Barker E, Roginsky A (2019) *Transitioning the Use of Cryptographic Algorithms and Key Lengths*. (National Institute of Standards and Technology, Gaithersburg, MD), NIST Special Publication (SP) 800-131A, Rev. 2. https://doi.org/10.6028/NIST.SP.800-131Ar2

[48]   Kent S (2005) *Extended Sequence Number (ESN) Addendum to IPsec Domain of Interpretation (DOI) for Internet Security Association and Key Management Protocol (ISAKMP)*. (Internet Engineering Task Force (IETF)). Request for Comments (RFC) 4304. https://doi.org/10.17487/RFC4304

[49]   Pauly T, Touati S, Mantha R (2017) *TCP Encapsulation of IKE and IPsec Packets*. (Internet Engineering Task Force (IETF)). Request for Comments (RFC) 8229. https://doi.org/10.17487/RFC8229

[50]   McDonald D, Metz C, Phan B (1998) *PF_KEY Key Management API, Version 2.*
         (Internet Engineering Task Force (IETF) Network Working Group). Request for
         Comments (RFC) 2367. https://doi.org/10.17487/RFC2367

[51]   Salim J, Khosravi H, Kleen A, Kuznetsov A (2003) *Linux Netlink as an IP Services
         Protocol.* (Internet Engineering Task Force (IETF) Network Working Group).
         Request for Comments (RFC) 3549. https://doi.org/10.17487/RFC3549

[52]   Shafer P (2011) *An Architecture for Network Management Using NETCONF and
         YANG.* (Internet Engineering Task Force (IETF)). Request for Comments (RFC)
         6244. https://doi.org/10.17487/RFC6244

[53]   Srisuresh P, Holdrege M (1999) *IP Network Address Translator (NAT) Terminology
         and Considerations.* (Internet Engineering Task Force (IETF) Network Working
         Group). Request for Comments (RFC) 2663. https://doi.org/10.17487/RFC2663

[54]   Moriarty K, Morton A (2018) *Effects of Pervasive Encryption on Operators.*
         (Internet Engineering Task Force (IETF)). Request for Comments (RFC) 8404.
         https://doi.org/10.17487/RFC8404

[55]   Korver B (2007) *The Internet IP Security PKI Profile of IKEv1/ISAKMP, IKEv2,
         and PKIX.* (Internet Engineering Task Force (IETF) Network Working Group).
         Request for Comments (RFC) 4945. https://doi.org/10.17487/RFC4945

[56]   Kuhn DR, Hu VC, Polk WT, Chang S-jH (2001) *Introduction to Public Key
         Technology and the Federal PKI Infrastructure.* (National Institute of Standards and
         Technology, Gaithersburg, MD), NIST Special Publication (SP) 800-32.
         https://doi.org/10.6028/NIST.SP.800-32

[57]   Cooper D, Santesson S, Farrell S, Boeyen S, Housley R, Polk W (2008) *Internet
         X.509 Public Key Infrastructure Certificate and Certificate Revocation List (CRL)
         Profile* (Internet Engineering Task Force (IETF) Network Working Group). Request
         for Comments (RFC) 5280. https://doi.org/10.17487/RFC5280

[58]   Santesson S, Myers M, Ankney R, Malpani A, Galperin S, Adams C (2013) *X.509
         Internet Public Key Infrastructure Online Certificate Status Protocol – OCSP.*
         (Internet Engineering Task Force (IETF) Network Working Group). Request for
         Comments (RFC) 6960. https://doi.org/10.17487/RFC6960

[59]   Esale S, Torvi R, Jalil L, Chunduri U, Raza K (2017) *Application-Aware Targeted
         LDP.* (Internet Engineering Task Force (IETF)). Request for Comments (RFC)
         8223. https://doi.org/10.17487/RFC8223

[60]   Barker E, Chen L, Roginsky A, Vassilev A, Davis R, Simon S (2019)
         *Recommendation for Pair-Wise Key Establishment Using Integer Factorization
         Cryptography.* (National Institute of Standards and Technology, Gaithersburg, MD),
         NIST Special Publication (SP) 800-56B, Rev. 2.
         https://doi.org/10.6028/NIST.SP.800-56Br2

[61]   Fu D, Solinas J (2010) *Elliptic Curve Groups modulo a Prime (ECP Groups) for
         IKE and IKEv2.* (Internet Engineering Task Force (IETF)). Request for Comments
         (RFC) 5903. https://doi.org/10.17487/RFC5903

[62]   Barker E, Chen L, Roginsky A, Vassilev A, Davis R (2018) *Recommendation for
         Pair-Wise Key-Establishment Schemes Using Discrete Logarithm Cryptography.*
         (National Institute of Standards and Technology, Gaithersburg, MD), NIST Special
         Publication (SP) 800-56A, Rev. 3. https://doi.org/10.6028/NIST.SP.800-56Ar3

[63]   Sheffer Y, Tschofenig H (2010) *Internet Key Exchange Protocol Version 2 (IKEv2)
         Session Resumption.* (Internet Engineering Task Force (IETF)). Request for
         Comments (RFC) 5723. https://doi.org/10.17487/RFC5723

[64]   Kivinen T, Kojo M (2003) *More Modular Exponential (MODP) Diffie-Hellman
         groups for Internet Key Exchange (IKE).* (Internet Engineering Task Force (IETF)).
         Request for Comments (RFC) 3526. https://doi.org/10.17487/RFC3526

[65]   Lepinski M, Kent S (2008) *Additional Diffie-Hellman Groups for Use with IETF
         Standards.* (Internet Engineering Task Force (IETF)). Request for Comments (RFC)
         5114. https://doi.org/10.17487/RFC5114

[66]   Kuhn D R, Walsh T, Fries S (2005) *Security Considerations for Voice Over IP
         Systems.* (National Institute of Standards and Technology, Gaithersburg, MD), NIST
         Special Publication (SP) 800-58. https://doi.org/10.6028/NIST.SP.800-58

[67]   Souppaya M, Scarfone K (2012) *Guidelines for Securing Wireless Local Area
         Networks (WLANs).* (National Institute of Standards and Technology, Gaithersburg,
         MD), NIST Special Publication (SP) 800-153. https://doi.org/10.6028/NIST.SP.800-
         153

[68]   Rescorla E, Modadugu N (2012) *Datagram Transport Layer Security Version 1.2.*
         (Internet Engineering Task Force (IETF)). Request for Comments (RFC) 6347.
         https://doi.org/10.17487/RFC6347

[69]   Frankel S, Hoffman P, Orebaugh A, Park R (2008) *Guide to SSL VPNs.* (National
         Institute of Standards and Technology, Gaithersburg, MD), NIST Special
         Publication (SP) 800-113. https://doi.org/10.6028/NIST.SP.800-113

[70]   Mavrogiannopoulos N (2018) *The OpenConnect VPN Protocol Version 1.1.*
        (Internet Engineering Task Force (IETF)). Internet-Draft draft-mavrogiannopoulos-
        openconnect-02. https://datatracker.ietf.org/doc/draft-mavrogiannopoulos-
        openconnect/

[71]   Krawczyk H, Eronen P (2010) *HMAC-based Extract-and-Expand Key Derivation
        Function (HKDF).* (Internet Engineering Task Force (IETF)).
        Request for Comments (RFC) 5869. https://doi.org/10.17487/RFC5869

[72]   Nir Y, Josefsson S (2016) *Curve25519 and Curve448 for the Internet Key Exchange
        Protocol Version 2 (IKEv2) Key Agreement.* (Internet Engineering Task Force
        (IETF)). Request for Comments (RFC) 8031. https://doi.org/10.17487/RFC8031

[73]   Nir Y, Langley A (2015) *ChaCha20 and Poly1305 for IETF Protocols.* (Internet
        Engineering Task Force (IETF)). Request for Comments (RFC) 7539.
        https://doi.org/10.17487/RFC7539

[74]   Nir Y (2018) *Using the Edwards-Curve Digital Signature Algorithm (EdDSA) in the
        Internet Key Exchange Protocol Version 2 (IKEv2).* (Internet Engineering Task
        Force (IETF)). Request for Comments (RFC) 8420.
        https://doi.org/10.17487/RFC8420

[75]   Simpson W (1994) *The Point-to-Point Protocol (PPP).* (Internet Engineering Task
        Force (IETF) Network Working Group). Request for Comments (RFC) 1661 and
        Standard 51. https://doi.org/10.17487/RFC1661

[76]   Hamzeh K, Pall G, Verthein W, Taarud J, Little W, Zorn G (1999) *Point-to-Point
        Tunneling Protocol (PPTP).* (Internet Engineering Task Force (IETF) Network
        Working Group). Request for Comments (RFC) 2637.
        https://doi.org/10.17487/RFC2637

[77]   Pall G, Zorn G (2001) *Microsoft Point-to-Point Encryption (MPPE) Protocol.*
        (Internet Engineering Task Force (IETF) Network Working Group). Request for
        Comments (RFC) 3078. https://doi.org/10.17487/RFC3078

[78]   Lloyd B, Simpson W (1992) *PPP Authentication Protocols.* (Internet Engineering
        Task Force (IETF)). Request for Comments (RFC) 1334.
        https://doi.org/10.17487/RFC1334

[79]   Simpson W (1996) *PPP Challenge Handshake Authentication Protocol (CHAP).*
        (Internet Engineering Task Force (IETF)). Request for Comments (RFC) 1994.
        https://doi.org/10.17487/RFC1994

[80]   Townsley W, Valencia A, Rubens A, Pall G, Zorn G, Palter B (1999) *Layer Two Tunneling Protocol "L2TP"*. (Internet Engineering Task Force (IETF) Network Working Group). Request for Comments (RFC) 2661. https://doi.org/10.17487/RFC2661

[81]   Rigney C, Willens S, Rubens A, Simpson W (2000) *Remote Authentication Dial In User Service (RADIUS)*. (Internet Engineering Task Force (IETF)). Request for Comments (RFC) 2865. https://doi.org/10.17487/RFC2865

[82]   Weis B, Gross G, Ignjatic D (2008) *Multicast Extensions to the Security Architecture for the Internet Protocol*. (Internet Engineering Task Force (IETF) Network Working Group). Request for Comments (RFC) 5374. https://doi.org/10.17487/RFC5374

[83]   Hardjono T, Weis B (2004) *The Multicast Group Security Architecture*. (Internet Engineering Task Force (IETF) Network Working Group). Request for Comments (RFC) 3740. https://doi.org/10.17487/RFC3740

[84]   Weis B, Smyslov V (2019) *Group Key Management using IKEv2*. (Internet Engineering Task Force (IETF) Network Working Group). Internet-Draft draft-yeung-g-ikev2-15. https://datatracker.ietf.org/doc/draft-yeung-g-ikev2/

[85]   Baugher M, Canetti R, Dondeti L, Lindholm F (2005) *Multicast Security (MSEC) Group Key Management Architecture*. (Internet Engineering Task Force (IETF) Network Working Group). Request for Comments (RFC) 4046. https://doi.org/10.17487/RFC4046

[86]   Weis B, Rowles S, Hardjono T (2011) *The Group Domain of Interpretation*. (Internet Engineering Task Force (IETF)). Request for Comments (RFC) 6407. https://doi.org/10.17487/RFC6407

[87]   Prasad S, Wouters P (2018) *Labeled IPsec Traffic Selector Support for IKEv2*. (Internet Engineering Task Force (IETF)). Internet-Draft draft-ipsecme-labeled-ipsec-00. https://datatracker.ietf.org/doc/draft-ietf-ipsecme-labeled-ipsec/

[88]   Migault D, Guggemos T, Nir Y (2019) *Implicit IV for Counter-Based Ciphers in Encapsulating Security Payload (ESP)*. (Internet Engineering Task Force (IETF)). Internet-Draft draft-ietf-ipsecme-implicit-iv-07. https://datatracker.ietf.org/doc/draft-ietf-ipsecme-implicit-iv/

[89]   Smyslov V (2018) *Intermediate Exchange in the IKEv2 Protocol*. (Internet Engineering Task Force (IETF) Network Working Group). Internet-Draft draft-smyslov-ipsecme-ikev2-aux-02. https://datatracker.ietf.org/doc/draft-smyslov-ipsecme-ikev2-aux/

[90]   Boucadair M (2018) *IKEv2 Notification Status Types for IPv4/IPv6 Coexistence.*
         (Internet Engineering Task Force (IETF) Network Working Group). Internet-Draft
         draft-ietf-ipsecme-ipv6-ipv4-codes-02. https://datatracker.ietf.org/doc/draft-ietf-
         ipsecme-ipv6-ipv4-codes/

[91]   Tjhai C, Tomlinson M, Bartlett G, Flurher S, Van Geest D, Garcia-Morchon O,
         Smyslov V (2019) *Framework to Integrate Post-Quantum Key Exchanges Into
         Internet Key Exchange Protocol Version 2 (IKEv2).* (Internet Engineering Task
         Force (IETF)). Internet-Draft draft-tjhai-ipsecme-hybrid-qske-ikev2-03.
         https://datatracker.ietf.org/doc/draft-tjhai-ipsecme-hybrid-qske-ikev2/

[92]   Grance T, Hash J, Peck S, Smith J, Korow-Diks K (2002) *Security Guide for
         Interconnecting Information Technology Systems.* (National Institute of Standards
         and Technology, Gaithersburg, MD), NIST Special Publication (SP) 800-47.
         https://doi.org/10.6028/NIST.SP.800-47

[93]   Souppaya M, Scarfone K (2016) *Guide to Enterprise Telework, Remote Access, and
         Bring Your Own Device (BYOD) Security.* (National Institute of Standards and
         Technology, Gaithersburg, MD), NIST Special Publication (SP) 800-46, Rev. 2.
         https://doi.org/10.6028/NIST.SP.800-46r2

[94]   Harkins D, Carrel D (1998) *The Internet Key Exchange (IKE).* (Internet Engineering
         Task Force (IETF) Network Working Group). Request for Comments (RFC) 2409.
         https://doi.org/10.17487/RFC2409

4782